CW00348165

In Hind

A compendium of Business Continuity case studies

In Hindsight

A compendium of Business Continuity case studies

EDITED BY ROBERT A CLARK

IT Governance Publishing

IT Governance Publishing
IT Governance Limited
Unit 3, Clive Court
Bartholomew's Walk
Cambridgeshire Business Park
Ely
Cambridgeshire
CB7 4EA
United Kingdom

www.itgovernance.co.uk

First published in the United Kingdom in 2014
by IT Governance Publishing.

ISBN 978-1-84928-591-9

This book is dedicated to my brother-in-law, Tom Feeney –
an inspiration to us all

ABOUT THE EDITOR

A Member of the Business Continuity Institute and an Approved BCI Instructor, Robert Clark is also a Fellow of the British Computer Society and a Member of the Security Institute. In 1973 he joined IBM as a computer operator. Big Blue was one of those forward thinking organisations that practised business continuity management (BCM) before the expression had even been coined; but back in the 1970s, with the exception of periodical fire evacuation drills, BCM was simply referred to as disaster recovery and was entirely focused on protecting the IT environment along with the associated electronic data.

It was less than twelve months into his 15 year IBM career that Robert first became exposed to BCM. Both local and overseas disaster fall-back trials were regular features in the IBM calendar and often involved testing its recovery capability by transferring UK operations to Germany or the Netherlands. During his time with the corporation, the closest the operation came to a real disaster fall-back was in 1974 during the UK miners' strike when power interruptions became commonplace.

His 15 years with IBM were followed by a variety of positions, including 11 years with Fujitsu Services (formerly ICL) working with clients on BCM related assignments. In 2005 he was tasked with validating Fujitsu's own BCM state of readiness across Europe. He has managed and delivered BCM solutions in the public sector, for large corporations, SMEs and central governments, gaining experience in several industries including banking, insurance, oil and gas, airline, manufacturing and retail across ten different countries.

He is now a freelance Business Continuity Consultant and has spent much of the last three years in Malta, where he has promoted BCM both through consultancy assignments and BCI licensed training.

As a member of Toastmasters International, Robert is no stranger to public speaking. An experienced keynote speaker, he promotes BCM whenever the opportunity presents itself.

CONTRIBUTORS

Robert A. Clark MSc FBCS MBCI MSyI
Freelance Business Continuity Management Consultant at
www.bcm-consultancy.com

Carl Dakin QGM MSc FdA MSyI
Business Continuity & Security Consultant

Tony Duncan MSc FdA
Security Consultant

Owen Gregory MSc BA (Hons) MBCI MBCS
Services Planning, Business Continuity and Service
Continuity Practitioner

Jon Sigurd Jacobsen MSc FdA MSyI
Managing Director, SOS Event Security AS, Norway

Neil Swinyard-Jordan MSc FdA MSyI
Security Consultant

Catherine Feeney MSc JP FIH Cert Ed
Senior Lecturer in Tourism, Hospitality and Events
Management at Manchester Metropolitan University

We would like to thank Abdullah Al Hour, author of
Business Continuity Management: Choosing to survive, ir.
H.L. (Maarten) Souw RE, Enterpise Risk and QA Manager,
UWV and Thejendra BS, author of *Disaster Recovery and
Business Continuity* for their helpful comments during the
review process.

FOREWORD – MARTIN CADDICK, LLB MBA MBCI MIOR

It has to be admitted that most books about business continuity are dull. They shouldn't be, because the context is the stuff of news headlines. Not only do disasters excite interest, but even the process of business continuity planning – and understanding what really matters to your business – is hardly tedious.

This book is an exception to the rule. It takes a series of case studies, familiar to us from news reports, and digs deeper into what went wrong. Where other books bore us with methodology and process, this book catches our interest; and in doing so, it brings out why business continuity and crisis management really do matter and just how all-pervasive the consequences of a disaster can be.

The scale of some of the examples, such as the Piper-Alpha disaster and Hurricane Katrina, demonstrates how important this subject is. Yet we seem doomed to repeat many of the mistakes. Had the lessons from Bhopal been applied by the West Fertiliser Company in Texas, the 2013 explosion could have been avoided.

I am constantly amazed by the number of executives who dismiss potential disasters as being too unlikely to consider, or who put off dealing with known risks because they have other things to worry about. This book is full of these people, and what happens in the case studies provides ample evidence to counter their complacency.

We live in a world where we are becoming increasingly interdependent thanks to ever-faster travel and communication. It is well-nigh impossible to foresee what combination of events might cause disaster next, nor what the range of consequences might be. The importance of being well prepared grows by the day.

The contributors to this book have taken the time and trouble to think about what lessons can be learnt from each case – not just the things that could be done better, but also things that were done well. With a little of the imagination a good business continuity or crisis manager needs, nearly all the lessons identified here can be applied in other contexts, making this a useful book for such professionals.

The nature of this subject means that we spend a lot of time dealing with catastrophes and their consequences. It is almost impossible now to avoid being struck by a so-called 'black swan' event at some point in the life of a business, and our success is measured in terms of 'less bad' rather than 'good'. But the good news is that resilient organisations do survive disasters, and often improve their standing because they demonstrate their ability to manage crises well, inspiring confidence and loyalty in their customers and employees.

PREFACE – PHILLIP WOOD, MBE MSC FSYI CPP PSP AMBCI MINSTLM

Normally the preface to a book is written by its author, and I have not written a word of this one. I am very proud of *In Hindsight*, however, mainly because the authors are presenting a wider perspective on business continuity and its links to other activities, disciplines and functions. This approach is much needed in what is believed by many to be a solely IT-focused management process, which in my view business continuity is not. In reading through these case studies and the observations and analysis that the contributors make, hopefully you will agree that the wider linkages between the various elements of effective organisational resilience are recurrent and necessary to ensure anticipation, response and recovery when things do go wrong.

With an eclectic and varied background (and representing various disciplines), Robert Clark and the team of contributors have taken a broad view of some typical and not-so-typical events that have taken place and highlighted lessons from them. The title *In Hindsight* says a lot: my own specific academic interests revolve around how effectively humans manage and plan for unwanted events and there is much written about looking forward in general literature, with horizons, swans and 'megatrends' being referenced and quoted. All of this is thought-provoking and necessary. But it is equally necessary to look back in detail at what has happened before, as the contributors to *In Hindsight* have, and to highlight the frailties, omissions and sheer lack of effective thought that has brought organisations to the brink of disaster and beyond.

The causes of problems vary, and that is reflected in the range of cases covered in the book. So you will read about volcanoes, faulty cars, natural disasters, terrorism and diseases; and you will be relieved to see that there is discussion of IT-related issues. But you will also read about the *impacts* and lessons learned. The causes of the issues that are covered by the team of contributors are examined and analysed, and there are judgements made about the effects and efficacy of response, leading to either successful or unsuccessful outcomes. You will revisit some events that you have perhaps read about previously (you may even have been involved); and there are others that may not have come to your attention. For example, how much do you know about the effects on business of a public transport strategy for Malta? Importantly, there are no bombs, bullets, deaths, power outages or other 'headline' elements to that case study; simply failures to understand the continuity implications of immature strategies. Conversely, what can the catastrophic loss of life at a music festival or as the result of corporate planning and implementation failures teach us about the hubris and stupidity of humans? If you haven't considered it before, think about the recurrent theme in the majority of these cases; humans can be vain, negligent, lazy and often stupid – and that has a high cost in every sense.

You will read case studies here not from dedicated academics and not from contributors who are all resilience practitioners in their daily lives. What *In Hindsight* provides is a collection of analysed learning experiences, seen through the eyes of contributors who live with, work in and may have been affected in some way by some of the case areas that they have highlighted. Whether your interest is in 'disaster recovery' in its application by the IT world, or in real disasters that involved real people and real casualties, you will find something to learn in this book. If you are interested in tourism or terrorism, you will find them discussed here. Importantly, for me, the book and the case studies highlight the types of activity that underpin our daily lives, and therefore should be absolutely the focus of reading and learning. Businesses, consultants and managers spend a lot of time proposing ideas and planning strategies, and there is much to understand from where humans have forged ahead with their own objectives, priorities and perspectives – and failed.

As a fellow student of the issues highlighted in *In Hindsight*, I have found it to be an interesting, thought provoking and stimulating collection of studies and I have learned a great deal in reading it. Learning is the key to understanding, and understanding allows us to make the right decisions. So, whether you are a resilience professional or not, reading this book may help you to make the right decisions in the future. There is a saying: 'Hindsight is a wonderful thing'. It is true.

LIST OF FIGURES

CONTENTS

Contents

Contents

Contents

Contents

Contents

Contents

Contents

CHAPTER 1: INTRODUCTION – ROBERT CLARK

In September 2010, I started out on one of the most enjoyable journeys I have ever undertaken. It was not to some strange, far off and exotic land but a return to somewhere I had not been to since my teenage years – a return to the world of academia. Two years later I graduated from Buckinghamshire New University with a Master of Science degree in Business Continuity, Security and Emergency Management. Attaining a master's degree was the fulfilment of a promise made many years before not only to myself but to my mother Vera as well. I am very grateful that, at the age of 94 years, she was there with me to witness my graduation.

Unlike many who embark upon a master's degree I had no first degree, although I justified my place on the course by the commercial business continuity experience I had gained throughout my career. Naturally, I did not make this journey alone and found myself studying in a cohort of six mature students that quickly bonded not just academically but socially too. We came from different backgrounds bringing with us our own experiences of the real world and we quickly learned to draw on each other's strengths. Our university head of department, Phil Wood, once remarked that he always learned something from our group discussions, such was the diversity of knowledge that we collectively brought to the table.

Although we did not appreciate it at the time, we started preparing the content of this book towards the end of 2010. It was then that work commenced on the business continuity case studies which subsequently became the basis for this book.

These studies are diverse and cover many of the mainstream threats that business continuity practitioners are called upon to address. Some are based upon our personal experiences while others cover multiple threat scenarios. One such example is the 2005 Buncefield oil depot disaster, and the study even considers the question of whether it was caused by a cyber attack.

Each study looks at the events that occurred, interprets and analyses the facts while reaching appropriate conclusions and recommendations. Where similarities existed between the original case studies, they have been combined and, where appropriate, extracts from our dissertations have also been included. One such example is 'A Tale of Three Cities' which is a comparison of the terrorist attacks on Madrid (2004), London (2005) and Glasgow Airport (2007). Here the common theme is not just terrorism but the targeting of the respective transport infrastructures of the three cities.

In business continuity, we can all be guilty of thinking only of major incidents that could have a detrimental effect on our organisations. To that end, a chapter has been included which focuses on a series of smaller incidents, each of which still had the potential to have big impacts on organisations.

Amongst the studies is a contribution from Catherine Feeney, senior lecturer in Tourism, Hospitality and Events Management at Manchester Metropolitan University. Although she was not a member of the cohort, Catherine was invited to submit a chapter that focuses on the pandemic threat with specific emphasis on the impact that the 2003 SARS outbreak had on the tourism industry.

With the graduation now long since over and with a master's degree in the bag, that tiny cohort is spread across the world in several different countries. But it is good to know that our academic efforts may also be of practical use to anyone who has an interest in, or is actively involved with, business continuity, information security or risk management. It is my hope that through this book and the experiences of those that it chronicles, more and more people will come to realise the importance of business continuity.

In 1974, I first became involved in business continuity management (BCM). In those days it was simply called disaster recovery and was solely about protecting an organisation's information technology assets and electronic data. The mainframe dominated the computer world. The Internet was in its infancy and the threat from cyberspace was something you were more likely to read about in a science fiction novel than in the pages of a serious computing journal. It was to be almost another ten years before the personal computer was to arrive on the scene and over 20 before the commercialisation of the World Wide Web. Even the formation of the Business Continuity Institute did not happen until 1994. In fact, business continuity management and the Internet are about the same age.

My first involvement with BCM was as a computer operator with IBM and I was based in a computer room, or data centre if you prefer, which was about the size of a soccer pitch. Located at Havant in the UK, ten IBM System 360 mainframe computers and all their respective peripheral units filled that room. Among those mainframes were the computers designated to process all of IBM World Trade's customer orders and manufacturing logistics transactions. That included anything that was ordered by a client outside of the USA along with all the associated manufacturing instructions. It should come as no surprise that this operation was considered mission critical by IBM.

To ensure the continuity of this mission critical operation, two or three times a year a full disaster recovery test would be performed. This necessitated undertaking what we referred to as a 'disaster fall-back test' and involved transferring the operation to an IBM location in Germany or the Netherlands. Testing would occur over a weekend to minimise any disruption to the host location and, allowing for travel time, would be done and dusted over a four day period.

By the mid-1980s IBM recognised that the 'IT environment' represented only part of the story and other aspects of its business, such as its staff, properties and even supply chain were also crucial. This started to be reflected in the various scenarios that were tested and rehearsed.

With so many businesses detrimentally affected, culminating in around 600,000 job loses, the 9/11 terrorist attacks in 2001 were a major factor in emphasising the importance of BCM globally. This was further accentuated by the subsequent launching of BS 25999 in 2006 which was adopted as the established BCM standard across many parts of the globe. Finally, after evolving for around 40 years, 2012 saw BCM finally come of age when it joined the ranks of the international standards, taking its place alongside the likes of quality management and risk management. The Business Continuity Management System, or ISO22301 as it is known, was up and running.

Through my consultancy work, I still find myself amazed at the degree of naivety that exists in both public and private sectors and the excuses offered for not embracing business continuity, which have long since lost any originality. Recently, I became aware of the German division of a multinational company finding itself under pressure from its corporate headquarters to implement business continuity management. Not sure how to go about this, they approached their Dutch colleagues and asked if they could have copy of their plan so they could adapt it. In fairness, they had had no BCM training and had no in-house expertise that they could draw upon. Even so, they could not understand that, while they were prepared to share their plans, the Dutch said 'of course the plans won't work in Germany'.

Even though the products and services that both the Dutch and Germans offered were very similar, their respective business impact analysis and threat assessment exercises generated very different results. This ultimately affected what BCM strategies they each needed to adopt and how their subsequent business continuity plans (BCPs) shaped up. Or to put it another way, for business continuity one size does not fit all! Furthermore, even the most comprehensive of BCPs are effectively useless unless they are thoroughly tested and maintained.

But do you know what threats your organisation is facing and which of those could present a risk to its survival? If you have not performed a threat analysis exercise as part of your business continuity arrangements, the answer is most probably no. In fact, do you know how long your organisation has to recover from a serious incident (e.g. a fire, flood, IT failure, supply chain failure, product recall, loss of expertise, etc.) before its very survival could be placed in serious jeopardy? Is it several months, a few weeks, maybe two or three days or perhaps just a couple of hours? Five of the companies featured in this book ceased trading after catastrophes that they were unprepared for.

Most went with barely a whimper although one collapsed in the most spectacular fashion. A sixth company narrowly survived a catastrophe because of what can best be described as an 'Act of God'.

The threat matrix that follows in *Figure 1* includes 27 threats which are relatively common and would not look out of place in the results of a BCI member survey. They all appear in at least one of the case studies in this book; most appear several times. Around half of the incidents resulted in physical injuries and fatalities. Trauma was also not uncommon. Yet only one chapter, *A Tale of Three Cities* (p. 215), devotes its attention to terrorism which helps illustrate that the workplace can be a very dangerous place.

THREAT MATRIX	
ADVERSE PUBLICITY	**CHANGE OF GOVERNMENT**
• *Northgate / Buncefield*[3] *(p. 39)* • *Toyota (p. 151)* • *Devil in the Detail (p. 289)* • *MV Full City (p.133)* • *Barings Bank (p. 29)* • *Love Parade (p. 57)*	• *Madrid Train Bombing*[1] *(p. 220)* • *Arriva Malta (p. 273)*
CHEMICAL RELEASE	**CIVIL UNREST**
• *Bhopal (p. 121)*	• *Hurricane Katrina (p. 251)* • *Madrid Train Bombing (p. 220)*

CYBER THREAT	DATA LOSS
• *Northgate / Buncefield*[2] *(p. 39)* • *Devil in the Detail (p. 289)*	• *Aztec Chemicals (p. 91)* • *Northgate / Buncefield (p. 39)*
ENVIRONMENTAL DAMAGE • *MV Full City (p. 13)* • *Bhopal (p. 121)* • *Northgate / Buncefield (p. 39)* • *Aztec Chemicals (p. 91)* • *Piper Alpha (p. 103)*	**EXCLUSION ZONES** • *Aztec Chemicals (p. 91)* • *Northgate / Buncefield (p. 39)* • *London 7/7 Bombing (p. 228)* • *Madrid Train Bombing (p. 220)* • *Glasgow Airport Attack (p 238)* • *Bhopal (p. 121)* • *SARS Virus (p. 133)*
EXPLOSIONS (NON-TERRORISM) • *Aztec Chemicals (p. 91)* • *Northgate / Buncefield (p. 39)* • *Piper Alpha (p. 103)*	**FIRE** • *Aztec Chemicals (p. 91)* • *Northgate / Buncefield (p. 39)* • *Piper Alpha (p. 103)* • *Devil in the Detail (p. 289)* • *Åsta Train Accident (p. 205)* • *Glasgow Airport Attack (p. 238)*

FLOODING / ADVERSE WEATHER	FRAUD
• *Hurricane Katrina (p. 251)* • *Gloucestershire Floods (p. 169)* • *Devil in the Detail (p. 289)*	• *Barings Bank (p. 29)* • *Devil in the Detail (p. 289)*
FUEL CRISIS	**INDUSTRIAL ACTION**
• *Northgate / Buncefield (p. 39)*	• *Arriva Malta (p. 273)*
IT / TELCO FAILURE	**LOSS OF STAFF / EXPERTISE**
• *Northgate / Buncefield (p. 39)* • *Arriva Malta (p. 273)*	• *Northgate / Buncefield (p. 39)* • *Devil in the Detail (p. 289)* • *Arriva Malta (p. 273)*
MALICIOUS DAMAGE	**MALWARE / COMPUTER VIRUS**
• *Devil in the Detail (p. 289)*	• *Devil in the Detail (p. 289)*
PANDEMIC	**PRODUCT RECALL**
• *SARS Virus (p. 133)*	• *Toyota Vehicle Recall (p. 151)*

POTABLE WATER SHORTAGE	POWER FAILURE
• *Gloucestershire Floods (p.169)* • *Hurricane Katrina (p.251)*	• *Alexander L. Kielland (p.103)* • *Piper Alpha (p.103)* • *Hurricane Katrina (p. 251)* • *Gloucestershire Floods (p.169)*
SUCCESSION PLANNING	**SUPPLY CHAIN FAILURE**
• *Devil in the Detail (p. 289)*	• *Volcanic Ash Cloud (p.185)* • *Northgate / Buncefield (p.39)* • *MV Full City (p.13)* • *Aztec Chemicals (p.91)* • *Piper Alpha (p. 100)* • *Toyota Vehicle Recall (p.151)* • *Gloucestershire Floods (p.169)* • *Arriva Malta (p.273)*

TERRORISM	THEFT/INFORMATION SECURITY
• *London 7/7 Bombing (p.228)* • *Madrid Train Bombing (p.220)* • *Glasgow Airport Attack (p. 238235)*	• *Devil in the Detail (p. 289)*
TRANSPORT	**DISRUPTION**
• *Herald of Free Enterprise (p.79)* • *Åsta Train Accident (p. 205)* • *Northgate / Buncefield (p.39)* • *Volcanic Ash Cloud (p.185)* • *Arriva Malta (p.273)* • *SARS Virus (p.133)*	• *Hurricane Katrina (p. 251)* • *Gloucestershire Floods (p. 169)* • *London 7/7 Bombing (p. 228)* • *Madrid Train Bombing (p. 220)* • *Glasgow Airport Attack (p. 238)*

Figure 1: Occurrence of threats within case studies

Notes

[1] A change of Government did not cause the Madrid bombing. It is widely accepted, however, that the bombing caused the governing Conservative Party of Prime Minister José María Aznar to lose the general election on 14 March 2004, three days after the bombings, an election they were expected to win comfortably. In Malta, there was a great deal of speculation that the performance of Arriva Malta was fundamental in bringing the Government down.

[2] Although there is no evidence that Northgate Information Solutions suffered a cyber attack during its recovery from the Buncefield oil depot explosion, it remained vigilant and continued penetration testing of its systems. The question must be asked, however, as to why no consideration was apparently given by the official enquiry to the possibility of a cyber attack being the root cause of the disaster.

[3] Even though there is no record of Northgate Information Solutions receiving any adverse publicity as a result of the Buncefield disaster, reference is made to the BP Deepwater Horizon oil spill in the Gulf of Mexico. BP CEO Tony Hayward's on camera comment '*I'd like my life back,*' was a public relations disaster.

Figure 2 below indicates which of the case study incidents resulted in fatalities.

CASE STUDY INCIDENTS THAT RESULTED IN FATALITIES		
• *Bhopal (p.121)* • *Piper Alpha (p.103)* • *Alexander Kielland (p.100)* • *Åsta Train Accident (p. 205)* • *London 7/7 Bombing (p. 228)*	• *Madrid Train Bombing (p. 220)* • *Glasgow Airport Attack (p 235)* • *Gloucestershire Floods (p. 169)* • *Toyota Vehicle Recall (p. 151)* • *Herald of Free Enterprise (p. 79)*	• *Love Parade (p. 57)* • *SARS Virus (p. 133)* • *Hurricane Katrina (p. 251)*

Figure 2: Case study incidents that resulted in fatalities

CHAPTER 2: THE MV 'FULL CITY' INCIDENT – NORWAY'S WORST EVER OIL SPILL – JON SIGURD JACOBSEN

'This [oil spill] happened close to our summer house. The day after we had bathed from a beautiful stony beach, it was covered with crude oil!' – (Thor, 2009).

The MV *Full City* was a Panama registered bulk carrier with a gross tonnage of 15,873 tonnes. It was capable of taking a cargo weighing around 11,000 tonnes creating a deadweight tonnage of 26,758 tonnes. Built at Hakodate, Japan, it was completed in 1995, Chinese crewed and Chinese owned by the Roc Maritime Inc. It has twice made headline news. In 2011, it was attacked by Somali pirates in the Arabian Sea although it was swiftly rescued by a combined United States, Turkish and Indian naval force.

This case study, however, examines the earlier headline news event involving the same ship when it ran aground some two years previously, leaking its fuel oil in the process. It considers whether the incident was preventable, what the environmental impact for the surrounding area was, as well as the local response capability and the supply chain issues affecting YARA International ASA that had chartered the vessel.

At the time of this earlier incident, the ship was being operated by the China Ocean Shipping Company, known as COSCO. A Port State Control inspection had been performed in Kaliningrad, Russia, prior to the incident. This highlighted four inconsequential faults with no apparent relevance to what subsequently happened. It can therefore be concluded that the vessel was considered seaworthy.

On 23 July 2009, MV *Full City* received orders to transport mineral fertilizer, on behalf of YARA International ASA, from the Norwegian Port of Herøya to Puerto Quetzal in Guatemala. Loading was due to commence early in the morning on 1 August. In preparation, the ship needed to be at anchor the previous evening off the island of Såstein approximately three nautical miles from the mouth of the Langesund fjord. The following morning it was scheduled to have sailed up the fjord to Herøya to be loaded with its cargo.

Langesund and surrounds is an area of outstanding natural beauty and the location of the nature reserve of Lille Såstein, a nesting area for seabirds. The region incorporates the Norwegian counties of Vestfold, Telemark and Agder which have a combined population of over 500,000 inhabitants. It also has a coastline of approximately 4,000 kilometres, including all the islands. The tourist and fishing industries provide an important income for this region.

The incident

On July 30th the *Full City* bunkered off Skagen in Denmark and was fully fuelled when it arrived in the mid-afternoon at the anchor buoy off Såstein Island. It was understood to be carrying circa 1,005 tonnes of heavy oil and 120 tonnes of diesel oil. The anchorage was located approximately 0.9 nautical miles from the coast. Late in the evening the weather deteriorated and gale force and possibly even storm force winds were forecasted. When the storm finally broke, the subsequent height of the waves was believed to be between four and six metres. By 23:51 the *Full City* had slipped its anchor and the local automatic identification system, which can recognise a vessel as well as its course and speed, detected that the ship was drifting.

Roughly 18 minutes later the Captain of *Full City*, Zong Aming, took command of the bridge. Driven by the strong winds, the ship was drifting with a speed of between two and three knots and was by now only 0.3 nautical miles from the coast. Realising the seriousness of the situation, the captain gave the order to immediately start the main engine. His intention was to manoeuvre the ship away from danger but he failed and it ran aground at 00:23. The engine room flooded, stopping the main engine.

Shortly afterwards a rescue operation commenced and 16 of the 23 crew were airlifted from the stricken vessel by helicopter. The remaining seven crew members stayed on board the ship with the aim of damage control. With the vessel now badly damaged and well aground on the sandbanks of Såstein Island, it started shipping its engine oil. Strong winds and rough waves continued to damage the *Full City* through the night.

Following the event an investigation took place, and its stated purpose was as follows:

> *'The sole objective of this marine safety investigation is to reveal the circumstances and causes and contributing factors, with the aim of improving the safety of life at sea and avoiding future accidents. It is not the purpose of this investigation to determine liability or apportion blame.'* – (Accident Investigation Board Norway, 2009).

This did not prevent the Norwegian police arresting and charging the *Full City's* Captain, Zong Aming, and the

Officer of the Watch, Oilanng Lu, under anti-pollution and maritime safety laws. A study conducted over ten years by the Transportation Safety Board of Canada, which examined over 4,000 commercial marine incidents, had concluded that over 25% involved vessels running aground. Moreover, Mazaheri states that as many as 80% of commercial marine incidents can be attributed to human error. Midgård takes a different view. She claims that marine accidents are mainly caused by two combinations – either bad weather in combination with ships which are in a poor condition or bad weather in combination with human failure. Consequently, the finger of blame was always likely to point at the captain and whoever was the officer of the watch.

When the enquiry subsequently revealed that the anchor fluke had broken off during the storm, explaining why the captain mistakenly believed the ship was safely moored, he and the senior officer pleaded not guilty. Despite their pleas of innocence, both men were given short jail sentences having been found guilty of breaking both maritime safety laws and anti-pollution laws. Both sentences were suspended owing to the time they had already been detained.

The local response

This operation was initiated under the pollution legislation and was led by the Coastal Directorate. Local authorities (IUA) took the regional lead within their territories. Also involved were the Norwegian Coast Guard, the armed forces and local civil defence, fire brigade and municipalities. From the private sector, support came from NOFO, Exxon Mobile's Slagentangen refinery, with the

Swedish Coast Guard also providing assistance. A number of non-governmental bodies, the World Wildlife Fund, plus volunteers both local and international were also present. Unemployed Norwegians were also encouraged to participate in the clean-up.

The operation was divided into two main phases. The acute phase was carried out in the first 13 days with the primary goal of addressing the threat from oil that had not yet made shore. The second phase dealt with cleaning the polluted coastline.

'I am very glad to hear that the Norwegian Coast Guard believes the situation will return to normal for the areas affected by the oil spill.' – Helge Pedersen, Coast Affairs Minister.

Despite Pedersen's optimism the ensuing clean-up operation continued well into 2010 and was calculated to have needed some 18,000 man-days effort, including support from the many volunteers. The estimated cost was €25 million. Winter working conditions such as limited daylight hours, drift ice and temperatures as low as −20° Celsius were not conducive to achieving a swift resolution.

Despite being the fourth oil spill in Norwegian waters in five years, the clean-up operation was not without its critics. Poor operational control, lack of local experience, safety issues for personnel plus private contractors demanding large pay-outs were among the issues raised by critics. Moreover, no regard appeared to have been exhibited for the chain of command. In fact, without international support the local Norwegian effort may have proved inadequate. When considering the health and safety issues inherent in dealing with an oil spill, practical experience is worth far more than formal academic qualifications alone.

'This government has increased spending on oil spills on land, but unfortunately, they have forgotten that there is an urgent need to establish a state-run cargo ship emergency response unit in southern Norway.' – Marius Dalen, Bellona Oil Industry Advisor.

A further weakness originated from the lack of mutual understanding of how each of the bodies involved were operating, and a lack of collaboration was similarly evident. This flaw seemed to go both vertically and horizontally within the participating organisations, with each apparently following its own agenda.

It also transpired that the IUA Departments in the counties of Telemark, Vestfold and Agder each used different management systems. Moreover, they were unprepared to deal with a scenario of this magnitude, especially as their plans were outdated. This only served to introduce inefficiencies into the overall management of the situation.

The environmental damage

'The swimming season at Krokshavn and Steinvika is definitely over for this year.' Jon Pieter Fløo, Mayor of Telemark

The incident occurred at the height of the summer tourist season. At the time it was reported to be the worst ever oil spill in Norwegian waters. Approximately 10,000 m of booms plus a further 10,000 m of absorbent booms were deployed in an effort to restrict the oil dispersal. Even so, the oil pollution was observed across an area from Stravern to Grimstad, a distance of around 150 km. This was the fourth serious oil spill in Norwegian waters over a five year period, with incidents having also occurred at Rocknes (2004), Glomma (2006) and Server (2007).

The oil spill occurred very close to a seabird breeding ground. A variety of birds were put at risk by the oil spill, with an estimated 2,000 birds having to be destroyed.

'The accident could not have happened at a worse time. Although the nesting season is over the birds are still vulnerable, as from now until the end of August most of them are on the sea with their young.' – Norges Naturvernforbund.

An international response team was quickly formed with the objective of catching, cleaning and rehabilitating as many of the affected birds as possible. Support came from Belgium, Germany, Sweden and the UK. Local support was considered to be weak as the authorities lacked knowledge about how to deal with incidents of this nature. Moreover, there were insufficient numbers of suitably trained personnel in Norway.

The islands around Stråholmen, home to a colony of seals, are located in the contaminated area. While the mammals were exposed to the oil, however, it is believed the incident occurred just before they shed their winter coats. This fortunate timing enabled them to self-clean and no subsequent adverse effects have since been observed.

'The most serious threat of oil spills to fisheries and aquaculture activity is the economic loss arising from business interruption.' – (Clean Caribbean and Americas, 2004).

Marine researchers were concerned about the potentially harmful effects that the pollution would have on the local marine life. Both the oil and un-cleaned ballast water escaping from the vessel threatened the local breeding grounds for fish, shell fish and shrimp. Serious oil spills can expose marine life to both toxins and carcinogens that are known to exist in petroleum products. The Norwegian Food Safety Authority (NFSA) recommended that mussels and fish from the area that smelled even remotely oily should not be consumed.

Immediately following the *Full City* incident, a study of the effects of the oil spill on marine life was conducted by the Norwegian Institute of Marine Research. Over an eight month period, their findings showed a steady decline from the initial high concentration of contamination detected in local mussels to a level acceptable for human consumption. At his point, the NFSA withdrew its recommendation not to consume them. The institute's research also focused on fish in the area, although they could find no evidence of any contamination nor could they demonstrate that the fish had been adversely affected in any way.

Supply chain issues

YARA International ASA is the world's largest manufacturer of plant nutrients and supplies food and renewable energy for the world's increasing population. It has offices in more than 50 countries and makes yearly shipments of more than 20 million tonnes of plant nutrients to over 120 countries. The Norwegian state is the company's largest single shareholder. YARA's Porsgrunn factory, near Herøya, covers an area of 1.5 km^2 making it

Norway's largest industrial site. *Figure 3* shows its current annual production volumes:

PRODUCT	QUANTITIES
Ammonia	500,000 tonnes
Nitric Acid	1,320,000 tonnes
NPK Fertilizer	2,000,000 tonnes
Calcium Nitrate Fertilizer	810,000 tonnes

Figure 3: YARA Porsgrunn product output

A replacement vessel, *Universal Amsterdam*, was chartered and the Guatemala order despatched on 14 August 2009, less than two weeks after the originally planned shipment. The gross weight of the order was around 11,000 tonnes. Had the order been cancelled, it would have represented a potential sales loss of no more than 0.55% of YARA's total Porsgrunn NPK fertiliser annual production. Not a significant amount for the company to lose.

There is no information available regarding the impact of late delivery for the recipient in Guatemala of the fertiliser shipment, or on their downstream supply chain which was presumably the local agricultural industry. With the shipment arriving less than two weeks later than scheduled, however, even if the recipient was operating a just-in-time supply chain model the impact may well have been minimal. It is also unlikely to have resulted in a significantly reduced yield from the crops the fertiliser was intended for.

Conversely, the owners of the MV *Full City* would have not only forfeited the YARA shipment income but also any potential future revenue lost while the vessel remained in an unseaworthy state. It was a full six weeks before the ship was towed to Gothenburg, Sweden, to undergo extensive repairs. It was still in Gothenburg in April 2010, over eight months after the incident. To compound these losses, the Norwegian authorities imposed a US$39 million fine on the *Full City* owners, COSCO Shipping. Two years after the incident, six COSCO owned bulk carriers, including the *Full City*, were reported as being up for sale as the owners looked to deal with serious cash flow problems. Renamed the *Rising Eagle* in November 2011, the ship has new owners and now sails under the flag of Saint Vincent and Grenadines.

Insurance claims

Compared with the 2010 BP Deepwater Horizon oil spill in the Gulf of Mexico, where combined insurance settlements are expected to amount to billions of dollars, claims from the *Full City* oil spill were never going to be in the same league. One hotel complex in Langesund, however, did register a claim for 35 million Norwegian Krone – approximately US$4.5 million.

Lessons learned

Let us first put this event into perspective. Although it was Norway's biggest spill at the time, only approximately 200 tonnes of oil escaped from the *Full City,* since the remainder was pumped into a barge during the salvage operation to avoid any further pollution. When compared with other oil spills involving ships, this quantity of oil

rather pales into insignificance as illustrated in *Figure 4*,
below:

SHIP	LOCATION	DATES	OIL SPILT (TONNES)
Full City	Langesund, Norway	2009	200
Hebei Spirit	Taean, Republic of Korea	2007	11,000
Prestige	Galicia, Spain	2002	63,000
Sea Empress	Pembrokeshire, UK	1996	72,000
Exxon Valdez	Alaska, USA	1989	37,000
Amoco Cadiz	Brittany, France	1978	223,000
Torrey Canyon	Isles of Scilly, UK	1967	119,000

Figure 4: Examples of groundings resulting in oil spills

Moreover, while not resulting from an incident involving a
ship, the BP Deepwater oil rig accident in the Gulf of
Mexico resulted in excess of 500,000 tonnes of oil
escaping. As the Norwegian authorities seemed to struggle
to deal with such a comparatively small quantity of oil, how
would they have coped with some of the far greater oil
spills that have been inflicted on other nations?

2: The MV 'Full City' Incident – Norway's Worst Ever Oil Spill – Jon Sigurd Jacobsen

Was the incident preventable?

'The captain is ultimately responsible, under the law, for all aspects of operation such as the safe navigation of the ship.' – (Aragon & Messner, 2001).

Captain Zong Aming was reported to have retired to his cabin prior to the incident, leaving Oilanng Lu on duty as the officer of the watch. This was one of a number of key factors which undoubtedly contributed to the incident.

- The Captain ignored warnings not to anchor too close to the shore as gale force or even storm force winds were forecast.

- The officer of the watch, Oilanng Lu, was undertaking this duty for the very first time. Consequently, he would not have had first-hand experience of being in charge of the watch while dealing with weather of the ferocity encountered, even while at anchor.

- From the time the *Full City* slipped its anchor to the arrival of the captain on the bridge was a full 18 min. Given the circumstances, this represents either a breakdown in on-board communication, a general absence of urgency displayed on the part of the captain and the officer of the watch or a lack of appreciation of the seriousness of the situation.

- While it is true to say that the breaking off of the anchor fluke was an unexpected event, the captain's responsibility for the safety of his ship and crew under international maritime law is clear. Moreover, had he taken local advice and anchored the ship further from the shore, maybe there would have been sufficient time to avoid running aground.

2: The MV 'Full City' Incident – Norway's Worst Ever Oil Spill – Jon Sigurd Jacobsen

What went well

- Although the YARA fertiliser shipment to Guatemala was delayed by the grounding of the *Full City*, the company simply organised a replacement vessel.
- Swift support from the international community to assist with the environmental clean-up. Without it Norway would have struggled.
- The initial damage limitation phase (preventing as much oil as possible coming ashore) was completed within the first two weeks.
- The majority of the fuel oil was pumped out of the *Full City*, preventing further contamination.

What could have been done better

- Every organisation involved seemed to work to its own agenda, often appearing to be unaware of how others were functioning and in what way they should interface with each other.
- Absence of respect for the chain of command.
- Animal/bird rehabilitation was not part of the official response plan.
- The local volunteers lacked experience particularly regarding the handling of wildlife.

What did not go well

- Media communications were badly managed with mixed messages being broadcast and inappropriate levels of expectations being set.

- Local authorities' response plans proved inadequate and out of date while testing and training of personnel proved ineffective.

- The clean-up of the coastline proved more complicated and more expensive than expected. Allowances had not been made for winter weather conditions and limited daylight hours.

- When inclement weather is forecast, the coastal directorate should have the authority to enforce ships anchoring too close to shore to relocate to a safer distance.

Other observations

- YARA's route to market from Porsgrunn passes through the port of Herøya. A serious incident in the port such as a protracted strike could cripple its supply chain.

Conclusion

In some ways, Norway was quite fortunate; compared with other sea based oil spills, this was not a major league catastrophe. The *Full City* was a comparatively small cargo ship rather than an oil tanker carrying hundreds of thousands of tonnes of petroleum products. Furthermore, the proximity of the oil spill to a populated area with relatively good infrastructure made the clean-up operation a lot easier that it might have been. Had the disaster occurred in a more remote and less accessible part of the Norwegian coast, far greater challenges would have presented themselves.

Maybe Norway has just been unlucky, but four oil spills in a five year period would suggest that the writing is on the wall. It is only a question of when and where a similar and perhaps more devastating event will occur next. With that in mind, the Norwegian government should take steps to prepare their response. Appropriate training programmes should be introduced to improve response to both environmental clean-up operations and wildlife rescue endeavours, and a national level response plan should be developed and suitably validated to deal with similar emergencies in the future.

CHAPTER 3: BARINGS BANK COLLAPSE – OWEN GREGORY

This study analyses the collapse of Barings Bank and will demonstrate both the failure of internal controls and the problems initiated by deregulation within the financial industry. The infamous failure of the bank in 1995 was by no means the first time it had courted disaster.

In 1762 Francis Baring established a merchant bank in Mincing Lane, in the City of London, trading in cochineal, copper and diamonds. Barings Bank also became an 'acceptance house', guaranteeing the supplier would be paid by the buyer through the provision of Bills of Exchange.

After surviving near financial disaster in 1774 and 1787 Barings grew to become one of the finest merchant banks in Europe, even helping to broker the Louisiana Purchase in 1802. In 1890, however, a scheme involving buying large sums of Argentinian debt went badly wrong when the Revolución del Parque caused the South American country to default on its payments, and lack of confidence in Barings almost caused its foreclosure.

'There was no getting away from the almost unthinkable consequences if Barings did go down, not only would the failure of the City's leading acceptance house inevitably bring down a host of other firms, including all the discount houses, but the very status of the bill on London would be threatened, and thus the pre-eminence of the City as an international financial centre.' – David Kynaston (Fay, 1996, p. 11).

Barings was saved by the intervention of the Governor of the Bank of England, William Lidderdale. This earlier event provides a useful insight into the events that caused the collapse of Barings some 105 years later – the Barings collapse of 1995 started with a 'Big Bang' and ended with an earthquake.

Big Bang Day

27 October 1986 was named 'Big Bang Day' in the City of London, because the deregulation of the financial markets on that day affected almost every financial institution. The deregulation ended the role of the specialist financial institutions that concentrated on specific tasks in the financial system and would:

> '. . . *allow for the existence of financial institutions that could engage in a wide variety of activities and in a variety of types of markets, thus having a much greater customer appeal than that hitherto associated with small niche players such as Barings.'* – (Stein, 2000, p. 1217).

At the time of the Big Bang Day, the author was working as an IT developer for Union Discount Company of London Limited (Union). From his first-hand experience, he recalls that the level of reporting insisted upon by the regulatory authorities increased hugely. An automation of risk reporting from organisations was required to allow membership of the deregulated institutions. In line with this, Union was required to create near real-time reporting as part of the regulatory controls. This constituted a method of electronic transfer for risk and exposure measurements which were electronically sent to the regulators on a frequent basis throughout the trading day.

The information in the new exposure-control system was also to be monitored within the organisation to ensure that no exceptional risks were attributable to trading. This included exposure in positions taken in all trading including the derivatives market. The system seemed to be sound as, although companies recorded losses and gains in their year-end statements, nothing untoward really occurred that would worry the financial regulators of the institutions in the City.

In July 1989 Baring Securities employed a new member of the back office staff, settling futures and options contracts. His name was Nick Leeson. In early 1992 Leeson was given the opportunity to manage the Baring Securities back office in Singapore despite wild excesses outside of work, as he impressed bosses at the bank with his diligence.

Soon after his arrival in Singapore Leeson requested that the company should apply for him to be licensed as a front office derivatives trader as well. The majority of Leeson's trading took place on the Nikkei-225 stock market using a technique called arbitraging, which involves taking advantage of the difference in prices by buying contracts listed on one exchange (e.g. Osaka Securities Exchange) and selling them on another (e.g. the Singapore Monetary Exchange). This method reduces the risk of encountering large losses in a single position. It is also known as hedging. One such gamble on the Nikkei-225 allegedly earned Barings US$150 million in the final quarter of 1994.

On the 23 January 1995 the Kobe earthquake occurred while Leeson was in a derivatives position that required the market to remain in the 18,500-19,500 range. The Tokyo stock market fell 1,000 points to under 17,800 and in attempts to redeem his positions Leeson:

'. . . *went on a massive buying spree in the hope that it would push up the Nikkei futures market, but to no avail. Leeson's huge losses seem to have arisen as a result of his failure to hedge his positions. Instead, gambling on a rise in the Nikkei-225 stock market average. . .when the nature and scale of his operations became known, he had incurred a loss of nearly £1 billion, which exceeded the bank's capital.*' – (Bhalla, 1995, p. 660).

On 28 February 1995 Peter Baring observed that while the arbitraging continued, '*It was in principle a low-risk business.*' The management of the risk associated with a single operative having both dealing and settlement capabilities did nothing to control trading risk, however – in fact it generated a risk for which no control was in place.

James Bax, a director of Barings Singapore, warned London in March 1992, shortly after Leeson was granted the dealing license, that:

'*We are setting up a structure which will subsequently prove disastrous.*' (Bhalla, 1995, p. 660).

It was management failure that did not terminate the risk. The failure of information systems and reporting is also to be blamed for an unacceptable trading position not to be recognised. The Barings directors claimed that Leeson withheld information by posting losses to a 'settlement errors account', number 88888 – but any true consolidation of the Singapore accounts should have included account 88888 in its calculation and allowed immediate treatment of the situation.

This shortfall in the reporting information displays a lack of accountability, supervision and control. In October 1993

Peter Baring had noted that, *'derivatives need to be well controlled and understood'* – clearly the intent was unmatched by the control.

Year end 1994 saw Leeson reporting a £102 million profit to the British tax authorities although in reality he had cost the bank £200 million. Had Barings been aware of the true extent of its exposure, the subsequent collapse may well have been avoided as the bank still had around £350 million of capital.

It seems highly likely that deregulation resulted in a greater level of stress being generated, furthering the drive for the production of profits for investors and greater dividends for shareholders. Bonus payments were also tied to the performance of the banking departments and, for the purpose of profit-making, increasing the risk in trading was regarded as the norm. Baring's risk taking, especially in the case of the Singapore operation, was a case that quickly went out of control with devastating effects. The Bank of England refused to bail out Barings, as it had done 105 years before.

Barings was declared insolvent on 26 February 1995, and KPMG were appointed as administrators. At the same time, the Bank of England commenced its own investigation and their findings were published in July of the same year. Lord Bruce of Donington remarked that:

> *'Barings' collapse was due to the unauthorised and ultimately catastrophic activities of, it appears, one individual (Leeson) that went undetected as a consequence of a failure of management and other internal controls of the most basic kind. . . . . Management teams have a duty to understand fully the businesses they manage.'* – Lord Bruce of Donington (Hansard, 1995).

The majority of Barings Bank was sold to ING, a Dutch financial group, for £1 sterling and over 200 years of banking history was ended.

With the benefit of hindsight, a number of commentators and, indeed, Leeson himself, credited much of the responsibility and autonomy that he attained on the bank's own inadequate internal risk management practices. Those who raised concerns about his status and modus operandi were invariably ignored.

Lessons learned

The lessons that can be taken from the collapse of Barings can primarily be sub-divided into three factors – human, operational and technical failings. The **human factors** that were prevailing and contributed towards the situation included:

- Post-deregulation opportunity for higher earnings, in a growing market, for successful job candidates.
- Success of individuals in gaining profit for organisation increased personal bonus prospects (bonus related to profitability), leading to a trading risk increase.
- Demand from investors to receive greater returns in deregulated trading.
- Fast moving jobs market led to employees 'jumping ship' for better opportunities to earn.
- Loss of knowledge base as employees moved to other opportunities.

From an **operational** perspective the following observations were made:

- Growth of organisations operating in the City of London stretched the regulatory capabilities of the Bank of England.

- Survival-of-the-fittest mentality, defining successful organisations as those able to produce returns and quickly adjust to the change in the market conditions.

- Mergers, take-overs and acquisitions rife.

- Evolving market requiring changes to the method of operations.

- New investment types requiring new risk and control methods.

- Globalisation permitting round the clock operations, requirement for subsidiary organisations to be geographically distributed.

- Globalisation leading to geographically distant events affecting performance of local markets away from the event origin.

- Allowing the same individual to deal and settle trades; including the rejection of a director's concern over such.

- Rejection of internal audit reports.

- Manager of the derivative business based in London while trading carried out in Singapore.

- Removal of restrictive practices leading to additional competitiveness and subsequent greater risk taking in a newly overcrowded market.

- Pressure from increasing numbers of foreign banks needing a presence in the London market.

- Movement out of historically 'niche' markets into new investment types – leading to companies operating outside of their 'comfort zone' and expertise.

- Risks of external influence on the markets not anticipated.

Finally, the following **technical** observations were made:

- Increasing use of, and dependence on, information technology – still then an emerging technology.
- Evolving markets needing evolving information systems – markets growing faster than the control capabilities.
- Capability to hide true positions on a trading account from management.

What could have been done better

- Senior management did not heed warnings about the introduction of new risks.
- Failure of reporting meant that they not recognise the serious financial trouble the bank was in. Had they been made aware at year end 1994, they could have acted to prevent a collapse.

What did not go well

- Deregulation, combined with financial incentives for risky behaviour, made a disaster more likely.
- The internal risk management practices at Barings proved completely inadequate.

Conclusion

The analysis of risk, and any mitigation of the risks that can be identified, is the primary function involved in either business continuity management or emergency planning.

In the case study above the absence of levels of risk management either caused or increased the impact of the particular event.

Barings Bank collapsed due to a risk introduced by the management of the company. Despite warnings from a local director in Singapore three years prior to the eventual demise of Barings, no actions were taken to treat or terminate the risk. In this case the blame must lie with poor management, creating a situation that would eventually cause the downfall of a respected banking institution. Nick Leeson was provided with the means to adversely affect the operation of the bank and did so with disastrous consequences.

The conclusion is that risks must be constantly monitored to ensure that the correct actions can be carried out for their immediate mitigation. As part of risk mitigation a sound business continuity plan, emergency plan or combination of the two must be in place to cover both the public and private interests as necessary.

CHAPTER 4: NORTHGATE INFORMATION SOLUTIONS, A VICTIM OF THE BUNCEFIELD OIL DEPOT DISASTER – ROBERT CLARK

'No one lost their life because of the Buncefield explosion. But many people lost the lives they had before it happened.' – Jacqui Campbell.

In December 2005, the Maylands Industrial Estate at Buncefield near Hemel Hempstead in the UK housed some 630 businesses employing over 16,000 people. Located on the estate and positioned next to the Hertfordshire Oil Storage Limited (HOSL) was Northgate Information Solutions' head office. It processed the payroll systems that paid approximately one in every three UK employees. It also provided other IT services to clients including local authorities, the British Labour Party and commercial organisations such as Tesco and Manchester United Football Club. Any failure of service delivery to its clients was considered unacceptable.

The fifth largest oil storage depot in the UK, HOSL, or Buncefield as it was often referred to, had a capacity of 60 million gallons (273 million litres). Operated by Total, it was linked by pipeline to other oil depots and refineries. It stored oil based products including petrol and kerosene, the latter being used to supply regional airports. Heathrow Airport, in fact, depended upon Buncefield for 50% of its daily intake of aviation fuel.

During the evening of Saturday 10 December 2005, an operation started to transfer unleaded fuel to Buncefield Tank 912 via the Thames/Kingsbury pipeline at a rate of around 550 m³/h. From approximately 3:00 am onward on

11 December, the gauge recording the level in the tank did not change. It is estimated that around 5:20 am the tank had reached its capacity and began to overflow. The safety system in place to shut off supply and avoid overfilling failed and the pumping operation continued. Moreover, between 5:50 am and 6:00 am, the pumping rate actually increased to 890 m^3/h. The inevitable combination of the fuel and air resulted in a combustible mixture being created. This finally ignited at 6:01 am causing a series of explosions and fires which subsequently destroyed the oil depot while also resulting in serious damage to neighbouring Maylands Industrial Estate.

The resulting disaster is estimated to have cost in excess of £1 billion. Among the first firemen to arrive was Sub Officer Jon Batchelor who quickly declared the scene a major incident. It was probably the biggest fire in Europe since World War II and the largest of the explosions registered at 2.4 on the Richter scale. Amazingly no one was killed but 43 people were injured and widespread damage was caused to nearby homes and businesses. Several large businesses were affected by the incident including Fujifilm, ASOS and DSG. Others that were not physically damaged went bankrupt because they were located in the exclusion zone imposed around Buncefield by the emergency services and were unable to operate. Twelve months later, the redundancy count at the Mayfield Industrial Estate directly attributed to the disaster had reached 900.

In the middle of this destruction was the now decimated Northgate Information Solutions head office. It was extremely fortuitous that only four members of staff had been in the building instead of the 500 plus employees who were based there during the working week.

4: Northgate Information Solutions, a Victim of the Buncefield Oil Depot Disaster – Robert Clark

More than 2,000 local residents were evacuated and local roads and motorways were closed along with many local schools, as fears about the potentially harmful effects of the smoke increased. With 50% of its daily fuel supply cut off, Heathrow Airport had to ration supplies to aircraft. Some aircraft were diverted to Stansted or other European destinations while short haul flights were asked to refuel before arriving at Heathrow.

Despite an al-Qaeda threat against oil refineries and storage depots issued only four days prior to the Buncefield disaster, a 9/11 style plane crash or a conventional terrorist attack was ruled out very early in the investigation. The official inquiry's final report endeavours to explain why the petrol transfer operation was not halted when the receiving tank had reached capacity. Volume two of the final report describes how the Supervisory Control and Data Acquisition system (SCADA) should have turned off the petrol flow, although it acknowledged that local controls can override this'. Nowhere in the report can any reference be found to the possibility of a cyber attack being considered as the primary cause of the overflow. Prior to Buncefield, several incidents had occurred which have been referred to as cyber physical events. Some resulted in the actual destruction of oil and gas pipelines. Reports of compromised SCADA systems now abound including the very high profile Stuxnet attack on the Iranian nuclear programme. Furthermore, some six years after Buncefield Shell IT Manager Ludolf Luemann warned of the danger of cyber attacks on the oil industry, remarking that:

> *'If anybody gets into the area where you can control opening and closing of valves, or release valves, you can imagine what happens. It will cost lives and it will cost production, it will cost money, cause fires*

*and cause loss of containment, environmental
damage – huge, huge damage.'* – (BBC News, 2011).

Before the first explosion occurred, a vapour cloud was
seen on CCTV drifting across the adjacent industrial estate.
There were in fact several explosions but the main one was
colossal and appears to have been centred on the Northgate
car park.

The Fire Brigade treated Northgate as a separate incident
and had the explosion occurred during office hours,
extensive fatalities would have been almost inevitable. The
force of the blast was such that a fireproof safe located at
the back of the building on the second floor was recovered
from the front of the building on the ground floor. Fire and
Rescue Service crews from St Albans and Redbourn
conducted an initial search of the premises. One crewman
described the interior of the Northgate building:

*'It looked as if you had picked it up, shaken it on its
side and then put it back down very carefully.'*

Disasters do not always happen between the hours of nine to
five, from Monday to Friday, and Buncefield was no
exception. Quickly invoking its well-rehearsed recovery
plans, the Northgate crisis management team met within three
hours of the disaster and immediately activated their data
centre fall-back contract with SunGard, who offer managed
recovery services. Client data was retrieved from the secure
storage facility and restored to the SunGard servers.

Northgate's reaction

With many of Northgate's client systems being payroll,
recovery priorities needed to be set keeping in mind that, by
its very nature, payroll is cyclic and recovery time

objectives will vary during that cycle. Within two days the first payroll run was successfully completed. Over 200 of Northgate's clients were directly affected and around 100 of their consultants worked around the clock in twelve-hour split shifts over a ten day period to resolve the crisis. What was also extraordinary was that during the recovery, Northgate's staff still found time to counsel concerned clients about their own contingency plans. While acknowledging the enormous staff commitment, Business Recovery Director Mark Farrington also stated:

> *'Had we lost any of the thirty core support staff that knew the systems best, we would have been stuck.'* – (Information Age, 2006).

It is not uncommon to see statements in business continuity plans which make assumptions that all of an organisation's staff will be available to support a recovery. This even fails to acknowledge legitimate absenteeism for staff holidays, sickness or for any other acceptable reason. While Northgate's reinstatement of its clients' services seemed to proceed comparatively smoothly, had the explosion occurred during office hours it is highly likely that key staff would have been injured or killed. Although comprehensive documentation was available, which is of paramount importance in a recovery, of equal import is relevant knowledge and know-how held by staff. Moreover, it is quite likely that some employees that were perhaps not physically injured would have been traumatised. In the case of the 1996 Manchester IRA bombing, some employees whose company premises were caught in the blast were reported to be still receiving trauma counselling two years later even though the entire area around the vehicle borne improvised explosive device had been evacuated before the blast. It is sensible that every business continuity plan should make provision for trauma management and counselling plus informing next of kin in the event of injuries or fatalities. Farrington also flags this point and stressed that staff welfare and counselling services should be considered as an option.

In fact, Northgate had planned and rehearsed for what they considered to be a worst case scenario – 'apocalyptic' seems an appropriate word to describe the disaster. But while their recovery might be considered textbook, in his appraisal of the recovery Farrington cited several 'lessons learned'. Of particular note are his recommendations pertaining to staff and testing for multiple scenarios that should include loss of personnel. Testing strategies should always allow for situations that include the loss of employees, which could be for any one of a number of reasons such as a fire, explosion or pandemic. Some organisations factor in succession planning when developing their testing scenarios. But to be comprehensive, a succession plan needs to look at all levels of an organisation and not just the top echelon. Somewhere in their lower ranks may exist individuals who are of key importance to that organisation. Consequently, Farrington's point about the potential impact of losing any of the core staff is well made.

Planning where to locate its staff both during and post recovery seems not to have received quite the same level of attention as the disaster recovery itself, another point not lost on Farrington. His post-disaster recommendation that adequate provisions are included in the plan to provide key staff with an alternative working location is sound. This was particularly emphasised by the fact that, seven weeks after the incident, around 10% of Northgate's staff still had not been relocated. Some employees were accommodated in hotels while others worked from home. When offices were finally located for the finance and administration staff, however, suppliers were very supportive and reacted quickly to help fit out the new premises. The goodwill built up over many years certainly paid off.

As part of any business continuity plan, it is advisable not only to identify your key members of staff, but also to understand how quickly you need to get them back to work and how you intend to achieve that. The urgency that is applied to this activity needs to be driven by the pre-determined recovery time objectives that an organisation is working towards.

The majority of the Northgate's clients' services were restored in December and 180 client payroll runs successfully transferred £1.4 billion via BACS within eight days of the disaster. The incident also disrupted Addenbrooke's Hospital in Cambridge as Northgate supported the system used for patient admissions and discharges. Fortunately, the hospital had contingency plans in place and switched over to a manual system. That said, it should be appreciated that as a first responder the hospital is regulated by the UK Civil Contingencies Act 2004 and must have a valid business continuity plan in place.

As part of building a resilient IT capability, Northgate had invested heavily in redundancy including an in-house high availability solution. This was supported by dual backup generators plus an uninterruptable power supply and three internet service providers. Northgate's data centre plus its in-house redundancy was destroyed in the carnage along with its entire desktop environment. Also destroyed were voice and data communications, including the call centre for which no redundancy arrangements had been made.

4: Northgate Information Solutions, a Victim of the Buncefield Oil Depot Disaster – Robert Clark

Having a dependable fall-back partner already in place was a crucial aspect of the business continuity strategy. In this respect Farrington recognises SunGard's significant contribution, referring them as a *'reliable and capable recovery partner.'* CEO Chris Stone echoed these sentiments and said that SunGard had *'acted in an exemplary fashion.'* What is not clear is how efficiently and effectively the desktop environment was recovered, particularly as the workforce was initially rehoused using multiple sites, including some staff being based at home.

Farrington points out that recovery plans may just assume that only one client or one system has been affected by an incident. But in Northgate's experience, everything needed to be recovered. While recovery time objectives for restoring an individual client or system may be achievable, meeting a combination of similar or even identical objectives may prove impossible if there are insufficient numbers of skilled employees available to accomplish this. It is conceivable that more staff may be required than for normal business operations if recovery time objectives are to be met.

The recovery of data by Northgate was hampered as the overnight backups created immediately before the blast were lost. They were not due to be removed to an off-site storage facility until one hour after the explosion occurred. No explanation could be found in terms of how this data was subsequently recovered – one can only assume that it was. Nevertheless, given the circumstances, it appears that there was really very little Northgate could have done that would have mitigated this situation short of having previously adopted a potentially expensive mirroring solution as part of a data management strategy.

The only serious technical issue identified was the time needed to restore full connectivity. Northgate's three suppliers, BT, NEOS Networks and Cable & Wireless, struggled to quickly restore a comparable level of service to the SunGard site. Although most clients' systems were live again within a few days of the explosion, one month on only 50% of Clients had had their telecoms restored to the pre-disaster level. Even so, it is unclear how long it took to restore the status quo, but we do know it took more than a month. Had a testing exercise with suppliers included a scenario for redirecting connectivity, it may have provided Northgate with early warning of the probable elapsed time issues that they ultimately experienced. Nevertheless, the cost of such a test may well have been considered prohibitive. The only potential solution to this is to 'pre-wire' a warm or hot standby site. This is something that would need to be considered as part of the business continuity budget at Northgate's disposal. Farrington's telecoms concern was shared by CEO Chris Stone.

When reviewing the recovery progress made by 2007, Northgate CIO John Lockett summed it up by saying:

> *'The situation Northgate is in now is one where the company has come out of a spell in intensive care, is out of hospital and is recuperating.'* – (Lockett, 2007)

Farrington also recorded eleven other aspects of the overall activity that worked extremely well during the recovery. He specifically felt that the *'Business Continuity, Disaster Recovery and Crisis Management plans and their rehearsal were invaluable.'* After normal resumption of operations, they took the lessons learned from Buncefield and revisited the business continuity plans for their other sites. Moreover, Northgate remained vigilant throughout the recovery period. Penetration testing of the restored systems continued on a 'business as usual' basis to guard against any opportunist cyber attacks. What remained of their Buncefield premises was protected 24/7 to facilitate salvage of all surviving key assets while discouraging any would-be 'disaster tourists'.

Communications

During the recovery, communications were quite correctly seen to be of vital importance. This was a multi-faceted exercise. Northgate quickly issued a statement to the City aimed at reassuring stakeholders and the financial markets. Moreover, an 0800 number phone line was set to communicate the message of the day. Northgate's CEO Chris Stone made videos to communicate with the staff although it is not clear how these were distributed and viewed. Account managers were responsible for appraising clients. With all their careful business continuity preparation it is perhaps astonishing that Northgate had not created a communications plan in advance of any possible disaster.

'Four hostile newspapers are more to be feared than a thousand bayonets.' – Napoleon Bonaparte.

One of the most critical aspects of communication during a disaster is addressing the media. A wrong word here or there can make a substantial difference as to how the story is reported or what messages are sent out. In the case of the 2010 Deepwater Horizon oil spill in the Gulf of Mexico, BP's CEO Tony Hayward said on camera that *'I'd like my life back'*. The incident had claimed eleven lives and Hayward's remarks were nothing short of a public relations disaster. Little evidence can be found of how well Northgate performed in front of the media. It must be remembered, though, that the plight of this one company was undoubtedly very much overshadowed by the scale of the overall disaster. Northgate to all intents and purposes was a comparatively small disaster within a far bigger disaster. Conversely, HOSL received praise for responding quickly to support those affected by the incident as a goodwill gesture. They provided a round-the-clock counselling service, funding for voluntary organisations that were helping the local Buncefield residents, and organised emergency repair work for properties damaged by the blast.

Recovery of the Year

As for Northgate's clients, it was reassuring to learn that at least Addenbrooke's Hospital did not rely solely on Northgate for its patient system and had taken ownership of appropriate manual contingency measures. Since other clients were seeking contingency related advice from Northgate, however, it can only be assumed that they were not so well prepared in this respect.

In all, more than half the 630 businesses on the Mayfield Industrial Estate were disrupted by finding themselves inside the initial exclusion zone. A total of six buildings on the estate, including Northgate's, were condemned and subsequently demolished. A further 30 needed major repairs to be undertaken before they could be reoccupied. It was not possible to quantify the knock-on effect that the disaster would have on the supply chain although it was estimated the estate's contribution towards the regional GDP was around 2%. Five weeks on, 88 businesses had still not been able to return to their premises.

The disaster resulted in thousands of insurance claims of which 749 were business related and over 3,000 were raised by individuals. Northgate's own financial liability was limited by its insurance cover which included business interruption insurance, building contents and cover for the head office building itself. The company set up a team to handle the claim for losing its head office building and, along with the emergency services and local authorities, Farrington stated that Northgate enjoyed a *'terrific response'* from the insurers. By May 2006 the insurers had agreed to write a cheque to the value of £30 million to cover the cost of constructing a new head office.

It would be difficult to argue that the oil industry's safety track record is an impressive one. Far from it! Being located close to an oil depot or an oil refinery is not good news as it only serves to increase the threat profile that an organisation is facing. Despite the claims of Chris Hunt, Director General of the UK Petroleum Industry Association, the Buncefield disaster was not unprecedented. There had been similar incidents at Newark, New Jersey in 1984, St Herblain, France, and Naples, Italy in 1995 . Moreover, in another case of overfilling by BP in Texas in 2005, 15 fatalities resulted. What was unique about Buncefield was the scale of disaster.

What Northgate was confronted with on that December morning was almost as close to a worst case scenario as one could get. Without question, its staff magnificently rose to the challenge they were presented with. So, when the 2006 Business Continuity Awards were announced, Northgate's achievement was appropriately recognised when it received the accolade of 'Most Effective Recovery of the Year'. This was well deserved and the recognition received should act as a lesson and inspiration to other, less prepared organisations.

There is no question that Northgate and its staff should be immensely proud of what they achieved. A job very well done. But while not wishing to take anything away from what was accomplished, is this really a good example of a textbook business continuity case study? When you consider the acknowledged shortcomings in Northgate's plans, the whole exercise appears to have been an IT-driven rather than a business-driven recovery. In other words, was it the tail that was wagging the dog? Without question, the IT disaster recovery element of the activity went remarkably well and the commitment to testing and exercising clearly paid off. But the recovery of Northgate's actual business including the relocation of the staff seemed to be made up as they went along.

What is particularly obvious was that Northgate took its responsibilities as an IS supplier very seriously along with its obligation to its clients. This commitment was reflected by client confidence in Northgate. While it lost two small accounts immediately after Buncefield, by way of compensation it won around £100 million worth of new contracts.

Lessons learned

Buncefield was registered as a hazardous site and was subject to the Health and Safety Executive's Control of Major Accident Hazards (COMAH) regulations. One must question the wisdom of siting either commercial or domestic premises near to COMAH sites because of the greater risk this presents to the properties and their inhabitants. Moreover, the increased risk will invariably not go unnoticed by insurers and will usually be reflected by increased premiums. Planning authorities would be wise to take account of this and resist the development of land in close proximity to such hazardous sites. Northgate quickly took note following the disaster and, while still located in Hemel Hempstead, the new head office is now almost one mile (1.6 km) away from Buncefield.

What went well

- The immediate reaction of the Northgate crisis management team, initiating the recovery process within three hours on a non-working day, was impressive. Even CIO John Lockett, who was holidaying in Brazil, had joined the CMT within 24 h.

- The gargantuan commitment from staff.

- The IT disaster recovery aspect of the operation went exceptionally well, with the first client payroll run completed within 48 h. The company acknowledge that regular testing of the plan had certainly helped raise the level of awareness and competence amongst employees.

- Northgate had clearly recognised that it was necessary to complement their on-site ICT capability, including the in-house redundancy, with the extra layer of resilience that SunGard offered. The company found SunGard to be '*a reliable recovery partner*'.

- Data backups were kept in a secure, off-site location thereby facilitating a fast recovery.

- The '*terrific response*' from the emergency services, local authorities and Northgate's insurers. It is said that you find out how good your insurer is when you need to make a claim. Clearly, Northgate had chosen well.

- Northgate's reputation as an IS supplier remained intact. Not only did all but two (small) clients demonstrate their confidence by remaining with the company, but an extra £100 million worth of additional contracts was won shortly afterwards.

- The continued level of vigilance for both information security and physical security to deter hackers and would-be disaster tourists.

- At least one of Northgate's clients, Addenbrooke's Hospital, recognised its obligation to maintain accountability for its business continuity arrangements and successfully activated its contingency plans.

What could have been done better

- The communications plan was a case of 'it will be alright on the night' as no preparation had been done prior to the disaster. Even so, the information available pertaining to Northgate's performance in this respect would suggest that they did a good job.

- No provision had been included in the plan to address any staff losses. Only the timing of the event saved Northgate from a potentially catastrophic loss of life which may have robbed it of the key employees needed for the recovery.

- Clearly defined roles and responsibilities need to be in place before a disaster with appropriate levels of governance.

- Methods to address employee welfare issues and trauma counselling should be an integral part of the plan.

- Testing should accommodate multiple-scenario situations rather than single events. In the case of Northgate, everything needed to be recovered.

What did not go well

- The re-establishment of the pre-disaster level of online service to clients took well over a month despite the involvement of three ISPs.

- The relocation of Northgate's employees seemed very ad-hoc with the plan being made up after the catastrophe occurred. This resulted in some employees having to wait weeks to be relocated. While the company strived to meet the recovery time objectives for ICT, the recovery of the non-ICT aspects of the business were just not in sync.

- There was no backup in place for voice and data communications.

Other observations

- The creation of an exclusion zone is done at the discretion of the emergency services. They decide how big the zone should be and when the restrictions can be lifted. Businesses untouched by the explosion went bankrupt as they found themselves within the exclusion zone and had no plans for dealing with such a scenario. Exclusions zones may last for just a few hours or for a few days. In the case of the 1996 Manchester bombing, an exclusion zone was in place for several weeks.

- Northgate acted upon lessons learned and ensured they were reflected in the plans for all of its premises.

- Locating a business close to a COMAH site brings with it additional risks to both business and employees and may attract higher insurance premiums.

Conclusion

Perhaps the summary of this major incident is best left to the Business Continuity Institute's Technical Director, Lyndon Bird. He observed that the incident happened at the most inopportune time when demand for oil based products traditionally peaks. It is perhaps disappointing that he makes no mention of the potential human tragedy that could have unfolded had the timing of the event been different. Should the explosion have occurred during the working week, the fatality count could have been appalling in Northgate alone. One can only speculate how much more difficult their recovery would have been had key staff been lost. Byrd adds that:

'It [Buncefield] provides more messages and lessons than all the other annual incidents put together. This is what Business Continuity is all about.'

Northgate's recovery was solid, and allowed the company to survive the disaster. In one sense they were lucky, however, because their recovery plans did not fully take into account areas other than IT. The risk to life posed by the massive oil facility in the area was not factored into the plans, nor was the need to communicate effectively with the media. Fortunately, the company has survived and used the Buncefield incident to hone their response while taking positive steps to reduce the potential for disaster, for example by moving their headquarters. They have rebalanced and improved their recovery approach by giving greater consideration to the areas where they were weakest.

CHAPTER 5: THE LOVE PARADE: DUSSELDORF
2010 – TONY DUNCAN

'An event where people wanted to party, dance and have fun, turned into a terrible tragedy.' – Horst Bien, Duisburg's Chief Prosecutor, 2014.

The Love Parade was a free-to-attend music festival that originated in Berlin in 1989, where it was held annually until 2003. In 2007, the Love Parade was moved to the Ruhr, approximately 330 miles west of the German capital, and hosted by the city of Essen, attracting a crowd of 500,000. The following year it moved to the Ruhr city of Dortmund where an even larger crowd of around 1.6 million attended. In 2009, the Love Parade was planned to be held in Bochum but was cancelled over safety fears.

In 2010 the event was held in a disused railway freight yard in the German city of Duisburg on 24th July. This study reflects on the resulting disaster that occurred at the event culminating in the deaths of 21 people, injuring approximately 500.

Rainer Schaller created Lopavent to take over and run the Love Parade in 2006, paying a reported €3,000,000. He initially saw this as a massive advertising platform for his McFit gymnasium chain; by 2010 in Duisburg, however, there were 40 sponsored floats at the Love Parade of which McFit took just two.

Duisburg 2010

Along with its close neighbour Essen, Duisburg was nominated as a City of Culture for 2010 and came under pressure to host the parade. City Mayor Adolf Sauerland said:

'We want the Love Parade and will do everything in our power to host it. The party will not be cancelled by us.'

The Love Parade organisers, Lopavent, were granted a permit for a crowd capacity of 250,000. Planning for the ingress and egress of such large numbers for this event proved difficult. Consequently, it was decided after several multi-agency planning meetings to incorporate a dual purpose ingress/egress method. The access control facilities would be opened and closed to facilitate the ingress and egress of patrons from the site. The ingress point was also the main egress point. There was a secondary, egress only ramp to the side of the main ramp. This does not appear to have been well signposted and did not perform as expected.

'The Duisburg police and fire departments registered their discomfort with the plan. But at a July 15 meeting with all those involved in granting the permit, nobody spoke up. Five days later, however, the police voiced concern as to how access routes might be affected should the event site become full.' – (Becker, et al., 2010).

Despite several pre-event statements from Lopavent that the expected crowd would not, at any time, exceed the permitted capacity of 250,000, the organisers estimated that the event drew approximately 1.4 million people. This figure was later challenged by Ramon van de Maat, a Duisburg police spokesman:

'It would have been impossible for so many people to get to the city in such a short timeframe with the

*transport options available. And there wasn't
enough space at the freight station to accommodate
such a crowd.'* – (Diehl, et al., 2010, p. 4).

The venue was situated on the other side of town from the
train station, in an effort to stagger visitors' arrival. Even
so, the rate of build-up of attendees was far more than
expected. The police and security agencies closed the main
ingress/egress point and formed barricades to regulate
pedestrian movement with the intent of reducing this initial
pressure. Despite this, a critical mass crowd formed in the
tunnel and surrounding areas between 13:00 and 15:00
ultimately resulting in a stampede.

Pre-event issues – contingency, safety and security planning

There were several multi-agency planning meetings along
with site visits. These meetings were well attended by
representatives of the city, event organisers, emergency
services and security providers for the event, along with
relevant experts in crowd management, police and fire
safety officers.

Event planning meetings were addressed by all the involved
parties but concerns over ingress and egress plans from
various agencies were either not well publicised or ignored.
A senior police officer from the city of Köln (Cologne) who
inspected the Duisburg site ahead of the festival told the
Express newspaper:

*'There were 12 to 13 inspections. And every time we
went there we agreed that the plan would result in
chaos, that people would be injured and killed. But
the warnings had been ignored. We were always*

told that this wasn't up for discussion. The city administration was adamant that the Love Parade must go ahead.'

Some reports indicated that the expected attendance would be well in excess of the permitted 250,000 but no real contingency planning to address this possibility was evident.

'Due to the late approval of the event, the security concept may have been finished 'last minute'. The likely consequence is that contingency plans may not have been sufficient and could not have been exercised enough. There was probably not enough time to ensure good coordination between organisers and police force.' – (Helbing & Mukerji, 2012).

The data in *Figure 5* was provided by the event organisers but should be treated with a degree of caution as entry to the events was free. It originated from very modest beginnings in 1989 when there were less than 200 attendees. Even so, the figures suggest that it was extremely unlikely that the participants would be as low as 250,000.

There were no events held in 2004, 2005 or 2009.

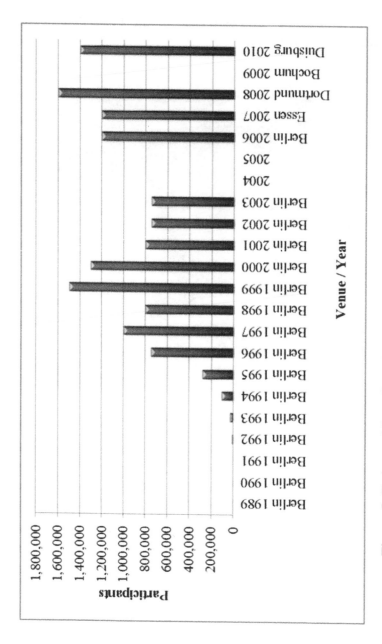

Figure 5: Estimated Love Parade attendances 1989–2010 Incident timeline

Figure 6, below, shows a map of the Love Parade arena during the 2010 event.

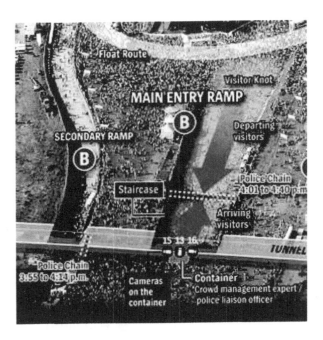

Figure 6: Map of Love Parade arena

There are a number of accounts in the public domain of what exactly happened and when. This has led to slight variations in the actual timings reported. Therefore, the times shown in *Figure 7* should be regarded as approximate.

TIME	DETAIL
~11:00	Crowd density and pedestrian arrival rates build up from an early stage with gate opening times being

	delayed for approximately one hour due to essential maintenance work being carried out on the site. The west side of the tunnel systems shows signs of extreme congestion and instances of aggression were reported by security staff.
12:02	Event access control facilities opened (delayed from 11:00).
13:00	Crowds build up and congestion continues, prompting the event's crowd management expert, Carsten Walter, to order the partial closure of 10 out of 16 gates. Crowd pressure initially eases but a failure of communication sees the police commander order the reopening of these gates, resulting in the ingress crowd surge.
14:00	The event officially starts and there is a change in shift for police. Another officer replaces the liaison officer assigned to Carsten Walters.
14:30	Police liaison officer and Carsten Walters try, without success, to contact the police commander for assistance and clarification of orders. It takes a further 45 min for the police commander to be in direct contact with the crowd management expert.
15:55	Police commander orders the formation of three separate police chains – one in each of the east and west tunnels and one on the ingress/egress point. This results in a further increase of egressing patrons on the site side of the police chain as well as a build-up of crowd mass within the tunnels due to continuing arrivals and static queues.
16:30	The crowd has become a critical mass and visitors in tunnel start panicking and screaming for help.

16:35	The crowd rushes towards the open access points, causing a stampede resulting in 21 fatalities and approximately 500 injured persons.
17:15	The Duisburg City operations room appears blissfully unaware of the unfolding crisis and believes the Love Parade a big success.
18:00	Organisers decide not to stop the event in case a mass exodus causes more difficulties.

Figure 7: Love Parade timeline

Risk management

> 'The making of the Love Parade 2010 tragedy began, not at the festival's tunnel entrance, but with the risk assessment and crowd management for the event many months before. And if there was one monumental error that set this tragedy in motion, it was arguably the outrageous miscalculation of the anticipated festival attendance by Rainer Schaller's (Lopavent) festival organization.' – (Crowd Management Strategies, 2010).

It is not known which model the risk manager used to assess the event. A key parameter for crowd management risk assessments is a reasonably accurate estimate for the crowd size. Even if the average of the Essen and Dortmund events had been used, the estimated crowd size would have been closer to one million. By starting with a substantially flawed estimate, the risk assessment conclusions were always going to be unsound.

Without a tenable foundation to work from, neither the organisers nor public safety agencies had any chance of creating a viable safety plan for the event. This also applies to suitable emergency and contingency plans. Furthermore, with the formal approval and sign-off being given so close to the proposed date, there was little opportunity to rehearse and exercise the plans.

'From this one unbelievable error in planning, Love Parade 2010 was set on its tragic course.' – (Crowd Management Strategies, 2010).

The probability, consequences and manageability of all aspects of the event, which ought to have been more closely examined, would have been:

• The arrival, ingress, and egress of visitors to the site with additional control measures being used to bring the residual risk down to acceptable levels.

• Implications and control measures for the increase in capacity relative to the site capacity calculation.

Professor Michael Schreckenberg, a 'local panic researcher' from the University of Duisburg-Essen whose area of responsibility is the 'Physics of Transport and Traffic', was invited to review the Love Parade arrangements. His observations and recommendations, however, appear to have been largely ignored.

'The city of Duisburg paid no attention to my advice that the tunnel should be submitted to a more detailed study.' – Michael Schreckenberg.

The risk manager needs to have taken better note of all relevant stakeholders' concerns. A primary objective of risk assessments is to identify potential threats and hazards across all the critical relationships that are necessary to successfully manage the event. It would appear that vital concerns that challenged the wisdom of holding the event were ignored.

'The police and other experts were pushed up against the wall with political pressure during the preliminary planning. Their objections and reservations weren't taken into consideration and critical voices were muzzled. The political ambition of city leaders and the economic interest of the organizer to adorn the city with such a mega event, suffocated any professional discussion over the risks.' – Konrad Freiberg, Head of the German Federal Police Union.

Government and non-governmental agency/ stakeholder engagement

The event organiser, taking the role of a non-governmental stakeholder, was able to exert a large amount of pressure on local governmental agencies to allow the event to be held. On learning that its application was being rejected due to unfiled documents, Lopavent's lawyers sent an urgent letter to the mayor's office requesting the granting of permits. They cited the potential economic and intangible damages involved for both the organiser and the city if the event was cancelled. The permits were issued to the event organiser on the 21 July 2010 – three days before the event was to take place.

'Permission would come from the city, certainly with high tax revenues and public image playing a decisive role.' – Wolfgang Sterneck, (St John, 2010).

The various stakeholders involved showed an inconsistent approach to the event, even though there were developing crowd management issues from early on in the event day. The interior minister, who was visiting the site, was told of the close cooperation of the agencies involved in the planning and implementation phases of the event. He was advised that there was no cause for concern even as reports of crowd collapses were coming in. It is not known whether communication or motivational issues were to blame for not involving this key stakeholder.

Legal aspects

> *'The organisers and politicians involved had ruthlessly disregarded the doubts and warnings raised by experts in advance of the event. . . Official permission for the Love Parade was 'unlawful' and 'should never have been granted.'* – (Henning, 2011).

The minutes of multi-agency meetings and group correspondence revealed that city officials had started the planning procedure with a strict interpretation of the laws concerning the staging of events. As planning activity continued, this interpretation was replaced by a more flexible approach. This can be seen with the calculation of both event capacity and emergency egress width that, against the advice of certain public departments, were a departure from federal German law.

By granting the permit for the event to proceed, the city was in breach of the law which stipulates how wide the escape routes need to be for such an event.

> *'For 220,000 partygoers, the escape routes should have been 440 meters wide; for 250,000, 500 meters.*

At the Duisburg site, however, the escape routes were a mere 155 meters wide.' – (Becker, et al., 2010).

What is more, allowing two large flows of people moving in opposite directions at the same time is a recipe for a disaster.

Both fire protection and Department of Public Safety experts were unanimous in that the approach to the proposed Love Parade site did not comply with existing regulations. Should an emergency occur, only a limited number of people can pass through a bottleneck such as the Duisburg tunnel. Furthermore, the tunnel was the only route available for emergency vehicles to also enter or leave the site. The general consensus of these experts was that a departure from existing laws could not be justified.

'The regulations regarding assembly sites were criminally ignored. The people who signed the approval are to blame.' – Michael Böcker, Fire Brigade Union Chairman.

Communications

The need for fast and effective communications at an event the size and significance of the Love Parade is crucial. But a number of issues were experienced with defective walkie-talkies, making event staff and police dependent upon mobile phones. To further compound matters, the local mobile networks had become overloaded and both forms of communications proved unreliable.

For large events, it was common practice for police to request a prior right of cellular radio communication from network suppliers. This was not requested, with budget constraints understood to be the key factor in the application not being made.

It also appears that the event team's police liaison officer had neither a walkie-talkie nor a mobile phone! Moreover, there was no functioning public address system or megaphones available in the area of the tunnel and ramp to communicate with the crowd.

> *'The situation in the crowd is difficult also, because no one has an overview of the scene, and the noise level (as well as the overload of the mobile phone network) make communication largely impossible.'* – (Helbing & Mukerji, 2012, p. 25).

It also transpired that some of the police radios were outdated and spare parts were unobtainable. Dead spots were commonplace and the range of the radios was often unpredictable, making it difficult to reliably reach officers in emergencies.

> *'Often officers take their private mobile because it's the only way to stay in touch. But the mobile phone network collapsed on Saturday.'* – Andreas Nowak, Police Federation North Rhine-Westphalia.

The finger of blame

Not surprisingly, no one party seemed willing to accept responsibility for the tragedy. Not the city of Duisburg – and certainly not North Rhine-Westphalia Interior Minister, Ralf Jäger.

The German Press reported that Love Parade founder DJ Dr Motte accused organisers of being only concerned with making money, and not taking responsibility for the people attending the event. In view of the economic arguments used in pressurising city officials to authorise the event, there may be substance in Motte's allegation.

As part of an interim report on the incident, commissioned by city officials, the Duisburg mayor claimed that the city had no overriding responsibility for security at the event and particularly not for the flow of visitors. Although the 32 pages of this report seem to exonerate the city, its 358 page annex section reveals that the city had approved highly questionable safety plans just three days before the event.

Finding himself under pressure in the aftermath, Duisburg City Mayor Adolf Sauerland continued to defend the event's safety plan, referring to it as *'solid'*. He was almost immediately contradicted by Ralf Jäger, Interior Minister, North Rhine-Westphalia:

> *'At no time did the security plan created by Lopavent for the event work correctly and at some point completely collapsed.'* – Ralf Jäger.

In an interim report also released by Jäger, attention was drawn to a series of failures where repeated warnings about safety and security issues had been ignored by officials.

> *'Seldom have so many experts warned so clearly of the risks of holding such a mass event on a site that was completely unsuitable.'* (Schaer & Crossland, 2010).

The Köln police force were handed responsibility for the investigation. They quickly asserted that criticism levelled at their Duisburg colleagues by event organiser Rainer Schaller was premature. Moreover, Duisburg Police Force had earlier stated that they had no official responsibility for pedestrian flow at the ingress/egress point. Nevertheless, it was alleged that they were the main instigators of the action taken which pre-empted the tragedy, without due reference to those stakeholders responsible for this area.

'At this point we're not yet in a position to say what the trigger was for the whole thing. One cannot seriously determine it yet, but we would prefer it if Herr Schaller didn't engage in speculation.' – (Diehl, et al., 2010, p. 2).

In February 2014, almost four years after the tragedy, ten people were charged with 'negligent manslaughter' and 'causing bodily harm'. The accused include four staff of the music festival organiser Lopavent and six members of the city administration. Excluded from the indictment are the former mayor of Duisburg, Adolf Sauerland, and the head of Lopavent, Rainer Schaller, although both are expected to testify as witnesses.

Lessons learned

For every disaster involving a crowd, whether considering Bradford (1985), Kings Cross Underground (1987), Hillsborough, Sheffield (1989), Mecca (1990) or Duisburg (2010), there are lessons to be learned or reinforced. Although the Love Parade event has been permanently cancelled, other large events around the globe can learn from Duisburg's experience.

Safety regulations are defined for a reason and should be observed. If they are found guilty of the offences for which they have been indicted, the ten individuals charged should be made an example of to deter others from similar acts.

German law clearly defines the parameters for the ingress and egress portals; these were ignored at Duisburg.

Moreover, it is dangerous to have two large crowds moving in opposite directions through the same portal at the same time. Where possible this should be avoided, alternatively, a directional flow separation technique should be utilised. At mass events, having staff experienced in crowd management on hand is crucial. Ideally, these events should be held in venues where local knowledge already exists.

Due attention should be paid to bottlenecks and single points of failure via a thorough threat analysis process. The resultant risk assessment needs to be based on realistic crowd expectation estimates and not just the capacity of the venue. In the case of Love Parade, based upon the organisers' own figures, no event since 1996 had fallen below 600,000 attendees. Without accurate crowd estimates, safety and security plans become unsound. Facilities for arriving and departing emergency services vehicles needs to be designed so as not to disrupt the ingress and egress of attendees to the event.

As part of their basic project management, it would be sensible for events of this nature to have a 'go/no-go' date in their timetable for safety, security and contingency plan sign-off and permit issuing. Adequate time must be allocated for testing and, if necessary, revising the plan. This clearly did not happen in Duisburg. If insufficient time is available for validation and plan rehearsals, serious consideration should be given to cancelling the event.

There were some severe errors in the establishing of efficient communication systems within the event planning structure. These errors resulted in the poor allocation of resources, culminating in an inadequate flow of information between stakeholders at important times. In fact, on the day, communications were shambolic. Walkie-talkies were unreliable, mobiles phones were negated by overloaded networks, a public address system had not been installed and megaphones were not available to communicate with the crowd. No one person seemed to have an overview of what was happening. People were dying while the city operations room thought the event was an enormous success.

It is important to have an efficient means of communications between organisers, emergency services, including the police, and the crowd. Effective walkie-talkies with mobile phones acting as a back-up should facilitate stakeholder communications. A repeat of the Duisburg Police Force's reluctance to request a prior right of cellular radio communication from the network providers should be avoided. Furthermore, an efficient PA system with megaphone back-ups should be readily available for addressing the crowd. That said it must be remembered that the level of decibels generated by a similar event could stretch any form of communication to its limit. It is worth not only testing this equipment, ideally in a noisy environment, but there is also merit in conducting a site survey that maps out communications along with associated resources.

It would be advantageous for all groups involved in an event like Love Parade to increase their knowledge of the key relationships and command & control functions necessary for successful management. An increased element of expert continuity and contingency consultancy should be presented to the various stakeholders, who can then identify their own critical relationships and function and embed this data into any future planning activity.

Finally, intelligence on the event should be collected from different stakeholders and collated to form a unified strategy. Relying on only one stakeholder for information relating to the event limits the opportunity for each stakeholder to examine relevant information and identify areas of concern.

What went well

- The organisers did not shut down the event following the fatalaties. This prevented further panic and another crush.

What could have been done better

- When formulating the plan, information should have been gathered from more than one event stakeholder.
- Expert concerns over plans for Love Parade were ignored.
- Communications equipment available was insufficient and unreliable. Police were forced to use the mobile phone network, which was not a suitable backup.

What did not go well

- Lopavent and Duisburg severly underestimated the size of the crowd. This made all of their contingency plans irrelevant.
- Regulations regarding the size of the ingress/egress point were clearly ignored.

- The ingress/egress points should not have been in the same place. A secondary egress point was not well signposted.

Conclusion

The Love Parade stampede is a quintessential example of a head-on collision. On one side, the sound advice put forward by health, safety and security professionals. On the other, the kudos plus the political and economic benefits that Lopavent and Duisburg would enjoy from staging a successful prestigious event. Professional ambition of city leaders and the organisers' economic interest seem to have dictated the direction of planning activity and the allocation of resources.

> *'On the one hand, Rainer Schaller wanted to see this (Love Parade) through as cost-efficiently as possible. On the other hand, Adolf Sauerland, the conservative mayor of Duisburg, also desperately wanted the Love Parade, in order to improve the image of the city and undoubtedly his own image as well.'* – Wolfgang Sterneck.

With the event being held in Berlin for 16 consecutive years while the crowd gradually increased in size from less than 200 in 1989 to over one million, the city had become experienced in managing all aspects of the event. Once it moved to the Ruhr area in 2007, it never stayed in the same place two years running. Each event was at a different location with a new set of safety and security issues to manage. What is not clear is just how experienced the Lopavent staff were at Duisburg.

Countless commentators have since claimed that Duisburg was a disaster waiting to happen. Many professional experts deserve recognition for expressing their serious safety and security apprehensions before the event took place. Sadly, their arguments went unheard.

'When one looks back, however, one now remembers first of all the fatalities of the last Love Parade, who were sacrificed on the altar of profit and greed.' – Wolfgang Sterneck.

From a legal perspective, it is clear that the event should never have been authorised. The law was unquestionably broken when the minimum exit size parameters for the expected crowd magnitude were totally ignored by organisers and city officials. Based upon the Duisburg tunnel width (155 m), the maximum crowd capacity permitted should have been less than 80,000. The site selected was simply not a suitable venue.

Comparisons were inevitably made with the cancellation of the Bochum 2009 event, when safety issues prevailed. Bochum's concerns were about whether the city's infrastructure could cope with the large influx of visitors that the Love Parade would attract.

Crowd Management Strategies, a consulting service which promotes effective crowd safety measures, believe that safety and security plans were compromised at the pre-event risk management stage. Without an accurate estimate of expected attendees, it was never going to be possible to produce a workable plan.

It is clear that there were no systems of accountability incorporated into contingency planning for the event. There was also no inclusion of basic command and control functions which would have helped identify chains of command, thereby facilitating the development of relevant stakeholder interrelationships.

Quite possibly the only right decision of any consequence made on the day was not to stop the event after the fatalities. It was wise to avoid a big surge of people leaving the event even though they would all be heading in the same direction.

With ten individuals now indicted for negligent manslaughter and causing bodily harm, it is surprising that the now-former mayor of Duisburg, Adolf Sauerland, and Lopavent owner Rainer Schaller have so far escaped the net.

CHAPTER 6: *HERALD OF FREE ENTERPRISE* – CARL DAKIN

Roll on/Roll off ships (Ro-Ro) are widely used across the globe. Despite their success and popularity the Ro-Ro concept has its critics, some of whom point to tragic accidents that they have been involved with such as the *Estonia* shipwreck in 1994 and the subject of this chapter, the capsizing of the *Herald of Free Enterprise* some seven years earlier.

> *'The World Casualty Statistics for 1994 published by Lloyd's Register of Shipping show that passenger/ Ro-Ro cargo loss rate per thousand ships was 2.3 – the same as the average figure for all ships.'* – (Global Security, 2014).

Despite only sampling 12 months of data, the Lloyd's Register findings suggest that Ro-Ros are no less safe than any other type of commercial ship.

On 6 March 1987, the *Herald of Free Enterprise* (*HFE*), set sail at 18:05 hours GMT from a berth in the inner harbour at the Port of Zeebrugge, Belgium. The ferry was crewed by 80 staff and was carrying 459 passengers and 131 vehicles. With a passenger capacity of 1,326 and maximum car capacity of 350, the vessel was only about one-third full.

The ferry departed the outer harbour and she approached the outer mole at 18:24, at which time her master, Captain David Lewry, increased to full power and the ferry accelerated to approximately 18 knots. Within four minutes the *HFE* had capsized and eventually came to rest with her port side on a sand bank. The tragedy resulted in the loss of 150 passengers and 38 crew members plus numerous injuries.

Two factors combined to minimise the death toll – the vessel was well below its maximum passenger capacity and it veered to starboard immediately before capsizing. The latter meant it came to rest on a sandbank and remained half-submerged rather than completely sinking in deeper water. Even so, the death toll represented one of the worst for a British commercial vessel in peacetime since the *Titanic* disaster of 1912.

The UK Government was swift to respond. Three days after the incident the Secretary of State for Transport, exercising his powers under Section 55 of the Merchant Shipping Act 1970, ordered a formal investigation to be conducted by the Wreck Commissioner. The findings of the formal investigation were outlined by the Honourable Mr Justice Sheen in his formal Report of Court (no.8074). Following a detailed analysis of the report a number of critical factors have been identified which contributed to the catastrophic failure of the *HFE*. This case study will examine the critical factors in the context of business continuity management (BCM).

The *HFE* and her two sister ships were built specifically for the Dover – Calais route operated by Townsend Thoresen. Her vehicle decks were configured in harmony with facilities at these ports, which allowed vehicle decks E and G to be loaded simultaneously. At the time of the incident Townsend Thoresen had recently become an acquired subsidiary of Peninsular and Orient (P&O).

Not for the first time, the company had assigned the *HFE* as a relief ferry for the Zeebrugge route. There is, however, no evidence to suggest a risk assessment was ever carried out or critical information with respect to the different facilities at this port were promulgated within the ship or to shore based management. Unfortunately, the berths at Zeebrugge were designed to receive the bow of a single deck ship and could unload only one deck at a time. Furthermore, the *HFE* incurred additional problems with offloading vehicle deck E under high water spring tide conditions. The vehicle ramp at Zeebrugge could not be elevated sufficiently to reach the deck and therefore the ship was required to take on ballast to increase her draught. The reduced loading/unloading capacity and the requirement to trim the ship by ballast incurred significant time delays.

Against this backdrop of impaired loading/unloading efficiency, the importance of maintaining the sailing schedule remained a key driving factor within the operational management team. This point is illustrated by Mr D. Shipley, the Townsend Thoresen operations manager at Zeebrugge, who wrote an internal memorandum, dated 18 August 1986, to assistant managers. The memorandum encouraged ships' crews to save time at Zeebrugge and sail at the earliest opportunity.

The memorandum emphasised the importance of maximum efficiency from the ship's crew in order to achieve targets. When considering the merits of efficiency over effectiveness it can be concluded that effectiveness – doing the right thing – is more important than efficiency – doing things right. Shipley, in his capacity as an operations manager, should have been aware of the loading and unloading difficulties for the various classes of ship operated by Townsend Thoresen. Equally, he should have been central to devising a risk assessment for the port which could have been incorporated as part of the company's BCM arrangements.

A common theme throughout the report is that the management of Townsend Thoresen were substandard, from the board of directors to junior officials.

'From top to bottom, the body corporate was infected with a disease of sloppiness.' – (Sheen, 1987, p. 14).

The investigation identified a failure on the part of the shore management and cited the lack of clear directions as contributory to the disaster. Although the company had a board of directors, the multiple and discrete management layers ashore and the hierarchy aboard ship inhibited the flow of information and the decision making process. This, in turn, created a culture whereby much of the critical information was managed by specific functions utilising a 'stovepipe' or 'silo' approach.

'An issue ignored is a crisis ensured.' – (Regester & Larkin, 2008, p. 95).

The stovepipe approach was illustrated in 1983 when the *Pride of Free Enterprise*, a sister ship to the *HFE*, is documented to have left Dover on at least two separate occasions with her bow and stern doors open. The master of the *Pride* sent an internal memorandum to all deck officers, bosuns and assistant bosuns highlighting the importance of ensuring the doors were secured before sailing *'and to give this their close attention.'* This critical information was not promulgated to other ships in the fleet or wider within the company, and it was not until June 1985 that one of the masters of the *Pride* raised the issue to senior shore-based management.

Dealing with the media

The severity of the disaster attracted an immediate and intense media response. Unfortunately Townsend Thoresen had not considered a media handling strategy, illustrated when a senior company spokesperson speculated on the cause of the disaster during a media interview soon after the incident. The spokesperson conjectured that the ship hit the harbour wall.

Media handling is a vital component to any crisis management (CM) plan and can be effective in reducing damage to reputation. This is especially true during the initial period after an incident when information can be limited, which encourages the media to urge so-called 'experts' to speculate. The formation of a CM team and giving some prior consideration to a CM plan would have identified the requirement to develop a media handling strategy. The importance of having an established CM team cannot be over-emphasised and plans should be rehearsed in order to minimise crisis impacts, particularly when communicating with the media. Even if a thorough CM plan was not considered to be important, some thought could have been applied to media handling and a simple list of do's and don'ts could have been imparted to a nominated spokesperson.

Irreparable reputational damage

The consequences of poor media handling can be catastrophic and, in the aftermath of an incident, can be more damaging than the incident itself. The harm caused to the Townsend Thoresen brand was deemed by P&O to be beyond repair. The public had lost confidence in the company and many were switching to rival Sealink. It was at this point that Townsend Thoresen effectively ceased to exist.

Absence of contingency arrangements

Evidence taken from members of the crew during the formal investigation revealed that contingency plans and a safe system of operation did not exist aboard the ship. Although the ship had formal 'Ship's Standing Orders', little thought had been given to their content. In addition, evidence from members of the crew indicated that procedures were often diluted or ignored in the interest of saving time. This was particularly apparent when analysing the procedures for leaving port and manning 'harbour stations'. The culture of poor leadership and bad practice is confirmed by the lack of compliance to standing orders.

'Approximately fifty percent of maritime accidents are initiated by human error.' – (Baker & Seah, 2004, p. 1).

The chief officer and assistant bosun had specific duties, notwithstanding their supervisory responsibilities as senior officers. This included the opening and closing of the bow doors, although the assistant bosun failed to close the doors on that fateful day. Even so, he admitted it had been his responsibility. Moreover, the chief officer failed to ensure the task was executed and to subsequently advise the ship's master of its completion, a series of failings that Sheen noted had led to the disaster.

A disaster in waiting

Sheen observed that there were no contingency arrangements in place that identified a backup for the assistant bosun in the event that he was not at his post when harbour stations were called. He also noted that this was not the first time a Townsend Thoresen vessel had sailed with its doors open, referring to the incident almost four years earlier involving the *Pride of Free Enterprise*.

The master is ultimately responsible for the safe operation of his ship. He was complicit with the bad practice aboard the ship, a fact supported by his and his deck officers' evidence. They concurred that when entering or leaving Zeebrugge, if trimmed by the head (i.e., when sea water ballast is increased in the forward ballast tanks) care must be taken to avoid the bow wave going above the bow spade. A deck officer should observe the bow spade and inform the master as appropriate, who would in turn reduce speed as necessary. During the minutes leading up to the disaster the master should have been cognisant that he was still significantly trimmed by the head. In nautical circles, it is widely known that this can adversely affect a ship's handling. Even so, he still elected to increase to full power.

The shore based management failed to effectively communicate clear direction to the ship and ensure that a safe system of operation was in place. Evidence of ship to shore and shore to ship communication was limited to written memorandums and a meeting between senior shore-based management and senior masters, which only occurred once in two years.

Shutting the stable door

Following the *HFE* disaster Townsend Thoresen initiated a refit programme of all its ships to include a panel of lights on the bridge to indicate the position of the doors. This was, of course, no consolation to the casualties aboard the *HFE* particularly as the risk of sailing with open bow doors had been raised some four years earlier by the master of the *Pride of Free Enterprise*.

The birth of corporate manslaughter

> '*In 1989, seven individuals, including Stanley, Sable, Lewry and deputy chief marine superintendent John Alcindor, and P&O European Ferries were charged with corporate manslaughter. The trial opened at the Old Bailey in September 1990 and though it collapsed after 27 days, it paved the way for the Corporate Manslaughter and Corporate Homicide Act 2007, which finally came into force in 2008, almost exactly 21 years after the Herald disaster.*' – (Allen, 2011).

Lessons learned

There is no question that Townsend Thoresen had not embraced business continuity. That said, we must remind ourselves that the incident actually occurred before any Publicly Available Standards (PAS) had been published for BCM. In fact, it was a further 16 years before PAS 56 (the predecessor to BS25999 and ISO22301) was released for general use. Even the Business Continuity Institute was not formed until 1994 and the holistic BCM approach in use today did not begin to fully evolve until the end of that decade. Therefore, there were no standards available in 1987 by which we can judge Townsend Thoresen on its BCM shortcomings.

The same is not true for crisis management. Although there is much debate around the date of its actual conception, it had been around for many years before the *HFE* disaster.

Effective crisis management should also include a communications plan, particularly for dealing with the media. Public relations case studies often tell of companies suffering severe or even irreparable reputational damage resulting from incompetent or misleading media communications. Townsend Thoresen was no exception and, having lost confidence in the brand name, the travelling public switched to a competitor ferry service.

In fact, business-as-usual communications within the company appeared very weak. Attempts by the master of the *Pride of Free Enterprise* to alert the company to the dangers of sailing with bow doors open fell on deaf ears. It is also clear that profitability was considered more important that the safety of the ship, its passengers and crew. Cost-effectiveness was seen as a higher priority than health and safety.

Contingency planning is also nothing new and has been practiced for centuries, particularly by the military. In many ways, making some form of contingency arrangements is simply applying common sense. For Townsend Thoresen there was certainly no excuse for not identifying a 'Plan B' in the event that the assistant bosun was not at his post when the doors needed closing. After all, they already had experience of one of their ships sailing with bow doors open, but chose to take no further preventative action.

The belated installation of warning lights on the bridge indicating whether the loading doors were open or closed was a positive move. As was Sheen's recommendation that CCTV be installed to provide an additional level of safety management on the vessels.

A standard set of company operating procedures with vessel specific annexes, designed by a suitably experienced and qualified consultant, were clearly missing from the ship. Consequently, there was very little to use as the basis for a programme of training and rehearsal for the crew. Moreover, this would have needed to be an ongoing programme because crew attrition rate was flagged as undermining the ship's efficiency. Greater effort should have been applied by Townsend Thoresen to encourage their retention.

Almost three decades on, we can of course benefit from hindsight.

'Undoubtedly lessons were learnt from the sinking of the Herald of Free Enterprise, and ferry travel is far safer as a result. The likelihood of such a disaster happening again is now very low, thanks to changes in both the structure of ships and an overhaul of attitudes to safety in ferry companies and their crews.' – (Radley, 2012).

What went well

- Following the disaster, Townsend Thoresen refitted their ships to prevent a similar accident from occurring.

What could have been done better

- The *HFE* was not designed for the port facilities at Zeebrugge. A risk assessment should have been carried out before the ferry began calling at the port.
- Although safety plans for the ship were in place, they were frequently ignored to save time. Shore management

failed to ensure that operational safety measures were being observed.

What did not go well

- The culture of sloppiness at Townsend Thoresen directly contributed to the disaster. Putting cost-effectiveness and staying on schedule ahead of safety concerns was a major contributory factor. The master of the *HFE* was complicit in this.

- A silo approach inhibited communication and the flow of critical information at the company. It prevented the warning by the master of the *Pride of Free Enterprise* being addressed.

- Officers aboard the *HFE* failed to communicate with each other regarding the closure of the doors.

- No media handling strategy was in place and incorrect statements were made to the media. This helped to ensure that the Townsend Thoresen name became tarnished, with the result that P&O discontinued the brand.

Conclusion

Sadly, it is nigh on impossible to find any positives from the Herald of Free Enterprise disaster. Instead, analysis illustrates that a series of failures compounded by human error led to the unfolding of a tragedy that could have been avoided.

CHAPTER 7: THE AZTEC CHEMICAL EXPLOSION, THE BIGGEST BLAZE IN CHESHIRE FOR 35 YEARS – ROBERT CLARK

During the time I spent working in Italy, I came across a business continuity strategy which was new to me, as its successful execution was dependent upon what I can only describe as 'divine intervention'. It is not a strategy for the faint-hearted, nor is it to be found in the pages of the Business Continuity Institute's Good Practice Guidelines.

When I was working in Crewe in the summer of 2007, although I did not realise it at the time, I may have witnessed a case of this 'divine intervention' in action. This chapter examines the consequences of an explosion at Aztec Chemicals in Crewe, UK. It resulted in the biggest fire in the county of Cheshire for 35 years while causing much local disruption. It also looks at the consequential impact experienced by Fujitsu Services, one of around 150 companies also located on the same industrial estate. The case study primarily draws on the personal experience of the author, who was working at Fujitsu, and an interview with Carl Chadwick, the financial director of Aztec, who was the senior manager on site at the time of the incident.

Formerly known as International Computers Ltd (ICL), Fujitsu Services is a property-rich, multi-national IT equipment manufacturer which also offered information services and consultancy. At the time of the incident it had around 20,000 UK-based staff. By comparison Aztec was a chemical retailer and aerosol manufacturer employing around 70 staff. Prior to the disaster, the entire Aztec operation was accommodated in a single building which combined its offices, sales operation and production facilities. It housed raw materials, some finished products and all the company's IT capability upon which it was totally reliant.

At 12.15 pm on Monday 4 June 2007, a comparatively new aerosol can shredding machine operated by Aztec Chemicals' sister company Greenway Environmental Ltd exploded. Flames shot across a storage yard, igniting nearby drums of solvent materials. The fire quickly spread to and eventually totally destroyed Aztec's premises. Thankfully there were no fatalities or injuries although one employee who was positioned very close to the initial explosion subsequently needed counselling.

Financial Director Carl Chadwick explained that when the fire started, he did not rely on the automatic fire alarm installed in the Aztec building and made three emergency 999 calls himself. He was dismayed that the fire and rescue service (FRS) '*took an age to arrive*', even though the fire station was only approximately one kilometre away. By contrast, the FRS's version of events differs significantly and they claim to have been on site within six minutes of the first call.

While no evidence has been found that contradicts either the FRS or Chadwick's account, the FRS's union was critical about the initial response. They claimed that it was the scene of one of Cheshire's largest fires in recent years and yet initially only a single pump was despatched. In their defence, the FRS said that around 98% of all automatic calls were false alarms. They did, however, acknowledge that 43 calls were received reporting the incident – why only dispatch one appliance when the sheer volume of calls was a strong indication that it was not a false alarm?

7: The Aztec Chemical Explosion, the Biggest Blaze in Cheshire for 35 Years – Robert Clark

A 200 m exclusion zone was quickly established as hazardous materials were stored on site including liquid petroleum gas. This was later extended to a 400 m zone. All businesses located within the zone, including Fujitsu Services, were evacuated.

'This was a major incident which could have been a lot worse if crews had not prevented flames from reaching cylinders containing 25 tonnes (25,000 kilograms) of Liquid Petroleum Gas, close to the original site of the fire. It is extremely fortunate that there were no injuries to members of the public or fire fighters.' – Paul Hancock, Cheshire Chief Fire Officer.

The fire covered an area of approximately 10,000 m² and some neighbouring buildings were damaged. But the FRS's primary attention was focused on cooling down the LPG canisters in an effort to prevent a potentially catastrophic explosion. This activity was apparently fraught with danger, not least because some old aerosol cans located awaiting disposal nearby started exploding. As Chadwick explained, the FRS let the fire in the building burn itself out while they concentrated on damage limitation. In retrospect, the disparity between the Fire and Rescue Service's six minute response time claim and Chadwick's recall of events seems irrelevant as, given the circumstances, saving Aztec's premises would never have been an FRS priority. At the peak of the incident there were 30 fire appliances in attendance and 100 firemen.

'I am often asked what single piece of advice I can recommend that would be most helpful to the business community. My answer is a simple, but effective, business continuity plan that is regularly reviewed and tested.' – Eliza Manningham-Buller, former Director-General of MI5.

7: The Aztec Chemical Explosion, the Biggest Blaze in Cheshire for 35 Years – Robert Clark

Aztec Chemicals was not well prepared for a disaster, let alone one of this magnitude. Chadwick explained that he had started developing a recovery plan but it contained very little detail and had never been tested. A daily data backup tape was created which an employee took home, returning it the next working day to replace with a new backup. On this basis, during the working day, both the company's primary and backup data would be in the same place.

'It's not until something like this happens that you realise that this [the backup process] was sheer stupidity.' – Carl Chadwick.

Aztec's backup approach did not follow business continuity best practise. Chadwick acknowledged that it was designed on the basis that a disaster would only occur outside of normal working hours. Should it occur during office hours, it was assumed someone would think to rescue the backup. On the day of the disaster, however, the employee designated to take the backup tape home had arrived late for work. He had inadvertently left the tape in his car – but along with the company premises, all the employees' cars parked in the Aztec car park had been totally burnt out. To further compound the issue, Aztec Chemicals had changed their insurer only four days earlier and had received no paperwork or policy documents when the incident occurred. Unsure whether or not they were covered, Chadwick contacted the new insurer and was relieved to learn that their cover was in place. David Flatley from surveyors Salisbury Hamer summed up the situation:

'You are probably talking about at least a couple of million pounds on structural damage, plus damage to plant and equipment. Then you are looking at about four to five million pounds in terms of

physical damage. The plant equipment came from the continent and it will cause serious disruption to business and also to employment. It's unlikely to be up and running within the next 12 months.' – (Crewe Chronicle, 2007).

The exclusion zone remained in place for three days. It was only when this was finally lifted that it was discovered that, miraculously, the car containing the tape had survived. In his haste to get into the building, its owner had illegally parked the car and it was spared the fiery fate that so many other vehicles had endured.

'We were unbelievably lucky – unbelievably lucky! Without that tape I just don't know how we would have recovered.' – Carl Chadwick

Within eight days of the fire, alternative local office accommodation had been found and occupied. A new voice and data network and telephone system were provided by Aztec's supplier Livewire Networks. Replacement computer equipment was procured from a large UK retailer and the data restored. By day ten, the company had been re-stocked and the chemical retail part of the business was operational again. Chadwick said: *'This was comparatively easy to achieve because of the nature of the business we are in.'* The company's insurer also made substantial funds available to cover the initial restart costs.

Even though the chemical retail aspect of Aztec's business was quickly recovered, there was no work for those employees who had been engaged in aerosol manufacturing. Aztec's handling of this situation was innovative. As Chadwick explains, *'We did a deal with a local employment agency and they found temporary work for our people until we needed them back.'* This avoided any redundancies, lay-offs or short-time working immediately after the incident and no recruiting and training worries when the aerosol business was ready to recommence.

Your competitors can turn out to be your best friends in a crisis

Twelve months before the disaster, Aztec had been discussing a joint venture with a Dutch aerosol producer that had spare capacity. Although this was never fully developed, when the disaster occurred the Dutch were approached again. *'We got them to sign a contractual agreement that they would not approach our clients,'* explained Chadwick. *'We didn't make any money but we kept the business going and never lost a single client'*. The lost income was covered by business interruption insurance.

While the Dutch took on the role of temporary drop-shippers for Aztec's aerosol business, the key challenge was in recovering Aztec's own aerosol production capability. This necessitated importation of plant equipment which had a delivery lead time of several months. Moreover, the new building housing the chemical retail operation was not suitable to also house aerosol production. Fortunately, more suitable local premises were acquired but the UK's Health and Safety Executive (HSE) demanded additional stringent safety measures to be introduced before production could restart. Chadwick commented, *'This is when the insurers decided to get tough,'* and while they agreed to pay for the replacement plant machinery, they refused to pay the £300,000 to cover the new HSE requirements. Aerosol production was finally resumed in March 2008, nine months after the disaster.

But HSE had not yet finished with the incident. Aztec's sister company Greenway Environmental Ltd subsequently appeared at Chester Crown Court along with the manufacturer of the exploding aerosol shredding machine, Pakawaste Ltd. Greenway pleaded guilty to breaching Section 2(1) of the Health and Safety at Work Act 1974 by *'failing to ensure the safety of its workers'*. It was fined £37,500 plus costs of £50,000. Preston based Pakawaste, pleaded guilty to breaching Section 6(1)(a) of the Health and Safety at Work Act 1974 by *'failing to ensure the shredding unit was designed and constructed to be safe'*. It was fined £50,000 plus costs of £87,030.

As for Fujitsu, when the 400 m exclusion zone was established, its nearby premises had to be evacuated and its staff withdrew beyond the new safety perimeter. Fujitsu's Crewe premises primarily provided 'hot desk' accommodation for its consultants but of specific concern was a critical client call centre located on site which has a recovery time objective measured in hours. A crisis management team conference call was hastily organised. Based upon input from the emergency services, it was decided to invoke the continuity plan for the loss of the Crewe office and all in-bound calls to the Crewe call centre were re-routed to the Manchester office. The call centre function remained at the Manchester Office until Thursday 7 June when normal operations were resumed at Crewe.

Those Fujitsu employees who did not have any specific business continuity related responsibilities to carry out were instructed to go home. This presented another problem, however, as the majority of the staff had arrived by car and the Fujitsu car park was located inside the exclusion zone. Some employees had also left personal items including house keys in the office. Police discouraged any re-entry into the building or the car park and threatened to formally caution anybody ignoring their instructions. Anyone apprehended disregarding this directive would not only have earned themselves a police caution along with a criminal record, but would have potentially put their life in jeopardy. Moreover, they would have been creating an unnecessary extra level of risk for the emergency services who may have had to rescue them had the situation suddenly deteriorated.

Lessons learned

Aztec now realised that only having one building presented a serious single point of failure. All the raw materials, production plant machinery and the IT capability was contained in one area. The very nature of the business and the requirement to handle hazardous chemicals dramatically increased the risk from a fire or explosion.

With the benefit of hindsight, the data backup process's shortcomings have not been lost on Chadwick. The company now keeps multiple backup copies in a secure offsite repository. Chadwick was clearly disappointed that the insurance cover fell substantially short of what the recovery actually cost. The major issue was the extra cost of meeting the HSE requirements for the new aerosol production premises. The insurers had underwritten cover which would finance the recovery of like-for-like and which excluded the revised safety specification that the HSE demanded. Aztec has since increased its business interruption insurance from 12 to 24 months. As the recovery was completed within nine months, however, this additional cover would have been of no benefit had it been in place before the disaster.

What went well

- The Aztec Chemicals resale business was operational again within two weeks of the initial disaster. This was only possible because of the miraculous survival of the backup tape.

- Subcontracting the manufacture of aerosol products to a Dutch competitor.

- Approaching local employment agencies to secure temporary employment for the workforce and avoiding redundancies.

- Fujitsu's seamless call centre fall back, making use of their Manchester site.

What could have been done better

- In retrospect, Aztec's Carl Chadwick realised their backup strategy left the company incredibly exposed. Data backups must never be kept on the same premises as the original data. At least one copy of the latest backup should always be kept in a separate, secure location.

- Chadwick also concluded that Aztec Chemicals was under-insured. Without, a detailed BCP, however, it would have been very difficult to accurately estimate what level or type of cover was required. It is quite acceptable for insurance to be an integral part of a business continuity strategy. There is no question that it can be a differentiator in terms of whether a company can successfully recover from a serious incident. It should never be used in isolation, however, or seen as a substitute for a properly developed and tested business continuity plan.

• The wisdom of the Fire and Rescue Service's initial decision to send only one fire appliance to the scene has to be questioned. Had a risk assessment been adequately performed, they would have known the nature of Aztec's business and the type of hazardous materials that were stored on site along with the inherent dangers.

What did not go well

• Clearly the positioning of the aerosol shredding machine had not been given due consideration. It created avoidable risks, including a serious health hazard.

Other observations

• Companies should have a comprehensive and thoroughly tested business continuity plan. If a plan is not tested, it is not worth the paper it is written on.

• Operating out of a single building created a single point of failure for Aztec Chemicals. This was exacerbated by their utilisation of hazardous and inflammable chemicals – a threat that was passed on to the company's immediate neighbours.

Conclusion

Two key factors enabled Aztec to recover. First, the successful retrieval of the company's data and, second, the business interruption insurance without which the recovery's financial burden could have proven insurmountable. Conceivably, there is a third factor. In the absence of a detailed recovery plan, without Chadwick's extensive company knowledge and ability to manage in a crisis Aztec may not have survived. Although supported by loss adjusters, he was the senior and most experienced employee available. Since the majority of the 70 strong workforce was split between shop floor and back-office functions, and the company's owners were incommunicado at the time of the crisis, it is difficult to see who else could have so successfully managed the recovery.

There is no question that Aztec Chemicals is extremely fortunate to still be in business. To reiterate Chadwick's assessment: '*We were unbelievably lucky.*' In contrast, Fujitsu were delighted that their continuity plans worked so smoothly.

CHAPTER 8: PIPER ALPHA AND ALEXANDER L. KIELLAND: A COMPARISON OF TWO NORTH SEA TRAGEDIES – CARL DAKIN AND JON SIGURD JACOBSEN

'The oil and gas fatality rate is 7.6 times higher than the all-industry rate of 3.2 deaths per 100,000 workers.' – (King, 2013).

The oil industry is a multi-trillion dollar business and the world's reliance upon its products grows year-on-year. But working in the oil industry, particularly off shore, is not without its risks as the following table chronicles:

YEAR	OIL RIG	LOCATION	EVENT	FATALITIES
1988	Piper Alpha	North Sea	Explosion and Fire	167
1980	Alexander L. Kielland	North Sea	Accommodation platform structural failure and capsize	123
1989	Seacrest	South China Sea	Typhoon	91
1982	Ocean Ranger	Canada	190 km wind / 20 m waves	84
1983	Glomar Java Sea	South China Sea	Tropical Storm	81
1979	Bohai 2	China	Storm caused capsizing while rig under tow	72

1984	Enchova	Brazil	Explosion and Fire	42
2005	Mumbai High North	Indian Ocean	Collision and fire	22
2007	Usumacinta	Gulf of Mexico	Collision in storm	22
1964	CP Baker Drilling Barge	Gulf of Mexico	Explosion	21
2010	Deepwater Horizon	Gulf of Mexico	Explosion	11

Figure 8: Offshore oil industry accidents

Source: Offshore Technology Market & Customer Insight, 2014

This case study considers the worst two of these accidents, the Piper Alpha (PA) and the Alexander L. Kielland (ALK) disasters. Although caused by human error and structural failure respectively, a combined total of 290 oil workers lost their lives. Analysis of a purposive sample of available publications on the PA and ALK disasters has been performed which identifies some of the critical elements around these tragedies. *Figure 9*, below, shows an overview comparison of the two disasters.

	PIPER ALPHA	ALEXANDER L. KIELLAND
Platform operators	Occidental Petroleum	Philips Petroleum
North Sea oilfield names	Piper oilfield (UK)	Ekofisk oilfield (Norway)

8: Piper Alpha and Alexander L. Kielland: A Comparison of Two North Sea Tragedies

Size of platform	13,000 tonnes	10,105 tonnes
Purpose of platform	Oil / gas production	Accommodation
Crew	228	212
Survivors	61	89
Fatalities	167	123
Primary fatality cause	Carbon monoxide poisoning	Drowning
Incident cause	Human error / explosion	Structural failure
Life boats/rafts successfully launched	None	One
Average sea temperature	July – 13°C	March – 4°C

'Water temperature of 15°C or below provokes the physiological reaction or cold shock and swimming failure. This likely contributes to over half of the deaths through drowning.' **(Tipton & Brooks, 2008).**

Figure 9: Overview comparison of the two disasters

Piper Alpha

'Even after the Deepwater Horizon explosion, Piper Alpha remains the industry's shorthand for horror.' – (Steffy, 2011).

Piper Alpha was a large North Sea oil platform operating in the British sector of the North Sea, approximately 120 miles north east of Aberdeen. It was part of a complex network of three rigs that were connected via sub-sea gas or oil pipelines, with PA being utilised as the hub or central platform in the network.

During the night of 6 July 1988 the platform suffered a critical failure that resulted in an explosion. This was followed by an intense gas and oil fuelled fire that very quickly led to the catastrophic loss of the platform. The collapsing time frame from the first explosion to the point of structural failure lasted approximately 22 min. The disaster was the world's worst offshore oil accident with a human cost of 167 lives. There were 61 survivors. It is believed that only two fatalities were caused by the initial explosion. Several also succumbed to injuries that were consistent with falling or jumping, such as broken necks. Around 80 died in the accommodation block from carbon monoxide poisoning while waiting for direction from management.

The cost of rebuilding the platform was in excess of £1 billion and the wider cost to the global offshore industry has been estimated at £5 billion. The PA disaster demonstrated beyond doubt that the catastrophic loss of an offshore platform could result from human error. This should be considered alongside the 'once in 100 year wave' scenario as a low probability but very high impact event and certainly should not be ignored by risk managers.

It is clear that Occidental Petroleum (OP) were aware that the PA super structure could not withstand a high-intensity fire, but OP dismissed the scenario as too unlikely to be taken seriously. Unfortunately, lack of foresight prevented OP from conducting any form of risk assessment that a fire or explosion event would have on the platform. This is illustrated by the apparent lack of consideration given to the position of critical functions aboard the platform, such as the control room. This was located above an area that would be most vulnerable in the event of a serious fire.

Ultimately, the layout of the topside facilitated the propagation of the fire, which quickly destroyed critical centres during the early stages of the accident.

> *'Many evacuation routes were blocked and the life boats, all in the same location, were mostly inaccessible. The firefighting equipment on board could not be operated because the diesel pumps, which had been put on manual mode, were inaccessible and seem to have been damaged from the beginning.'* – Dr Elisabeth Paté-Cornell.

With several crucial single points of failure, including the positioning of firefighting equipment and lifeboats, the chances of saving the rig and its operatives were severely reduced. Many of the survivors had no option except to jump into the sea, which for some was from a height of 175 feet (53 m). Some subsequently drowned.

Furthermore, OP added components to the platform structure over a long period of time which critically altered the characteristics of the platform by creating areas congested with pipe work and equipment. These built-up areas prevented the explosion and subsequent fire from venting. The unvented blast damaged the firewalls which became ineffective.

There were processes in place aboard PA designed to reduce the risk to the safety of the platform and its operatives. The processes were reliant upon human compliance and careful management, however, a target driven culture dominated within OP, often at the expense of safety. This was in spite OP's track record of various accidents including the death of a worker; the company considered these accidents to be small. Moreover, during PA's design phase, there had been no systematic assessment of potential hazards and therefore no thought had been given to an explosion being just as likely as a fire.

The frequent of small accidents tended to grab management attention but at the expense of potentially more significant albeit 'less likely' events. The corporate attitude towards accidents usually involves measures being put in place to reduce the likelihood of small accidents occurring if this can be achieved at an acceptable cost. Often no consideration is given to serious, catastrophic potential accidents that would have a huge cost to life and assets.

A serious accident involving many casualties was a rare event and therefore some corporations could not justify to themselves the effort and cost of reducing the risk. Furthermore, in the event of a serious incident the corporation will attempt to exonerate itself on the basis that it was a 'freak event' and the company was justified in ignoring the possibility.

To further illustrate the culture of productivity before safety and the paradigm within OP that serious incidents were rare events, it is worth considering the actions carried out by the Offshore Installation Managers (OIM) aboard the Tartan and Claymore platforms at the time of the PA incident. The OIM aboard the Tartan platform ordered production to stop once he realised the severity of the PA situation, but the OIM aboard the Claymore platform remained focused on production and even ordered the pressure in the pipeline to be increased when a fall in pressure was experienced during the incident. The Claymore did not stop production until an hour after the initial explosion aboard the PA.

High-risk work environments, such as offshore platforms, are heavily reliant upon effective safety procedures that are adhered to by all levels of the workforce. It is clear from research that PA had a process in place, 'Permit to Work (PTW)', but the effectiveness of the process was greatly reduced by lack of enforcement and poor management. The PTW process should have formed an integral part of risk assessment. Managers and knowledge workers should have understood the reasons for risk assessments and corrective actions, as well as and the consequences of critical failure from non-compliance with the process.

The PA disaster was a sequence of events that, once a critical tipping point had been reached, could not be reversed. With careful analysis, however, the key failures can be isolated so that lessons can be learned and solutions applied.

Following the disaster a public inquiry was chaired by Lord Cullen who based his conclusions on eyewitness evidence, supported by technical evidence and expert opinion. A common thread that runs throughout the evidence was poor management and lack of adherence to safety procedures. This can be illustrated by the PTW process that formed the basis for a safe working environment aboard the platform. The PTW process is a suitable method to ensure a 'safe systems of work' and should ensure full and detailed consideration of any task before work is commenced. The process includes a thorough risk assessment and requisite risk reducing measures that should precede any work, as well as detailed contingencies in the event of a problem.

It is widely acknowledged that the likely cause of the initial explosion was the activation of a pump which was under maintenance. A pressure valve had been removed for servicing and the valve opening was sealed with a 'finger tight' flange. When the pump was activated a combustible vapour cloud was released under pressure, which subsequently ignited. If the permit to work process had been correctly supervised and adhered to, the relief crew would have been aware that the pump was unserviceable.

In order to reduce the risk of critical failure during routine maintenance, greater thought should be applied to each task. Every task should be considered in the context of the whole operation. In the case of PA, there were only two pumps to perform a given role, enabling one pump to operate and the second to be a back-up. When there is reduced or limited resilience, work should be completed to ensure essential function can be maintained, even at a reduced rate. In addition, a time appraisal should have taken place to identify if the task was feasible within the time available or if the relief crew should have conducted a 'relief in place' to complete the task.

Effective communication is essential for every organisation and can take many forms, specific to requirement. In the context of PA the level of communication between the day and night crew could not have been fully comprehensive, otherwise the day crew would have ensured the night crew had a full understanding of the status of the pump under maintenance. Moreover, the pump that was under maintenance was subject to two discrete PTW. One permit was held in the control room while the other permit was held in the safety officers' office. It is highly likely that separate facets of management were unaware of either or both permits, thus demonstrating a simple but significant breakdown in vital communication.

Cullen made 106 recommendations to improve safety in the offshore industry. As illustrated throughout this case study, formal safety procedures can be in place, but without careful management, measuring, monitoring and testing, the processes are ineffective. Prior to the disaster the Department of Energy (DoE) provided a regulatory function across UK industry but the PA disaster illustrated beyond doubt that an independent body with legal authority was required to regulate and ensure minimum standards were met. Responsibility for regulating safety within the offshore industry was transferred from DoE to the Health and Safety Executive (HSE).

The Offshore Safety Case Regulation was brought into force in 1993. It attempts to ensure that the safety management system is adequate, namely: that equipment design and operation are safe; that potential risks to personnel have been identified and appropriate controls provided; and suitable safe refuge, evacuation equipment and contingencies are provided. Each installation is required to submit a detailed safety case that requires HSE endorsement.

The Cullen Report and the PA disaster have had a lasting impact on the offshore industry. Most countries now have regulations that are enforced by bodies with statutory powers. Many companies also encourage a safety-focused culture that ensures a safe worker environment and minimum impact on the environment. This safeguards brand name and reputation. An example of a company that has adopted the safe approach is Qatar-based RasGas.

RasGas, a subsidiary of Qatar Petroleum, started extracting liquefied natural gas in 2001. The RasGas magazine carries the strategic message from the top level of the company that high standards of safety ensure a safe working environment for workers and protect the environment. The company are keen to ensure operations are underpinned by a comprehensive competency assurance programme to ensure workers are trained and fit for task. Rigorous and frequent testing of safety systems occurs, including:

- fire-fighting equipment and drills
- evacuation drills and life craft
- emergency shut-down procedures

The effect of this safety driven culture has been no unplanned disruption to production and no 'lost-time incidence' during an eight-year period.

The RasGas example is underpinned by a BCM process that has enabled it to identify elements that are critical to business and areas vulnerable to risk. Although BCM was still in its infancy in 1988, had a similar approach been adopted by OP a thorough threat analysis exercise would have highlighted many of the underlying risks that ultimately contributed to the PA disaster. Moreover, the Cullen inquiry revealed there had been no emergency simulation training or exercises between the three connected platforms. Had both the Tartan and Claymore platforms promptly stopped production, the fire on PA may well have quickly burned itself out with minimal loss of life.

8: *Piper Alpha and Alexander L. Kielland: A Comparison of Two North Sea Tragedies*

The Alexander L. Kielland

Located in the Ekofisk field, 235 miles to the east of Dundee, Scotland, the Alexander L. Kielland (ALK) Platform was a semi-submersible mobile rig of the Pentagon type. The rig was a French-built model constructed between 1972 and 1976. The ALK was originally intended to be operated as a drilling rig, but was only ever used as an accommodation platform. Both a drilling tower and accommodation units were mounted at the main deck and there was accommodation for up to 360 people on-board. The owner of the platform at the time of the accident was the Stavanger Drilling Company.

On Thursday 27 March 1980, the walkway connecting the ALK to the Edda 2/7 C platform was removed and using the anchorage points the ALK was shifted a short distance. This was standard practice in the face of inclement weather.

Approximately half an hour after the relocation was completed, a steel beam bolted to a main pillar broke. Very rapidly, all the other steel connections bolted to this main pillar also broke. This led to instability of the main pillar and it was reported to be listing at an angle of 30°–35°. One anchor temporarily remained in situ preventing further listing, and when that finally failed the ALK capsized. There were 212 people on board the ALK platform of which 123 perished.

The ALK accident was the first offshore accident with this magnitude of casualties. In fact it has only ever been surpassed by the Piper Alpha disaster. It occurred as a combination of bad weather, the failure of a steel connection bolted to a main pillar, and a lack of resilience within the original platform design to compensate for this failure.

8: Piper Alpha and Alexander L. Kielland: A Comparison of Two North Sea Tragedies

While examples abound of offshore oil and gas rigs succumbing to explosions, fires, extreme weather conditions and collisions, it is very rare for a working rig to be lost simply because of severe structural failure.

The ALK situation was further compounded by the lack of safety training that the crew had undertaken. All staff on the platform should have attended a three week safety course, both theoretical and practical, although there was no such requirement for visitors. Furthermore, all key staff on the platform should have undertaken a six month safety course and the platform executive had to hold a ship master's certificate. The course content focused on firefighting, the operation of rescue boats and rafts, and overall knowledge of safety. The training had, however, fallen well short of the requirement and none of the platform executives had attended the mandatory six month course. It further transpired that only four crew members had attended the safety course.

The ALK was well equipped with life jackets, life boats and rafts which were positioned at various points around the platform. Each crew member was allocated their own lifejacket and survival suit which they kept in their cabins. As the ALK began to list, there was also a power failure which added to the ensuing confusion. With many of the crew in the cinema as the crisis began, it was simply too dangerous to return to their cabins to collect their survival suits and life jackets. Consequently, there were insufficient accessible life jackets available for the crew and guests onboard. In fact, only eight crew members are known to have been wearing survival suits, and only four were rescued alive.

'The 14 minutes between initial failure of the leg and the rig's eventual capsize left a window in

which most of the personnel on board could have escaped, given a more effective command structure. But it would seem that no one took charge on the night.' – (Officer of the Watch, 2013).

Many of the crew were thrown into the sea as the ALK capsized. The rig held twenty 20-man rafts and seven 50-man lifeboats although launching them from the listing platform proved almost impossible. Of the four lifeboats lowered only one was released from the cables and was adrift upside down. The survivors inside righted the lifeboat and proceeded to rescue 19 other survivors from the water while seven crew swam to the Edda 2/7 C platform.

The Norwegian Rescue Services took the lead in the rescue operation and a NRS helicopter was quickly on the scene. In addition to the Edda 2/7 C platform, support came from the police, national and local authorities, paramedics and hospitals, the fire department and ambulance services. Attempts to launch life rafts from the Edda 2/7 C were only partially successful as it was discovered that the releasing mechanisms had been incorrectly configured.

As a part of the rescue plan four supply ships and the Edda 2/7 C platform under the command of Philips were standing by with rescue boats, lifelines and a staff elevator. The ships were instructed to take up stations close to the ALK but owing to the severity of the weather, this instruction was not followed. It was a full hour before the first of these ships arrived on station and even then it rescued no survivors. It took a further three hours for all four ships to finally be on station.

The common factors

Although the causes of the Piper Alpha and Alexander L. Kielland tragedies are very different, there are clearly some common themes that contributed towards the high death tolls:

1. When the crisis began there was an absence of leadership taking control of the situation. On both platforms, men died while they waited for their respective management teams to provide direction, if only to instruct them to abandon the rigs. In both scenarios, the only possible means of survival was in fact to evacuate the rigs.

2. An absence of training and rehearsals for emergencies was a common denominator. Although training standards had been defined they were not followed.

3. Many crew members drowned, particularly from the ALK. Even summer temperatures in the North Sea can be cold enough that the best of swimmers can quickly find themselves in difficulty. Heart failure in the prevailing conditions is not unknown.

What went well

• Following the Piper Alpha disaster, responsibility for ensuring safety in the offshore oil and gas industry was passed to the Health and Safety Executive. They must approve a detailed safety case for each installation.

What could have been done better

- Although OP were at least aware that Piper Alpha was vulnerable to a high-intensity fire, they ignored the problem as it was considered an unlikely event.

- No risk assessment was carried out, resulting in critical functions being located in high-risk areas.

- Staff on the ALK had not attended supposedly mandatory safety training courses.

- Life jackets and life rafts became inaccessible to crew after power failure.

What did not go well

- Those safety procedures which had been put in place on Piper Alpha were ignored due to a culture which prioritised targets over safety.

- Communications between day and night crews were not comprehensive.

- Management teams on both rigs did not provide leadership during the disasters.

- Attempts to launch rescue lifeboats from the Edda 2/7C were less successful because they had not been properly configured.

Conclusion – could tragedies of the PA and ALK magnitude reoccur?

As illustrated by *Figure 8*, while offshore oil related fatalities continue, the number of casualties per incident has fallen drastically since the 1980s, implying that safety on rigs has greatly improved.

In the case of the ALK, the design fault and subsequent structural failure that caused its capsizing present a risk to rigs of a similar design. In fact, just ten days after the ALK tragedy its sister rig the *Henrik Ibsen* listed 20° in Stavanger harbour, forcing the crew to take to the lifeboats. Ironically, the *Ibsen* had been earmarked to replace the ill-fated ALK although questions were subsequently asked about the safety and stability of this particular rig design. Springing to the defence of its product, ALK manufacturer Compagnie Francaise d'Enterprises Metalliques said there were eleven rigs of this design all operating without any problems.

Ibsen was righted and is still in use although it has since been renamed. It is now constantly monitored with acoustic emission devices to detect any potential structural failure. This safety precaution should provide an early warning of any developing problems, making a repeat of the ALK tragedy less likely.

Conversely, the PA disaster was primarily the result of human error although a series of other issues undoubtedly made the incident far worse than it needed to be. Statistically the safety of the North Sea installations has been improving but more progress still needs to be made.

'This is a work in progress and the momentum for improvement must continue.' – Judith Hackitt, UK Health and Safety Executive.

In 2003, on the Forties Alpha platform, escaping gas quickly formed a huge and potentially lethal cloud around the rig. But unlike the PA disaster, no one died or was even hurt that day predominantly because strong winds helped to rapidly scatter the lethal gas cloud.

8: *Piper Alpha and Alexander L. Kielland: A Comparison of Two North Sea Tragedies*

'Unlike a similar incident on the ill-fated Piper Alpha platform, the gas did not ignite, so what could have been a major disaster for myself and everyone else on board was averted by sheer luck.' – Oberon Houston.

The HSE review of the UK's offshore installations has been critical after a major three-year investigation into safety on more than 100 offshore installations. HSE also noted one major gas leak in the North Sea in 2008 on a scale comparable to the one that caused the PA explosion. The previous year there were five. Arguably Cullen's key health and safety recommendation, which underpins this work, was the introduction of safety regulations requiring the operator/owner of every fixed and mobile installation operating in UK waters to submit a safety case to the HSE for their approval.

With the Forties Alpha platform and Houston's words in mind, let us hope that luck continues to prevent more Piper Alpha scenarios until HSE's work in progress comes to a satisfactory conclusion.

CHAPTER 9: BHOPAL: THE WORLD'S WORST INDUSTRIAL DISASTER – OWEN GREGORY

'Traditionally, the severity of accidents in chemical process industries has been gauged on the basis of the human lives [lost]. However, factors such as loss of assets, contamination of surroundings and the resultant trauma also contribute to a very large extent towards the adverse impact of such accidents.' – (Khan & Abbasi, 1998, p. 305).

The chemical release in 1984 in the Indian city of Bhopal is arguably the worst industrial disaster ever. Fatality estimates vary dramatically from the Madhya Pradesh State Government's estimate of 3,000 to Greenpeace's 8,000. In fact, Greenpeace claim that as many as 20,000 have suffered premature deaths since the disaster, a statistic supported by the US Government's National Center for Biotechnology Information.

Background

Following independence from Great Britain in 1947, the Indian Government attempted to increase wealth in the country. They planned to swiftly move away from a primarily agrarian economy by encouraging industrial development. The rapid development plan required collaboration from foreign firms to assist with:

'[. . .]the rapid industrialisation of the country, [but] it is necessary that the conditions under which they may participate in Indian industry should be

carefully regulated in the national interest.' – (Peterson, 2009, p. 1).

This regulation took the form of a limit on foreign shareholding in 'Indian' firms, rather than in terms of health and safety, business continuity and emergency planning. In one sense, this rapid expansion of Indian industrial capability made the country comparable with the UK during the industrial revolution almost 200 years before – it became vulnerable to accidents and tragedies.

'Developing countries confer upon Multi-National Companies a competitive advantage because they offer low-cost labour, access to markets, and lower operating costs. Once there, companies have little incentive to minimize environmental and human risks. Lax environmental and safety regulation, inadequate capital investment in safety equipment, and poor communications between companies and governments compound the problem.' – (Cassels, 1993, p. 279).

Union Carbide India Limited (UCIL), a part-owned subsidiary of the US-based Union Carbide Company (UCC), wished to establish a plant for making fertilisers and pesticides in the 1960s to support increased food production for a growing population and to support the supply of locally grown cotton for the increasingly important textile industries. Initially, the majority of chemical plants were located in the Bombay area, but the local government of Madhya Pradesh were keen to increase industry in the area and UCIL were provided with land for the proposed chemical plant.

9: Bhopal: The World's Worst Industrial Disaster – Owen Gregory

Circumstances contributing to the enormity of the tragedy

At this time the population of Madhya Pradesh was increasing at 2% a year. Bhopal was one of the fastest-growing cities in India during the 1960s and 1970s as unemployed people from the surrounding countryside came looking for better opportunities. By 1984 it was home to 900,000 people.

The increases in population led to problems with the haphazard settlement of unoccupied areas of land, including those around the many industrial complexes. Indeed, in 1975 a 'hazardous industry' district was created 15 miles from the centre of Bhopal. Despite the dangerous production process and highly toxic methyl isocyanate (MIC) produced on site, however, the UCIL pesticide plant remained classified as 'general industry' and it stayed within the metropolitan area. It is important to note that UCC wished UCIL to import ready-made MIC, but the Indian government insisted on local production for economic reasons.

In addition to the changes in production methods, cheaper locally produced alternatives to UCIL's pesticide products became available. This had two effects. First, the UCIL plant was only operating at 20% capacity in 1984. Secondly, the technical staff operators at the plant, who had been trained by UCC in America, were moving away from the Bhopal facility to other jobs across India, diluting the levels of experience at the Bhopal plant. It was against this background that the disaster occurred, thanks to the 62 tonnes of MIC on the Bhopal site at the beginning of December 1984.

A disaster in waiting

*'Shaving costs and maximizing profits took
precedence over ensuring the safety of plant
workers and the surrounding communities.'* –
(Chemical Industry Archives, 2009).

In the very early morning of 3 December 1984 at least
2,500 people were killed in the immediate aftermath of the
release of MIC into the atmosphere. The pressurised gas
release was caused by a water-contaminated runaway
reaction in Tank 610 of the UCIL plant. The resultant cloud
of highly toxic gas spread over a wide area including a
railway station, a hospital and a densely populated
settlement area.

*'Exposure to MIC has resulted in damage to the
eyes and lungs and has caused respiratory ailments
such as chronic bronchitis and emphysema,
gastrointestinal problems like hyperacidity and
chronic gastritis, ophthalmic problems like chronic
conjunctivitis and early cataracts, vision problems,
neurological disorders such as memory and motor
skills, psychiatric problems of various types
including varying grades of anxiety and depression,
musculoskeletal problems and gynaecological
problems among the victims.'* – (The Lancet, 1989,
p. 952).

The cause of the incident is not in dispute, but the reasons
why water might have entered MIC Tank 610 have been a
matter of much debate. UCIL and the Indian government
claim that the cause was the error of a technician, who
flushed a release valve without inserting a necessary slip-
blind (a method of preventing flows of liquid by sealing a
pipe at a point between two pipe flanges). If true, this

would be a fault with the training and operation of the plant.

An alternate cause put forward by UCC considers sabotage by a disgruntled employee. The suggestion was that they had placed a rubber hose on a release valve of Tank 610 in order to contaminate the tank's contents. Minor incidents of sabotage by employees had occurred previously at the Bhopal plant. No one was ever accused or charged with sabotage however.

Once the chemical reaction was underway, neither the efforts of the plant staff or the safety devices in situ could prevent gas venting. Some 40 tonnes of gas was released over a period of about two hours. The combination of factors that prevented an on-site solution to the problem included:

> '[. . .]the long-term storage of MIC in the plant, the potentially undersized vent gas scrubber, the shutdown of the MIC refrigeration units, the use of the backup tank [611] to store contaminated MIC, the company's failure to repair the flare tower, leaking valves, broken gauges, cuts in manning levels, crew sizes, worker training and skilled supervision.' – (Moreorless, 2011).

Moreover, a 1982 safety inspection had been virtually disregarded and both the government and UCIL had not heeded the complaints of the trade unions representing the Bhopal workers over the reduction in shift crews and supervision. Fault was not limited to UCC and UCIL – the Indian and state governments were found complicit in allowing a potentially dangerous process to be carried out in proximity to a densely populated area.

It was also found that after the gas release hospitals which had been inundated with the victims did not know what chemical poisoning or toxicity they were dealing with. There are also pertinent points that can be raised about the capability of the local hospitals to handle the size of the population seeking assistance, and about the immediate response from the local police force in evacuating the locality after the gas release.

The tragic human legacy

'Nearly 28 years after one of the worst industrial catastrophes in history, toxic chemicals abandoned on the site are still contaminating the groundwater.' – (Bouissou, 2012).

While various sources report conflicting number of initial fatalities, the pollution legacy lives on. As much as 12,000 metric tonnes of toxic waste still remains at the abandoned UCIL site, which has resulted in local groundwater pollution. Toxic substances are known to have infiltrated the soil long before the disaster, however. In 1982 UCIL acknowledged several leaks throughout the plant which also coincided with farmers reporting cattle dying after grazing close to the site.

'The contamination of soil and groundwater in and around the UCIL premises is solely due to dumping of the above mentioned wastes during 1969 to 1984, and the MIC gas tragedy has no relevance to it.' – (The Hindu, 2010).

Malformed children continue to be born near the site and many local inhabitants are being diagnosed with complaints such as anaemia, skins disorders and cancer. Moreover, hundreds of thousands have been left chronically ill.

There is no question that the MIC gas release caused so many fatalities and left a legacy of human suffering for those exposed to its toxic effects. Evidence suggests, however, that the disaster may have served to conceal another potent cause of this on-going tragedy. Either way, the blame can be firmly placed at UCIL's door.

Effects on the local economy

'Hopes were high that the mere presence of such a large, global company would attract large-scale industrial investment to the city. The gas leak changed everything. Since Union Carbide there has been no major investment by foreign companies here.' – Rajendra Kothari, 2009.

In fact by 2009, although India's annual growth rate was around 8%, Madhya Pradesh lagged behind at 4%. While many developed countries would have been delighted with the level of growth, for Madhya Pradesh and Bhopal this was simply not enough.

With loss of employees due to illness being acknowledged globally as a threat for many companies, the Bhopal workforce was decimated overnight, leaving many local organisations exposed. This includes not only fatalities but also the thousands of chronically sick, many of whom were left unable to work. Potential investors may well be deterred by a workforce left with a legacy of unremitting illness.

Although arguably adding insult to injury for the inhabitants of Bhopal, the Madhya Pradesh State

9: Bhopal: The World's Worst Industrial Disaster – Owen Gregory

Government is reported to have been considering promoting dark or thana-tourism at the BCIL site.

'The state's move to turn the defunct Union Carbide factory premises into a site for 'disaster tourism' could be inspired by the Chernobyl site in the former USSR where visitors pay homage to the victims.' – (Dutta, 2009).

Litigation

In the intervening years since the tragedy, litigation has continued. The defunct Bhopal chemical plant was handed over to the Indian government. UCC agreed to fund a memorial hospital at the cost of US$470 million, a figure agreed by the Indian Supreme Court.

UCC has since been bought out by Dow Chemicals who refuse to accept any liability for events prior to their ownership. As recently as 2012, the drive to secure further compensation for Bhopal victims cast a shadow over the London Olympics. Some in India were taking issue with Dow Chemicals being a top-tier sponsor for the event. In response, the International Olympics Committee stated that, *'Dow had no connection with the Bhopal tragedy. Dow did not have any ownership stake in Union Carbide until 16 years after the accident.'*

Lessons learned

The lessons that can be taken from this tragedy can primarily be sub-divided into three factors – human, operational and technical failings. The **human factors** that contributed towards the situation included:

- Attrition of skilled employees leading to low level of experienced staff compounded by limited training for plant personnel.

- Reduction of shift operating staff to minimum (ineffective) levels.

- Slow response to escalating situation.

- Process employed that could introduce water to the MIC tank.

From an operational perspective the following observations were made:

- UCIL production policies and procedures weak; adapted from UCC but with local differences.

- The Bhopal plant was a low profit plant in an unimportant division (pesticides) for UCC and UCIL.

- Plant established at a time when its economic viability was uncertain.

- Eight managers in 15 years.

- Move from alpha-napthol processes to use of methyl isocyanate did not trigger any concerns over manufacturing methods.

- Need for industry exceeding the need for proper planning and mitigation – failure of government oversight.

- Lack of disaster planning.

- Lack of information disseminated to local authorities and health organisations regarding the materials vented into the atmosphere around the plant.

- Potentially dangerous plant permitted in heavily populated area.

- Little or no management or government response to in-plant safety reports or complaints.

Finally, a number of technical failings that contributed towards the disaster:

- General conditions increasing probability of serious accident.

- Process design allowed for large tank storage of MIC; other process designs use smaller storage tanks or a flow process that uses MIC immediately after it is made.

- Manual, non-computerised, sometimes non-redundant, control/monitoring systems.

- Immediate enablers of massive leak on 3 December 1984 included:

- Lack of positive nitrogen pressure, allowing contaminants in through nitrogen line.

- Water entered tank through relief valve and process pipes.

- Water by-passed either the blow-down valve or the safety valve.

- Both flare tower and gas scrubber off-line, no redundancy as each safety device operated with no substitute on failure.

- No empty tank for operators to shunt MIC into when they realise there is a problem.

- Tank over-full (75%-80% of capacity when manual says 50% max).

- No investigation of what kept water flowing out of drain valve when water flushing was begun on 2 December 1984.

9: Bhopal: The World's Worst Industrial Disaster – Owen Gregory

Conclusion

The analysis of threats and risk mitigation or contingency measures is the primary component of business continuity management or emergency planning. In this case study the absence of appropriate levels of risk management both caused and increased the impact of the event. It is clear that the organisation's risk appetite was profit driven, culminating in caution being thrown to wind vis-à-vis the health and safety of its employees and the local population.

The Bhopal chemical plant did have a series of safety devices established, but their suitability and operability were found to be lacking when the MIC runaway reaction commenced. Undertrained employees and inadequate staffing levels seriously constrained an appropriate response to an on-going situation. The unaddressed risks, associated with the plant itself, must be laid firmly at the door of UCIL. But even before the MIC release, UCIL toxic waste had been contaminating the local land and groundwater for around 15 years.

UCC should not be excused from a level of responsibility as they had the major capability for on-going training of the plant operations staff. Even so, it seems that as soon as the Bhopal plant became uneconomical to run the remaining 62 tonnes of MIC was left without necessary safety measures to control any untoward event.

The Indian government and the state government cannot be absolved of blame. They not only failed to follow up on an inspection that revealed safety flaws, but also permitted hazardous processes to be carried out immediately adjacent to a dense human settlement.

The emergency response to the MIC leak was also flawed with no apparent pre-planning or preparation undertaken during the plant's existence. It seems that no lessons were learnt from a dioxin leak from the Seveso chemical manufacturing plant in 1976. Although the Seveso disaster did not have a fatal outcome of the same magnitude as Bhopal, the large numbers of those affected around the Seveso area was due to the proximity of the industrial plant to a populated area.

The conclusion is that threats must be constantly monitored and analysed to ensure that the correct actions can be carried out for their immediate mitigation. As part of risk mitigation a sound business continuity plan, emergency plan or combination of the two must be in place to cover both public and private interests as necessary.

CHAPTER 10: THE DEVASTATING EFFECT OF THE SARS PANDEMIC ON THE TOURIST INDUSTRY – CATHERINE FEENEY

'Looking at underlying drivers of disruption. . . concern over a future pandemic is consistently affirmed across sectors and geographies.' – (Bird, 2013).

Recent Business Continuity Institute surveys have demonstrated that pandemic is a threat taken very seriously across all sectors. The UK Government considers pandemic a 'Tier 1' threat to the country's economy and security, alongside terrorism, war and cyber threats. With the position of global watchdog against health threats, the World Health Organisation (WHO) advises us that we can expect more pandemics in the future. Unfortunately, the WHO is unable to tell us when they might strike, what form they might take, and what effect they might have on both humans and animals. History has taught us, however, that pandemics can devastate the population.

First highlighting tourism's position as a major global industry, this study goes on to look at the effects of a pandemic on the trade by considering the case of 'Severe Acute Respiratory Syndrome' (SARS) between 2002 and 2003.

By their very nature pandemics are unpredictable and have severe health risk implications. SARS is a highly contagious and potentially fatal condition for which there is no known cure. With a very mobile global population, SARS quickly spread from South-East Asia with cases being reported across the globe. The consequential threat this presented to the tourism industry was immense. The rapid and negative reaction of the travelling public during the crisis caused much hardship throughout the tourism industry.

The tourist industry – fragility versus resilience

History has demonstrated that tourism is a fragile industry when faced with health and safety threats to travellers. Consumer confidence will quickly evaporate in reaction to adverse events such as terrorism, natural disasters, high profile disasters, civil unrest and health concerns. London's 7/7 bombing is estimated to have cost the UK capital's tourist economy £4 billion. The 9/11 attack on the World Trade Centre saw close to 600,000 jobs lost, of which 279,000 were in the tourist industry.

The capsizing of the *Costa Concordia* in 2012 resulted in 32 deaths while the economic cost to the wider cruise industry ran into hundreds of millions of dollars. Even the author was offered a buy-one-get-one-free holiday as cruise companies struggled to fill their ships.

The cost in human fatalities from the 2004 Asian Tsunami was horrific with the immediate economic outcome being felt most acutely in the tourist industry. In the case of Thailand, the estimated 8,000 fatalities was a comparatively small percentage of the international disaster total of those reported killed or missing. Tourism accounts for 6% of the country's GDP, but in the six Thai provinces directly affected by the tsunami it was as much as 90%. Moreover, in the six months that followed the disaster, hotel occupancies in Phuket plunged from 63% to 27%.

Tourist behaviour with regard to Thailand can be compared to the reaction that Israel experienced in response to terrorism. During 2000 Israel welcomed close to 2.5 million visitors, but in October 2000 widespread and continued violence broke out when the PLO launched their Second Intifada. Over the four years of this conflict, tourist numbers dropped by 66%. Lost tourism income amounted to billions as hotel occupancy dropped as low as 20% and security costs soared, but it was not entirely a negative experience for the industry. To survive, hotel operations had to become lean, learning how to recalibrate their break-even occupancies from 45-50% to less than 30%. Paradoxically Israeli tourism benefited from the Intifada, becoming well positioned to exploit more peaceful times.

In the case of SARS, not just national but global tourism felts its affects.

Developing a strategy for resilience is essential to ensure a minimisation of disruption, and is particularly important for sustaining businesses in this essential global industry. It is paramount for tourist destinations and their products in the eventuality of customer exposure to health risks, especially in the case of a serious pandemic. Travel and tourism is heavily dependent on an intact environment, whether this is a natural, cultural, social or health environment. Although the sector is resilient it can be easily affected by negative events.

The economic importance of tourism in the emerging millennium

> 'The business volume of tourism equals or even surpasses that of oil exports, food products or automobiles.' – United Nations World Tourism Organisation.

10: The Devastating Effect of the SARS Pandemic on the Tourist Industry – Catherine Feeney

Sometimes referred to as a 'social phenomenon', the significance of tourism is considerable. It is now deemed one of the major arenas in international commerce, and represents at the same time one of the main income sources for many developing countries. There are various definitions of the tourism industry. For example:

> *'It [tourism] comprises the activities of persons travelling to and staying in places outside their usual environment for not more than one consecutive year for leisure, business and other purposes not related to the exercise of an activity remunerated from within the place visited.'* – (Dale, et al., 2005).

The importance of tourism growth to emerging countries is enormous:

> *'Modern tourism is closely linked to development and encompasses a growing number of new destinations. These dynamics have turned the industry into a key driver for socio-economic progress.'* – (Ambedkar, 2013).

This 'driver' presents itself as a significant business opportunity. Indeed, some nations have seen this as a panacea for managing some of their economic problems. Unfortunately, increased tourism is not always an adequate solution; the industry's significance for improving economic prospects is addressed by the United Nations World Tourism Organisation (UNWTO) in their statement that, *'The contribution of tourism to economic well-being depends on the quality and the revenues of the tourism offer.'* They do, however, offer support, acting to help developing countries benefit from sustainable tourism. The significant business case for, and proven economic impact of, tourism is outlined in *Figure 10*.

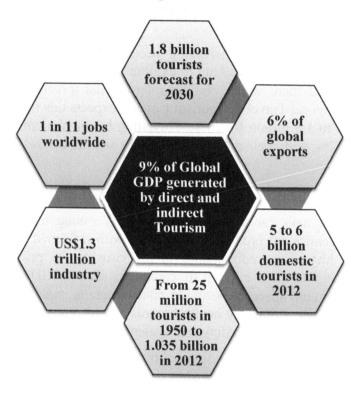

Figure 10: Facts and figures: why tourism matters

The UNWTO also state that that tourism is key to development, prosperity and well-being and provides opportunities for all nations. Despite the global economic downturn, tourism has continued to flourish although its growth has fallen short of predictions made at the turn of the century.

The tourism industry provides a diversity of sectors and products. 90% of the industry consists of small to medium enterprises (SMEs). The wide variety of products and services they offer creates difficulties when trying to develop homogenous solutions for the tourism business continuity.

Globalisation and increasing accessibility has produced travellers that are seeking to explore more exotic locations. In 2012 there were 1 billion international travel arrivals. The World Travel & Tourism Council expects this figure to rise to 1.8 billion by 2030. Travelling by air predominates at 52%, with road at 40%, water at 6% and rail at 2%.

Typical health issues threatening the tourism industry

Health risks can generate apprehension among travellers. Pandemics are predominately linked with influenza due to the historical predominance of the virus as the principal contagious disease. Even so, conditions such as AIDS, foot and mouth disease, pesticide contamination, malaria and West Nile virus pose health hazards and also stimulate far greater demand for safety and hygiene than ever before

Tourist anxiety is often fostered by the threat of exposure to communicable diseases. This can be further complicated when epidemiological investigations are unable to provide timely warnings to the tourism industry, SARS being a case in point. This can be further compounded by any inability among local and national public health services to respond to emerging threats. Countries, particularly developing nations, may need support from international non-governmental organisations (NGOs) such as the International Red Cross, Médecins Sans Frontières and the Disaster Emergency Committee.

10: The Devastating Effect of the SARS Pandemic on the Tourist Industry – Catherine Feeney

Background to managing crises in tourism

'SARS was actually a major trigger for the pandemic preparedness work for the travel, tourism and aviation sector.' – (Glaessar, 2010).

Prior to SARS, the majority of research on tourism crisis issues had concentrated on economic and financial events and impacts, although questions had been raised regarding the reactive nature of tourism research versus the need to develop better predictive capacity and theory generation. The necessity was recognised for swift responses and premeditative processes to reduce the impact of serious health crises affecting the industry. Until recently, however, the dearth of available literature on risk management in relation to health crises has made it difficult to monitor the industry's progress and responses.

Even so, the identification of major risks in tourism had not been totally neglected prior to the SARS outbreak. Several authors had identified noteworthy risks including terrorism, war and political instability, health, crime and cultural and language difficulties.

Academic texts used as sources for this chapter have primarily originated in the last 15 years. The release of these texts has perhaps been driven by the fact that some of the worst crises affecting the tourism industry have occurred during this time. Concern surrounding the spread of disease due to the phenomena of international tourism has now resulted in some much needed attention from political scientists.

Globalised tourism has raised concerns regarding how health issues are dealt with. Research points to a steady increase in international travel as a driving force in the global emergence and spread of infectious diseases.

The SARS pandemic – a catalyst for change

> *'Despite relatively few human casualties, SARS was an economic tsunami — creating US$30 to $50 billion in losses over a period of just a few months.'* – (TASW, 2011, p. 103).

SARS is an example of a major illness that provided a catalyst for the UNWTO to focus and develop strategies promoting efficiency in predicting and planning for challenging threats to health. Originating in Guangdong, China, in November 2002 it continued through 2003 with cases being treated across 26 countries. It presented a challenging situation due to the rapidity of the fallout around the event, which stalled travelling and seriously affected the tourism industry.

The Chinese authorities initially attempted to supress news of the virus to avoid any detrimental effects to their economy and prevent panic among their population. It was three months after the initial outbreak in Guangdong before the Chinese Ministry of Health advised the WHO that there were over 300 cases of the condition which we now know as SARS.

Unaware of the condition and its seriousness, Hong Kong was totally unprepared for the outbreak that followed. A Chinese doctor who had been treating SARS patients in Guangdong checked into the Metropole Hotel and infected several guests, most of whom were overseas visitors. They subsequently returned home to destinations that included Vietnam, Singapore and Toronto, taking the virus with them. In fact, SARS was already spreading even before the WHO knew of its existence.

On 12 March 2003 the WHO issued an unprecedented global warning about SARS. The message was unambiguous – this new mystery virus presented a threat to everyone on the planet. Strong recommendations were issued about travel restrictions to infected areas while airports introduced thermal imaging detectors, insisting that anyone who appeared to have a temperature should have a medical check.

'Although we had developed a war plan, we never thought we would have to use it.' – Dr Julie Hall, WHO.

The WHO launched its war plan, designed to identify, isolate and eradicate new diseases. It also persuaded some of the best microbiologists in the world to work together, something that was hitherto unprecedented. It was in a Hong Kong laboratory that the SARS virus was identified as being from the 'coronavirus' group and related to the common cold. Researchers concluded that it would spread like the common cold, via tiny droplets inhaled after an infected individual coughed or sneezed. Influenza is far more infectious than the common cold as it can hang in the air. It was concluded, however, that SARS can survive for up to 24 h on a surface such as a door handle or a lift button and this may have facilitated some of the cross-infection. This prompted recommendations to be more vigilant with regard to personal hygiene and in particular to more frequent washing of hands.

Quarantining victims plus anyone known to have been exposed to SARS was considered to be the only way to contain the disease. Hong Kong placed the residents of entire apartment blocks in quarantine while in Toronto as many as 10,000 people were 'invited' to go into isolation. Some schools and hospitals faced the same fate.

On the ground in Hong Kong most restaurants, bars and cinemas remained empty while the wearing of protective face masks became the norm. Airlines cancelled flights to and from the territory as passenger numbers plummeted as much as 77% in April 2003. Between March and May 2003, hotel occupancy rates dropped from 79% to 18%. The Metropole subsequently rebranded itself as the Metropark Hotel, perhaps in an effort to shed any lingering stigma from SARS.

'It looked like Hong Kong had no more future as it appeared as the epicentre of SARS and people would not want to travel there.' – Gary Ling, Reuters

For tourism, SARS presented a double threat. Similar to other industries, it needed to cope with the pandemic's effect on its own workforce but it also had to survive while its customers stayed away.

The WTTC has estimated the devastation to Asian tourism from the SARS outbreak. Up to three million people in the industry lost their jobs in the most severely affected jurisdictions of China, Hong Kong, Singapore, and Vietnam. Combined with the decline in tourist arrivals across the rest of Asia, even in countries that were largely or totally disease-free, this proved to be a particularly difficult time for the industry. The lack of cohesive planning was reflected in the region's wider tourism collapse, which the WTTC believes can be attributed more to how governments reacted to the perceived threat of the disease rather than to the real public health danger posed. The SARS outbreak resulted in a 1.2% decline in international tourism arrivals in 2003, with a 41% drop in East Asia during the month of April. The unprecedented WHO advice against non-essential international travel contributed significantly towards this.

The aftermath

Figures published seven years on demonstrate that a pandemic's economic and societal consequences can be enormous. The broad range of after effects illustrate that the results of the devastation cannot be accurately measured for several years after the event. In the final analysis, SARS affected 26 countries, had 8,098 cases, 774 deaths and caused economic losses of US$60 billion, far greater financial damage than was initially anticipated.

Figure 11, below, shows the points UNWTO identified when looking at the outbreak as a catalyst for activating change in the tourism industry:

| 1. | What are the key things that exist now that did not exist five years ago as a result of pandemic preparedness? | Three triggers spurred the development of pandemic planning and preparedness:

 • SARS
 • The 2009 Mexican 'Avian Flu' outbreak
 • The International Decade for Natural Emergency Plans (1990-1999) whereby 'National Emergency Plans' (NEP) were developed in many countries

 Major areas for activity around disease limitation included: communications, sensitivity, logistics and tourism. |

2.	What are the key achievements of pandemic preparedness for the tourism sector?	• Information management – importance of alerts • High importance of targeted, two-way communication, balanced information and case management
3.	What are the most critical gaps that remain in pandemic preparedness in the tourism sector?	• Branding and communication issues • Complacency • Fast and sincere reporting • International travel
4.	What are the key lessons that have emerged from the pandemic?	Pandemics are economically detrimental to the travel and tourism sector, particularly when insufficient information is published not only during but after an emergency is over (usually due to a dearth of available information). Also, the planning for threats from health risks has lacked a cohesive approach, and not just those arising in developing countries. The response to SARS and other pandemics included the development of strategic reaction that provided the framework for managing threats

		to a multi-faceted industry. Future research will provide more in-depth knowledge and resources to manage different situations. The transparency of the UNWTO, WHO and TERN enables the tourism industry to reflect and manage their business continuity and resilience strategic planning for the benefit of all.

Figure 11: The catalysts for change

Source: Glaesser 2006

Lessons learned

During the years since the SARS pandemic the UNWTO have been empowered through their experiences of dealing with serious health issues. This has enabled the development of a framework to manage health threats that affect large numbers of travellers.

The tourism industry was clearly not prepared for SARS and it suffered badly both economically and in terms of job losses. In the aftermath it has been more focused on preparing itself for any future significant health threats. Actions taken include the creation of the Tourism Emergency Response Network (TERN) in 2006, although the 2004 Pacific tsunami also influenced this.

10: The Devastating Effect of the SARS Pandemic on the Tourist Industry – Catherine Feeney

What went well

The diverse nature of the tourism industry, 90% of which is comprised of SMEs, meant that strong leadership was required from an international perspective. *'Singapore learned from the 2003 SARS pandemic the importance of addressing non-health issues and having a single, national-level mechanism for decisive decision-making.'* – (TASW, 2011, p. 41).

- A cohesive but collaborative approach emerged through leadership from the UNWTO. Their surveys show that the integration of travel & tourism into national emergency structures and national emergency plans and procedures has taken place from mid-2008. These surveys also revealed that for the majority of countries, particularly those depending heavily on tourism, an additional 'pandemic plan' was an essential preparation to run concurrently with the national emergency plan.

- The excellent collaborative development of TERN by the UNTWO is a positive step; the SARS outbreak showed the need for interconnected planning.

What could have been done better

- The industry failed to maintain an intact environment for travel and tourism during the pandemic. This could have been achieved through complete awareness of the pandemic situation and its restrictions, simulation exercises, strong communication at all levels (local, national and international) through various agencies, plus constant vigilance to enable preparedness for a pandemic and its consequences.

- Managing the external or macro environments to assist in providing resources would have enabled all affected countries to combat the pandemic with equal effectiveness. Promoting holistic planning for health crises is a global issue.

- Encouraging the remaining 28% of UN countries without a national emergence plan to create one is essential to maintain coherent global responsiveness.

What did not go well

- China's delay in alerting the WHO to the health crisis developing in Guangdong province left Hong Kong unaware and exposed to the pandemic.

- Of great concern to the UNWTO was the lack of assistance available to 'newly industrialised countries'. Managing pandemics in countries where public health departments do not have the depth of resources available in developed countries is difficult; these countries require support from the UN and NGOs to arrest the spread of contagious diseases.

Other observations

> *'SARS was not the killer disease that the WHO War Plan had been designed for. But maybe it was a dress rehearsal'* – (BBC World, 2003).

- World travel conditions for tourism have improved and grown exponentially. Consequently, there is a need for greater coordination among organisations responsible for containing communicable diseases. Support must continue for recently-established bodies which provide communication and ensure tourism can continue in affected areas. The role of public health organisations when managing a health crisis is crucial. Governments in cooperation with the relevant NGOs must provide a cohesive response to managing contagious outbreaks.

- Tourism thrives when it is safe to travel. Ensuring health and safety is beneficial to all stakeholders. Sharing information and methods of operation can prevent the dissemination of further strains of pandemic illnesses.

Subsequent improvements in tourism health crisis management

The UNWTO is responsible for monitoring and managing global health issues which might affect tourism. They have clear and established guidelines for dealing with such emergencies. Their coordination with various organisations, particularly the WHO, in the event of pandemics and health crises is paramount.

In 2006 the United Nations established the Tourism Emergency Response Network (TERN). TERN consists of the world's leading tourism associations who collaborate on strategies for managing crises.

The UNWTO developed initiatives for working closely with the travel trade after adverse events such as SARS and the 2004 Indian Ocean earthquake threatened tourism businesses on a national and global level. The UNWTO established the importance of TERN and has stated that it should be characterised by independence and interdependency, with each partner working towards the common goal of making travel and destinations safe for tourists.

It has established a set of basic guidelines. TERN should:

- Work closely with the UN System.
- Share real time information and ideas.
- Give clear, concise and geographically specific public messages.
- Establish close relationships with the media to better spread information as necessary.
- Be activated in response to regional and global emergencies of relevance for the travel and tourism sector, or at the request of a TERN member.

Under the umbrella of the UNWTO there is a panel of risk and crisis management programme members. They provide mitigation strategies, actions and instruments to evaluate risks of global and local importance. National organisations can disseminate this information to their health protection agencies, usually the public health authorities.

Conclusion

The process of managing threats and developing resilience to safeguard tourism has come a long way in the last 15 years. Closer collaboration with international governmental and non-governmental organisations has provided a more cohesive and constructive approach, enabling whole areas of the globe to better manage their communications and consequently their resources. Improved planning has helped the majority of countries to closely monitor events and ensure a safe environment for residents, travellers and tourists.

There is a vital lesson to learn from the SARS outbreak, which could help to reduce the impact of future pandemics on the tourism industry. Some research supports the argument that the tourism industry is not just a potential victim of pandemics; with the explosion of global travel it can also be part of the problem.

CHAPTER 11: TOYOTA VEHICLE RECALL – TONY DUNCAN

Product recalls can happen to almost any company regardless of who they are and in which industry sectors they operate. It is a threat that companies need to consider from a business continuity perspective. Over the years some big names have been forced to withdraw products from the marketplace, which has invariably been a costly experience and has sometimes caused damage to the company's reputation. The list is extensive and includes the likes of:

- Johnson and Johnson (Tylenol drug found to be sabotaged and laced with cyanide)
- Perrier (Perrier water tainted within benzene)
- Dell (Sony-supplied batteries used in Dell laptops had a risk of catching fire)
- Mattel (lead-tainted Chinese-manufactured toys)
- Fonterra (dairy products contained botulism causing bacteria)
- Coca-Cola (products sold in China contained chlorine)
- Beko (fridge/freezer units with faulty defrost timer that could catch fire)
- Tesco and other leading supermarkets (a variety of beef products contained horse meat)

The list goes on. This case study, however, focuses on the Toyota and Lexus vehicle defects that resulted in over eight million cars being recalled. This led to Toyota posting its first loss in more than six decades. The car manufacturer also experienced a 16% fall in stock price, wiping around US$25 billion off the corporation's market capitalisation.

Corporation background

The Toyota Motoring Corporation was first established in 1937 from the Toyoda Automatic Loom Works, the leading manufacturer of weaving machinery at the time. Patent rights to one of the weaving machines owned by the corporation were sold to finance investment and development of the first model of Toyota car.

With its headquarters in Tokyo, Toyota is the leading producer of automobiles in Japan with twelve manufacturing plants and a large number of affiliates. It also has approximately 52 manufacturing companies in a total of 27 countries, which produce the car brands Lexus and Toyota.

'There is no such thing as an entrenched and unassailable position in the automobile business. There never has been and I do not believe there ever will be' – L.L Colbert, Chrysler President, 8 June 1955.

Operations of the main Toyota corporation include elements of the financial services market as well as prefabricated housing and leisure boats. With the success of its brands based on reliability and quality, Toyota was rated as the number 1 car manufacturer in the world in 2008. In 2010 it is estimated that Toyota employed some 320,000 people.

The unfolding crisis

'The evidence that Toyota was expanding too much and too quickly started surfacing a couple of years

ago. Not on the corporation's bottom line, but on its car-quality ratings.' – (Ingrassia, 2009).

In 2009 rumours began to circulate regarding problems with electronic equipment and software contained within Toyota and Lexus brand cars. Although Managing Officer Hiroyuki Yokoyama did admit that the corporation had fallen short of standards expected by customers, he refused to confirm whether a recall was planned. Furthermore, apart from a 75 second interview given by Toyota's president, Akio Toyoda, the corporation did not enter into further discussions regarding the nature of the problems or their plans to resolve the situation.

But even before the rumours started gathering momentum, US insurer State Farm had raised its own concerns about Toyota accelerator problems to the federal regulator at least two years earlier. With a vast claims experience data base to draw on, the insurer was quite rightly concerned about the rise of accelerator related accidents. The regulator does seem to have been slow to react to this warning.

'Crisis Management experts told the Asian Productivity Organisation (APO) over the weekend that the crisis likely surfaced years ago but with the culture at Toyota, fast growing and wanting to beat the competition, no one wanted to break the news to the boss' – Matt Lauer, NBC Today Show, 2010.

After an economically hard year for the auto industry in 2008, sales of Toyota cars began to steadily increase. Reports of problems with their cars, however, also continued to increase leading to the recall of 12 models of cars between the autumn of 2009 and the spring of 2010. Toyota recalled approximately 8.5 million cars with eight million of those for potential floor mat, braking, accelerator pedal, unwanted acceleration or steering problems. The recalls made up 58% of total Toyota sales for that period.

Although Toyota reportedly knew about some of the problems the vehicles were experiencing, no definite conclusions had been reached about the cause. To be fair to Toyota, this may have delayed a recall as the company did not know what action to take until it understood the problem it was trying to fix. During this period of uncertainty, the corporation seemed to be more focused on minimising the effect of the incident than communicating with stakeholders with a view to resolving the issues.

Until the cause of the problem had been fully understood, it was never going to be possible to define a reliable solution. Consequently, many of the corporation's car production lines were shut down to avoid shipping more defective vehicles while engineers investigated the problems. It was eventually discovered that the fault was in the design of parts and not the manufacturing process.

Competitors and other groups regarded the Toyota recall as an extremely damaging incident to the main value that Toyota represented – quality.

Crisis management

The crisis management model in place when the recall incident went critical appears to have been totally inadequate for the nature of the incident. It is almost entirely focused on the supply chain and it is far from the action-oriented approach which is commonplace today within many large organisations. While it does make reference to risks such as earthquakes and fires, it makes no reference at all to dealing with a product recall. It even includes crisis management case studies which, in the heat of the moment, I doubt any crisis management team would have the time to read.

While there are implied levels of crisis management (i.e., country, area and corporate levels etc.) there are no roles and responsibilities identified within the document. Instead it refers to assigning crisis managers and then allocating a crisis team. The implication is that any crisis management team may have never met before and has probably never been involved in any rehearsals. Moreover, it points out that crisis management team members may find their 'day jobs' conflicting with their CM responsibilities. Surely when an organisation is seriously threatened, fixing the problem should take precedence over day to day activities?

The document also states that a separate 'outside communications manager' would provide visibility to the outside world. Presumably this includes the media and consumers. The existence of this role was clearly not communicated throughout Toyota as many corporation representatives made statements to the media that were uncoordinated and frequently in conflict with each other. This resulted in very mixed and confusing messages being disseminated.

Communications

In January 2010, Toyota launched a public relations campaign aimed at reassuring consumers, and after an outcry from dealerships reversed its decision to have replacement parts for affected cars delivered to factories, redirecting them to dealerships.

On 4 February 2010 Toyota announced an estimated cost of US$1.12 billion on warranty expenses, although this was widely regarded as an underestimation due to the fact that not all of the 12 models affected had been recalled by this point.

'Traffic to the news section of the Toyota European websites peaked at approximately 40,000 per day at the beginning of February 2010, which were ten times more visits than normal. . . on the day a major UK newspaper published the Toyota recall issue on its front page, almost 14,000 customers called Toyota Great Britain.' – Colin Hensley (Toyota, 2010, pp. 62–64).

So big had the story become that during the first week of February, the Toyota recall debacle had become the second most reported article in the USA, amounting to around 11% of the total news coverage.

'Deaths connected to sudden acceleration in Toyota vehicles have surged in recent weeks, with the alleged death toll reaching 34 since 2000, according to new consumer data gathered by the government.' – (Thomas, 2010).

By May 2010, the New York Times claimed that the number of fatalities had risen to 89 plus 57 injuries. As if this was not enough, Jim Lentz, President and CEO for Toyota Sales in the USA undermined consumer confidence in the brand. Appearing on the *Today Show* he wilted under cross-examination by host Matt Lauer and his appearance was described as like a deer caught in the headlights. A poll taken before the show reported that 37% of respondents said they would not buy a Toyota. Immediately after the show, this number leapt to 56%. Lentz's poor performance on camera arguably rates alongside the public relations disasters of BP's Tony Hayward and Freedom Industries' Gary Southern.

But in some ways, with respect to communications, Toyota was its own worst enemy. They did not have a communication plan that was observed across the corporation, particularly for media communications, which resulted in corporation representatives speculating on the cause of the problems.

'Rather than say that they are investigating the complaints and will issue a complete report at the conclusion of their investigation, Toyota representatives reacted to the complaints in ways that confounded marketing and crisis management experts. They confused everyone by jumping to conclusions and suggesting different causes in rapid succession.' – (Kalb, 2012).

To further compound matters, the US watchdog magazine *Consumer Reports* printed an article warning readers not to buy certain models of Toyota and Lexus cars due to problems with vehicle design and electronic stability control systems. The same day that the article was published Toyota requested that dealers halt sales on these vehicles and offered car loans to relevant customers.

Regulator penalises Toyota

On 7 April 2010, along with a statement that Toyota knowingly hid safety problems from government regulators, the U.S. Department of Transportation fined Toyota US$16.4 million. This is reportedly the highest ever civil penalty lodged, and the Department warned that further fines could follow. They also noted that had there not been a cap on the fines, penalty amounts could have reached US$13.8 billion. The authorities have to be challenged as to why it took them three years to reach this point, after being warned of the accelerator issue by State Farm insurer in 2007.

Supply chain management

'The reality is that auto suppliers make hardly any of their parts. They assemble cars from parts made by others.' – (Connor, 2010).

Prior to the recall, Toyota had been regarded as a model for supplier relationship management. Unfortunately, as planning for self-regulating and cyclical risk management was not a priority for corporation executives, the recall revealed a real failure in the comprehensive risk management process. It is evident that this corporation ignored the potential of extreme risk in return for the benefits gained with economies of scale, using the same supplier in the manufacturing process for several models of Toyota and Lexus cars. The failure in the supply chain also brought to light evidence of bad relation and stakeholder management.

'Your supply chain is only as strong as your weakest link.' – (Connor, 2010).

CTS, the US-based supplier of Toyota's troublesome accelerator, claimed that the problem had existed in 1999, years before the company started manufacturing the part for Toyota. But ADR International's CEO, Bill Michels, believes that Toyota should be commended for not trying to blame its suppliers for the massive recall problem.

Risk management failure

'Toyota's Recall Crisis was a failure in risk management.' – (Michels, 2013).

Had a comprehensive risk management process been followed and a threat analysis performed, the corporation would have been better positioned to manage the potential risks surrounding this incident. There are three classifications of supply risk that Toyota's risk management programme should have addressed – brand, commodity and disruption.

- ***Brand.*** The way the public and other stakeholders regard products in the marketplace and the images of quality that are associated with those products. Negative issues would dramatically impact on the corporation's brand image, whether the fault lay with the corporation or not.

  Potential risks to brands could be:
  o Small suppliers. Only Toyota is fully aware of who its suppliers are but the impact of the recall on the corporation was massive.
  o A company must have comprehensive and up to date information on supplier performance. If this is not the case there is an increased potential for a lack awareness of the risks involved.

  It is impossible to have full control of risks to the brand, so it is necessary for specific, forward thinking contingencies to be in place.

- ***Commodity.*** Although total control over brand management is virtually impossible, achieving some degree of control is a realistic expectation. There is, however, the potential for external factors to contribute to risks by affecting the price of goods and services. The price of elements at the base of the manufacturing process is directly related to the amount of profit or loss made by the corporation. Most organisations focus on the key elements but not on the secondary factors that may affect the commodity.

• **Disruption.** The potential for this type of risk comes from many factors including natural disaster, technical faults and operational contingency issues. The just-in-time supply chain model used by Toyota is vulnerable to both natural and man-made disasters. The best approach in combating this is to ensure that there is a comprehensive business continuity management process in place. This will assess threats and identify appropriate contingency and mitigation measures.

Unfortunately not all of these factors were assessed and incorporated by Toyota.

Strategic risk management

Toyota may have been more inclined to focus on the usual three categories of risk:

• hazards (fire, flood, earthquake, etc.)
• financial (currency fluctuations, banking influences, etc.)
• operational (production disruption, interrupted supply chains, etc.)

They should have recognised that strategic risks are potentially more costly to the main corporation and its stakeholders.

'Not all businesses face every form of strategic risk, but every business faces some. The seven major kinds of strategic risk are: project risk; customer

risk; transition risk; unique competitor risk; brand risk; industry risk; and stagnation risk.' – (Slywotzky, 2011).

The lack of awareness of strategic risk shown by Toyota could have resulted in severed ties between the corporation and suppliers and did result in the quality of their product being compromised. It could also have limited or even destroyed strategic control of elements of the manufacturing process.

Although there is no way to avoid strategic risk completely, there is merit in identifying, understanding, and implementing effective control measures that can mitigate potential risks.

It should be noted here that there were pre-incident attempts at strategic risk mitigation, with the corporation developing a process where resident engineers where deployed to the factories to be available in case of issues with the manufacturing process.

Reputational risk

Building a good reputation can be a long and painstaking process. By comparison losing it is relatively easy. Although Toyota had a reputation for superior product quality before this incident, it was their delay in initiating a recall, not the recall itself that created the primary risk to that reputation. After all, recalls are not uncommon for the automobile industry. But Toyota erroneously claimed at first that there were no problems with these vehicles, citing driver error.

Fortunately, they did realise in time the futility of getting involved in unconstructive arguments regarding who was to blame. They released a statement confirming their willingness to work through the incident with external stakeholders. Unfortunately, they should also have concentrated on keeping the public informed at all opportunities.

It should be noted, however, that the corporate leadership had the presence of mind to view the halting of production, a very costly course of action, as an investment in redeeming a positive reputation and a vital step in guiding the company towards recovery.

External stakeholder engagement

In this area, Toyota is different to many other similar organisations. It has no specific external stakeholder engagement policy and the only vague reference to one is contained within their corporation code of conduct, relating to incorporating stakeholders criticisms as appropriate into business activities.

There is no evidence of staff training in stakeholder engagement and no evidence of external stakeholder involvement in corporate decision-making. The corporation does not identify the methods in which stakeholders will be informed nor does it state how their involvement affects corporate policy.

It should also be noted that there was a substantial knock on effect felt by Toyota's main Japanese competitors, (Nissan, Honda, Mazda and Mitsubishi). All of these corporations saw negative repercussions along with falls in sales. Ford, in the US, however, saw a rise in sales and share price value.

Lessons learned

This incident was serious enough to knock Toyota from its number one spot in the automobile world, and the cost of rectifying the situation also plunged the corporation into the red for the first time in over 60 years.

The primary issues identified involve failures in risk management in Toyota's supply chain management process, and the lack of an effective communication strategy. Arguably, the corporation was also in a state of denial that it had a problem at all. But Toyota was big enough to survive and consumer trust in the brand and reputation has clearly not been irreparably damaged. Other organisations facing similar circumstances, regardless of industry, may not be so fortunate.

'There's no telling what the final costs associated with a major supply risk event will be. The only thing you know for certain is that an ounce of prevention will likely hurt a lot less than that pound of cure.' – (Minahan, 2010).

What went well

- Despite having to endure massive losses caused by the recall, Toyota recovered and regained the automobile manufacturers' number one position for both 2012 and 2013, beating off stiff competition from General Motors and Volkswagen. Other companies could do well to learn from the Toyota experience.
- Toyota accepted responsibility and did not try to hide behind supply chain failures. One can only respect this attitude.

- When a company chooses to outsource part or all of its operation, it needs to recognize that it still retains responsibility for its business continuity arrangements. This includes both its up-stream and down-stream supply chains. Toyota acted in accordance with this principle.

What could have been done better

- The reputation of a corporation is at risk when it is perceived to have been involved in arrogant or non-communicative behaviour. Even the appearance of a cover up can negatively affect external stakeholder behaviour and can even serve to shatter bonds with consumer groups and suppliers. Toyota was slow to react and its communication strategy appears flawed.

- The delay in releasing information was an error by Toyota although this may have been in part due to not knowing what the problem was and exactly what messages to communicate. Even so, to maintain a positive and public media image it is important to be transparent in all activities relating to areas of stakeholder interest. Negative aspects like vehicle faults should have been conveyed in full, via a clearly defined media and stakeholder management process, to effectively regain control of the crisis and reduce its impact on the corporation.

But Toyota needed to be clear about exactly who was authorized to speak to the media on the corporation's behalf. Moreover, every employee needs to know who has been appointed to this task whether at a corporate, regional or local level. It is just as they are made aware that enquiries from outside the corporation should always be referred to the corporation's official communication channels. This will ensure that a consistent set of messages are issued whether directly to the media or via some other means such as the corporation's websites.

It is clear that Toyota's customers were seeking information about what was happening. The 40,000 peak daily hit rate on the Toyota European news website and 14,000 phone calls in one day to Toyota GB bear this out. It would have undoubtedly helped Toyota's position if they had proactively contacted customers instead and offered some helpful guidance on what to do.

'One area for improvement, however, would be their social media strategy. So far @Toyota has re-tweeted one media item about the recall, and @toyota_europe hasn't mentioned it at all. Similarly, their Facebook page makes no reference to yesterday's announcement. @ToyotaGB is doing a great job, however, replying directly to customer questions, clarifying media reports with links to statements and directing people to more information. People use social media as a news source more than ever, and Toyota would benefit greatly from learning from team GB and incorporating social media into future crisis management plans across all international teams.' – (Cockram, 2010).

- Since Toyota ranked last out of 10 assessed corporations for addressing and responding to complaints, it is important for them to put systems in place to efficiently deal with complaints from stakeholders. These systems should incorporate relevant stakeholder information and behaviour into the early steps of crisis identification to initiate any incident mitigation processes. It is also advisable for organisations to realise that incidents can involve multiple internal and external stakeholders at the same time.

- The identification of the core values of the corporation and the development of relevant contingency planning incorporating these values will help the corporation to mitigate the impact on the areas in which it is strongest. If this is not effectively incorporated into the crisis management process it is possible that competitors will be affected, either reducing the corporation's standing in the market place or even negatively affecting the industry as a whole.

- State Farm, the largest US insurer, had contacted the US National Highway Traffic Safety Administration at least two years earlier regarding a worrying trend involving Toyota vehicles. This should have prompted Toyota to investigate while developing and implementing incident and risk management contingency planning in order to lessen the impact of any potential incident.

- In the right circumstances, it is quite acceptable for an organisation to decide to adopt a business continuity strategy which involves doing nothing until after an incident has occurred. This would normally be considered acceptable when the maximum tolerable periods of disruption can be measured in months. Toyota, however, allowed this situation to deteriorate for some considerable time before action was seen to be taken.

Toyota's crisis management process needs further development to look beyond just supply chain management. It also needs to be turned into an action oriented plan without unnecessary rhetoric. By also identifying plan owners and crisis management teams at corporate, regional and local levels it will enable the corporation to actively rehearse the various scenarios it may need to deal with in reality. Without rehearsing plans of this nature they are not worth the paper they are printed on.

What did not go well

- Confidence in Toyota across the USA was badly damaged by Jim Lentz's poor performance on the Today Show. Interviewer Matt Lauer had clearly done his preparation well. He was able to demonstrate that either Lentz was unaware that incidents had been occurring for several years rather than for just a few months prior to the recall or that Lentz was being less than honest about the situation.

Conclusion

Companies taking a long hard look at their supply chains have a number of serious questions to ask themselves:

- Does the scope of our supply chain management actually include all our strategic suppliers? Do we know our suppliers strengths and weaknesses? Are we in possession of sufficient supplier related information (e.g. supplier performance, and supplier profile data etc.) to be able to identify potential problems before they materialise?

- Do we have an effective supply chain management process in place that enables us to identify risks that may exist across the chain? Does our workforce have both an appropriate level of experience and sufficient bandwidth to deal with these risks?

- Are we managing our supply chain within an effective business continuity framework? Is an effective threat assessment being performed across the chain, both up-stream and down-stream, so that we have a good understanding of the risks they may present? Does the company actively develop mitigation actions and contingencies?

- Have we created appropriate BCM strategies? Have we developed and validated associated business continuity plans to create a level of confidence that incidents can be addressed as they arise?

- Do our strategic suppliers have business continuity plans in place and are they robust?

CHAPTER 12: THE GLOUCESTERSHIRE FLOODING, 2007 – CARL DAKIN

'The 2007 floods in Britain resulted in the largest civil emergency response since World War II.' – (UK Cabinet Office, 2010).

In 2007 the United Kingdom experienced some of the worst flooding in recent history. Following a very dry month of April, the summer was one of the wettest on record with heavy rain falling throughout June and July. Gloucestershire was seriously affected and on 20 July two months' rainfall inundated the area in just 14 h.

One of the vital industries that suffered serious impact from the flood was water services, including the provision of potable tap water plus the treatment of waste water and sewerage. Over 300,000 consumers serviced by the Mythe Water Treatment Works, owned by Severn Trent Water Ltd, had no tap water for more than two weeks.

This case study focuses on the critical impact to water services, as well as actions carried out by key stakeholders including the service providers plus appropriate first and second responders as defined in the UK Civil Contingencies Act (2004).

Background

Gloucestershire is an area of the UK that is prone to flood, according to records which go back as far as the 13th century. In recent times there have been at least seven serious floods recorded since the Great Flood of 1947, including the subject of this study.

12: The Gloucestershire Flooding, 2007 – Carl Dakin

'The event was estimated to have had a recurrence interval in excess of once in 200 years.' – (Roberts, 2012).

At approximately five miles (8 km) longer than the River Thames, the Severn is officially the UK's longest river. It rises in Wales and is fed by a number of major tributaries including the Warwickshire Avon with their convergence at the medieval town of Tewkesbury. The town itself is surrounded by flood plains and the Mythe Water Treatment Works is located on a man-made rise close to Tewkesbury.

Flood impact

'Climate change experts tell us that this is the sort of thing we need to expect for the future.' – (BBC News, 2007).

The impact of the adverse weather was felt across the UK. Around 48,000 households and over 7,300 businesses were flooded and several primary transport routes became inaccessible. Some people found themselves stranded, with one of the worst affected areas being Gloucester Railway station. Around 500 passengers found themselves marooned when train services were suspended while an estimated 10,000 motorists were stuck on the M5 motorway and adjoining roads. There were 13 fatalities recorded across the UK.

In the worst scenarios, the operation of critical services such as electricity and water supplies, including the Mythe Water Treatment Works, were compromised by flooding. Thousands of people needed evacuating and temporarily rehousing. In some cases, they were unable to return permanently to their own homes for several months.

'To put this into context, there were over 200 major floods worldwide during 2007, affecting 180 million people. The human cost was more than 8,000 deaths and over £40 billion worth of damage. But even against that backdrop, the floods that devastated England ranked as the most expensive in the world.' – Sir Michael Pitt, (Carmichael, et al., 2012).

Pitt also records that it was unclear whether it was safe or not to remain in flooded homes as health advisors were providing conflicting information. He notes that some victims probably needed counselling as they felt bereaved and were experiencing emotions such as disbelief, anger and blame. Twelve months later, research by the BBC revealed that some flood victims were still suffering with stress and anxiety although this was more to do with insurance claim-related issues and shoddy repair work by rogue builders.

Acute shortage of potable water

'We have never experienced an incident of this magnitude. Our crisis management procedures were not designed to manage a civil contingency of this scale.' – (Pitt, 2008, p. 193).

Evidence suggests that flooding on the scale experienced in 2007 had not been anticipated nor planned for. This is best illustrated by the events at the Mythe Works near Tewkesbury. The Mythe Works had suffered from low level flooding in the past but its operation had never been disrupted. The owner, Severn Trent Water (SWT), considered the disposition of the plant on man-made raised ground and recent improvements to site drainage to be adequate measures to militate against the level of flooding likely to cause disruption to operations. The scale of the flood in 2007, however, overwhelmed the site and it was forced to cease operation in order to prevent severe damage to critical machinery.

STW had to implement its plan to provide drinking water for up to 350,000 people, as mandated by the Department for the Environment, Food and Rural Affairs (DEFRA) under the Security and Emergency Measures Direction (DEFRA, 1998). Remarkably, as much as 6,000,000 l of water was delivered into the affected area on a daily basis, spilt 50-50 between bottled and bowser/tanker supplied water. The public were encouraged to recycle the plastic bottles and collection services were arranged.

Approximately 1,400 bowsers were located throughout the affected area. Unbelievably, some were vandalised and 150 went missing and may have been stolen. Although the police recovered the majority, there were still 20 bowsers unaccounted for five years after the flood. There were also reports of vans visiting bowsers and syphoning off the water. The public were asked to notify the authorities if they witnessed any such incidents.

Replenishment of the bowsers was initially slow as tankers had to be cleaned and disinfected before they could be used. This caused delays of up to 48 h before they could be deployed. Bowsers and tankers were also borrowed from other water companies in line with pre-existing reciprocal arrangements. In Cheltenham, twelve Portaloos were installed at the local shopping centre for the convenience of local shoppers.

The severity of the incident had not been anticipated by STW and its contingency to provide potable water via distribution points from bottled and bowser tank supplies proved to be a challenge for the company. It was able to meet the minimum requirement of ten litres per person per day, as directed under the Security and Emergency Measures Direction, but only with help from the armed forces and emergency services plus the private and voluntary sectors.

STW had not considered a protracted disruption to service of the magnitude experienced in 2007. They had also underestimated the psychological effect rationing would have on a public used to an average consumption of 138 l per person per day. Even so, STW recognised the threat to its reputation and the potential civil unrest resulting from public discontent.

'We expected it was going to be busy, but when we looked out the doors prior to when we opened up at 8 am there must have been. . . nearly 1,000 people outside waiting to come in. It looked like football crowds.' – Craig Lay, Asda Supermarket.

Police had to be called in to control crowds after one delivery of bottled water at the supermarket. In SWT's defence, they were meeting the minimum 10 l per day per person ration as dictated by DEFRA, albeit with support from outside the company.

Civil Contingencies Act

The Civil Contingencies Act (2004) defines category 1 responders (e.g. police, fire and rescue, local councils, etc.) and category 2 responders (e.g. utilities, transport and health bodies etc.) and legislates how they should prepare for and react in the event of an emergency. The Act requires that category 1 responders (e.g. Gloucestershire County Council, etc.):

'. . .maintain plans to ensure that they can continue to exercise their functions in the event of an emergency so far as is reasonably practicable. The duty relates to all functions, not just their emergency response functions.' – (HM Government, 2004).

Category 2 responders (e.g. Severn Trent Water, etc.) are expected to have plans in place that ensure they are able to support the category 1 responders during an emergency, where appropriate.

Prior to the 2007 floods Gloucestershire County Council (GCC) had already identified the requirement for contingencies to deal with civil emergencies. Although the Civil Contingencies Act requires Local Authorities (LA) to conduct risk assessments and develop contingency plans for vital services and assets, GCC had already developed and implemented a strategy in 2003. This was considered by many LAs to be 'best practice' and GCC were awarded a discretionary grant from the Cabinet Office to develop a BCM training package for LAs. This suggests that a good level of understanding existed within GCC to plan for potential crisis, developing an approach to BCM that was endorsed by central government and adopted by LAs throughout the UK.

Flawed business continuity approach

The impact of the flood had serious consequences across the community, with huge disruption to services and utilities. GCC initiated an immediate response. It handled the incident as a civil emergency within the framework of the Civil Contingencies Act, which had been incorporated into its business continuity management plan.

It quickly became clear that none of the first responders, including Gloucestershire County Council, had realised that the Mythe Water Works was such a significant single point of failure. With the exception of around 20,000 properties that it serviced, the vast majority of its 350,000 consumers were totally dependent upon its continued operation. Its closure was felt across the region including in Cheltenham, Gloucester and Tewkesbury.

Two points in particular are worth considering at this time:

- Firstly, assuming that SWT were fully aware that the Mythe was a massive single point of failure, a risk assessment should have shown its loss as having a very high impact on SWT's operation. Conversely, based upon the evidence presented, the probability of such an event was considered as very low. Since the assessment of the risk is derived from the probability of an event occurring and the corresponding impact, the resultant risk value would not have given much cause for concern. So while contingency plans were in place for alternative means of water supply, in line with legislation, insufficient focus had been given to mitigate the risk that actually materialised.

- Second, the fact that Gloucestershire County Council did not know that the Mythe was a single point of failure until after the commencement of the flooding suggests a major failure. It could be argued that GCC should have asked SWT about any exposures of this nature or that SWT should have been proactive in telling GCC. Had the oversight not occurred, perhaps contingency measures would have been better prepared.

Clearly, SWT had not planned to maintain the flow of potable tap water while experiencing a worst case scenario, which in this instance was the loss of the Mythe for an

The Gloucestershire Flooding, 2007 – Carl Dakin

extended period of time. While organisations are generally quite entitled to hide behind a 'risk appetite' and accept a risk, should this be the case for a vital service such as water supplier? In fairness to SWT, their contingency plans to comply with legislation worked.

The value of testing and exercising business continuity plans

Although GCC had embraced the concept of BCM and implemented a strategy, they failed to identify the need to train and prepare decision makers and key stakeholders before an emergency occurred. An integral part of the BCM lifecycle is testing and exercising the plan. This serves to validate the reliability of the plan, thereby avoiding the danger of having to test it in a live situation with the inherent risk of discovering that it does not work. It also gives the opportunity to raise levels of awareness while providing training for key staff.

It seems that GCC had embraced the concept of expecting and encouraging staff to 'think on their feet'. This could be considered an ad-hoc approach which forces personnel to rely on experience, which may be limited, and relies on correct decisions to be made under pressure, possibly with inefficient available information.

GCC described the ad-hoc approach in its guide to business continuity:

> *'1.7. Without plans, managers will have to rely on an 'ad-hoc' approach to deal with these, and the many other issues that will present themselves. This approach is essentially made up at the time of the incident.*

1.8. The benefit of an 'ad-hoc' response is that it requires little effort to set up or maintain. However, the ad-hoc approach is prone to failure. Individuals typically make incorrect assumptions, particularly in respect to:

- *their own responsibilities*
- *the responsibilities of others*
- *what facilities and arrangements can be relied upon during the event.'*

In the ideal situation, employees should not have to stop to think about how to react to a situation, they should just be able to get on with it. Ideally they will have attained an awareness level of unconscious competence through testing and rehearsals. As defined in the 2010 version of the Business Continuity Institute's Good Practice Guidelines:

'The awareness of staff may be defined at one of four levels:

1. *'Unconscious Incompetence' where staff are unaware of BCM issues. They do not know what they don't know.*
2. *'Conscious Incompetence' where staff are aware of BCM generally, but know little about its detailed requirements.*
3. *'Conscious Competence' where staff are cognisant of the BCM issue and are proficient (e.g. in following documented procedures) in supporting BCM.*
4. *'Unconscious Competence' where staff are instinctively fully competent in applying BCM in a variety of circumstances.'*

With GCC being a first responder, they had the responsibility of coordinating multiple agency responses, which in the case of the 2007 flooding would have included SWT. Any such response is always at risk of failure if insufficient testing and rehearsing is undertaken.

To consolidate and underpin the need for synergy across multiple agencies with equity in a contingency plan, training and testing should be carried out to ensure the BCM plan is fit for purpose, or identify areas of weakness so they can be remedied. But it is important to note that training is not necessarily the same as testing:

> *'Staff should be appropriately trained to recognize and discern between incidents and disasters, enabling them to make rational decisions. It is not unfeasible to imagine a diligent employee triggering the fire suppression system, after an alert, resulting in the dumping of litres of water over critical IT components. Appropriately training staff would, however, enable the employee to identify the real urgency of the situation and therefore make rational decisions regarding alternative actions to be taken.'* – (O'Hehir, 2007).

Training is vital to ensure personnel are familiar with emergency procedures, equipment and their role and responsibilities during emergencies. Training should include individual training specific to each person, followed by collective training involving the whole team, in order to ensure each team member has full comprehension of their role and how it fits into the larger plan.

This type of training approach is utilised to great effect by UK armed forces and can benefit a team that is required to function while under stress. Following analysis of the STW report for the 2007 floods, it is clear that STW were not included in any training, exercising or contingency planning prior to 2007. The lack of understanding among STW key personnel of roles and responsibility within the Gold command team is evident, which inhibited STW contribution to the Gold command team during the early stages of the incident.

Testing should be carried out separately and can take the form of individual assessment and collective scenario based exercises, but performance should be measured against agreed criteria. GCC have identified the requirement for training and testing; they are included in the GCC BCM lifecycle and occupy separate areas within the operational management phase.

Communications

GCC and STW implemented their communication plans and provided the media and local community with information updates on a regular basis. They utilised multiple communication channels, including the internet, customer service helplines and regular television and radio updates via the Gold media spokesperson. By channelling communications in this way, they ensured that messages were both consistent and accurate.

The importance of an effective media strategy must not be underestimated during a crisis. Without a continuous flow of information the media will seek alternative sources of information which is often speculative and inaccurate but is reported as authoritative. The media strategy utilised during the 2007 floods proved to be effective and helped to reduce public discontent by ensuring they were aware of the huge efforts being undertaken to resume a piped water supply.

Local authority websites also led the way by keeping the public informed on arrangements for bowser locations, where and when tankers would be sited and details of bottled water availability. They also kept the public advised on what was happening and provided helpful suggestions on how to manage their water rations.

Cheltenham Borough Council also included basic hygiene tips and encouraged people to make sure that the elderly had sufficient water to stave off any potential threat of dehydration.

Economic costs

> *'Overall costs to Severn Trent Water as a result of flooding at Mythe were estimated by the company at £29.6 million. This included the operational distribution of tankers and bowsers and quality testing some 23,000 samples after connection was resumed. The cost of bottled water supply and distribution to 350,000 consumers was estimated at £25 million.'* – (Environment Agency, 2010, p. 22).

The resultant disruption, economic loss and social distress turned the summer 2007 floods into a national catastrophe. Broad-scale estimates made shortly after the floods put the total losses at about £4 billion, of which insurable losses were reported to be about £3 billion.

What was commendable was the swift response from the insurance industry. They dealt with the equivalent of four years' worth of bad weather related claims in two months – over 180,000 claims, paying out £3 billion.

Lessons learned

In his official review of the 2007 flooding, Sir Michael Pitt makes 92 separate recommendations. Of particular note is:

> *'In the aftermath of the summer floods, Gloucestershire County Council set up a Scrutiny Inquiry to look at how the emergency services, local authorities and utility companies dealt with the event. The 11-week inquiry highlighted several critical local issues of concern, which included the inadequacy of flood warning systems, the lack of knowledge for the county's drainage system, and the vulnerabilities of single points of failure within the county's critical infrastructure.'* – (Pitt, 2008, p. xiii).

The 2007 floods illustrated the requirement to plan for worst case scenario, a scenario which must take into consideration all potential outcomes based on theoretical probability, not just past events. There is evidence to suggest that learning has resulted from the events of 2007 and procedures have been initiated to reduce risk. DEFRA in collaboration with GCC and consulting engineers developed the first edition of the Surface Water Management Pilot Plan (2010). The information contained within the plan is now available to all stakeholders and can be used to inform BCM as necessary, enabling stakeholders to have access to critical information specific to the management of surface water.

The Environment Agency early warning system should be incorporated into stakeholders' CM and GCC BCM plans in order to place on standby personnel and equipment which may be required in the event of serious flooding. The procedure should be developed to enable sufficient time to react, without repetitive false alarms each time there is heavy rain upstream. The requirement for advanced warning and preparatory activity is important due to the impact of flooding on the transport infrastructure. If a vital person or piece of equipment is not in place by a critical time, it will probably not get to its required location or will arrive after the critical tipping point has been passed.

Key personnel must be given suitable training to ensure they understand their role and responsibilities during emergencies. A collective training programme, involving all agencies and personnel with equity, should be developed and scheduled to enable a variety of events to be rehearsed. All nominated personnel must have the opportunity to participate. Although this type of programme can often be considered an unnecessary expense in terms of finance and man hours, the fact that STW had not participated in any type of civil emergency training or exercise was well documented in the STW Flood Report.

STW have already identified the need to re-evaluate the quantity of water required per person per day. STW have indicated an intention to include their findings in subsequent contingency plans and commence a programme of education to the public in order to fulfil public expectation. STW have also identified the requirement to communicate and collaborate with neighbouring water companies during crisis events in order to reduce impact on consumer needs.

What went well

- Gloucester County Council had implemented BCM before the Civil Contingency Act mandated it.
- They not only met the logistical challenge of supplying a daily minimum of ten litres of potable water to over 300,000,

but doubled it at the peak of their operation. SWT could not have achieved this on its own, however, and was clearly dependent upon other bodies such as the armed forces.

- Cooperation between water companies in providing additional tankers and bowsers for SWT to deploy.
- Communications worked well and the public were kept informed of the situation. Information regarding water supplies, including positioning of bowsers and tankers, was succinct.
- Flood victims were also encouraged to consider their neighbours' water needs, particularly if they were old or infirm.
- In the main, the UK Insurance industry responded quickly to support flood victims, with the Association of British Insurers stating that four years' worth of flood claims were handled within two months.

What could have been done better

- Replenishment of bowsers was initially slow as tankers needed to be cleaned and sterilised before they could be used for this task. As SWT had at least two days warning that the Mythe was likely to succumb to the flooding, they could have been more proactive in this respect.
- Health advice in terms of whether it was safe to continue living in flooded homes was inconsistent and confusing.

What did not go well

- The first responders were not aware that the Mythe was a massive single point of failure. More effective cross-agency communication and rehearsals may have allowed this exposure to be detected before the flooding commenced.

- The mindless theft of bowsers plus malicious damage was not foreseeable and SWT cannot be held to account for these actions. Reports of bowsers being siphoned from were also alarming. It is not clear whether any miscreants were caught and convicted but in war time this would have been considered akin to looting.

Conclusion

This risk of flooding is not going away any time soon. In fact since 2007, flooding not just in the UK but in many parts of the world continues to demand media attention. Climate change experts warn us that events like the 2007 floods may become the norm. We will need to get used to and find better ways of managing these situations.

The editing of this chapter took place in January 2014 while the UK was being almost constantly pummelled by torrential rain and very strong winds. Environment Agency flood warnings were regular features and in a number of coastal areas, on several occasions they reached the highest level – Severe (i.e., were potentially life threatening). Some parts of the UK seemed to be almost permanently underwater.

To further complicate the situation, Mother Nature also threw in tidal storm surges with at least one being on a par with the surge experienced in 1953. On that occasion Belgium, England, Scotland and The Netherlands were very badly affected and thousands of people lost their lives. Although the Cabinet Office have labelled the 2007 floods as causing the worst British civil emergency since World War II, once the floods have subsided, we may find that 2014 has some records of its own to claim.

CHAPTER 13: CLOSING THE EUROPEAN AIRSPACE: EYJAFJALLAJÖKULL AND THE VOLCANIC ASH CLOUD – ROBERT CLARK

The effects of the volcanic ash cloud that covered much of Europe in April and May 2010 were far reaching and swathes of its airspace were declared 'no fly zones'. This resulted in possibly one of the most disruptive events to have occurred in recent history for both businesses and travellers alike. The actual size of the eruption of the Icelandic volcano Eyjafjallajökull was considered by volcanologists to be relatively small, but the ensuing chaos across Europe was created by an amalgamation of the prevailing weather conditions and the absence of an aviation risk assessment model designed to address the composition of the resultant ash cloud.

This case study considers the effects of the crisis and has been based upon a combination of research plus the author's own personal experience and observations. In April 2010, he was one of an estimated ten million people stranded by the ash cloud. While attempting to return to the UK from the Italian island of Sardinia, he both witnessed and experienced first-hand the challenges that individual travellers faced in trying to reach their respective destinations.

The International Air Transport Association has a register of more than 500 active volcanoes in the world. In fact, there have been several occasions in recent years when volcanic activity has caused flight disruptions and airport closures. But most of these events have occurred in comparatively remote parts of the world, causing little

13: Closing the European Airspace: Eyjafjallajökull and the Volcanic Ash Cloud – Robert Clark

notable impact. In the case of Eyjafjallajökull, the ash cloud resulted in around 100,000 flights being affected over a six day period.

At the outset of the crisis, in addition to the European airspace disruption there were two other major factors of concern. Firstly, when Eyjafjallajökull had previously erupted almost 200 years earlier, it remained active for over twelve months. Furthermore, volcanologists warned that the problem could have seriously worsened if Eyjafjallajökull's much larger sister volcano Katla also erupted. Historically Katla has usually followed Eyjafjallajökull's lead. In short, the situation had the potential for drastic deterioration.

Volcanic activity that causes aircraft flight disruptions is nothing new. In the nine years between 1980 and 1991, there were seven reported incidents of aircraft experiencing temporary multi-engine failure resulting from an encounter with volcanic ash. The most severe case was over Indonesia in 1982 when a British Airways 747 suffered a failure in all four engines. There followed a 25,000 foot powerless decent over a 16 min period. Fortunately, the crew were able to restart the engines. In consequence, long standing recommendations to airlines have existed which advises them to avoid flying through ash clouds regardless of how dense they may be. This had in effect created a zero-tolerance mentality for aircraft encountering any type of volcanic ash cloud, regardless of the cloud's density or composition.

Like Mounts Fuji, Krakatoa and Vesuvius, Eyjafjallajökull is a stratovolcano, meaning it is conical in shape. Unlike those three examples, it is covered by an icecap measuring around 100 km^2. Between 3 and 5 March 2010, around 3,000 earthquakes were measured at the epicentre of the volcano which is often a sign that an imminent eruption is likely. By 20 March 2010, the Icelandic Meteorological Office reported the first eruption of Eyjafjallajökull since 1823. On 14 April, the volcano entered a second phase and generated the massive ash plume which drifted across Europe, paralysing its airspace.

'When the melt water from the Eyjafjallajökull glacier mixed with hot magma, an explosive eruption sent unusually fine grained ash into the jet stream.' – (Gislason, et al., 2010, p. 1).

The big unknown for the aviation industry in April 2010 was how damaging this fine-grained ash would be on aircraft that flew through the ash cloud. It was generally accepted that volcanic ash entering an aircraft engine would melt and form a glassy coating on the turbine. This, in turn, could cause the engine to stall but no data was available about levels of tolerance.

'Stalled engines aren't the only concern. It's like driving behind a truck that's kicking up stones on the highway only you are travelling at hundreds of miles an hour when the little particles smash into you.' – (Behar, 2008, p. 66).

The duration of the initial airspace closures was only six days although further spasmodic closures continued until 18 May. This not only had repercussions on the aviation industry and travellers but a host of other industries that rely upon air transportation as part of their supply chain.

One very high profile event that was affected early in the crisis was the state funeral of Polish President, Lech Kaczynski and his wife Maria, which took place on 18 April 2010. They had been killed eight days earlier when their plane crashed in Russia. Among the expected mourners who were unable to attend the funeral were US President Barack Obama, HRH the Prince of Wales, French President Nicolas Sarkozy and German Chancellor Angela Merkel.

Impact on the Icelandic community

Much has been said regarding the global impact of this event, but very little by comparison of the effect it has had on Iceland and its community. The population of Iceland long ago had to come to terms with living alongside volcanoes and other natural phenomena. Within the last 100 years alone, 16 of its 40-plus volcanoes have erupted. Volcanic ash is an acknowledged health risk and in worst case scenarios can result in asphyxiation. In general patients suffering from lung disorders such as chronic bronchitis, emphysema, and asthma should avoid coming into contact with it. Even people in good health should minimise their exposure and wear a face mask.

During and after the five weeks that Eyjafjallajökull was erupting, clear physical symptoms were observed amongst the local population in the southern Iceland area. Respiratory problems were common along with eye irritation, and long term monitoring of those exposed to the ash has been recommended. The situation might have been far worse, however, had it been a bigger eruption or had the prevailing winds not taken much of the ash cloud away from Iceland.

The crisis started early in the year when the majority of livestock was still being kept inside. The southern Iceland area supports 15% of all Icelandic cattle, 6% of sheep and

17% of all horses. Farmers needed to remain vigilant when livestock were returned to the fields as the volcanic ash that had fallen can be toxic. Moreover, flash flooding occurred as part of Eyjafjallajökull's icecap had melted. Some roads became impassable and low visibility due to ash fall also made driving conditions difficult. Little disruption was experienced around the transportation of milk from the area, however.

One definite benefit for Iceland has been the growth of volcano tourism, with local companies offering visit-the-volcano day trips. The local civil protection department publishes regular bulletins on which areas were safe and those to be avoided.

Impact on airlines

In addition to losing revenue from both passengers and freight, the airlines were also rather shackled by EU Rule 261. This obligated them to compensate passengers if they are not permitted to board, their flight is cancelled or it is subject to a long delay. This compensation can include hotel expenses, meals, etc., for an unspecified period. In the case of stranded passengers, in some cases this would have been many days. Furthermore, there was no guarantee that a passenger's airline carrier would be able to transport them to their destination as soon as the flight ban was lifted. Ten million stranded travellers would take some considerable time to rescue.

In 2010, the airline industry supported economies estimated to be in the order of US$3.5 trillion, utilising a workforce of 32 million. The six day no-fly zone that was experienced in April 2010 had significant global economic implications.

Had the crisis been allowed to continue, the cumulative effect would have been unthinkable.

Airlines felt that the authorities overreacted by introducing the no fly zones. Virgin Group Chairman Sir Richard Branson told the BBC that had planes been allowed to immediately assess whether the ash cloud was too dangerous to fly through, the ban would have been lifted far sooner. On the same programme, Ryanair CEO Michael O'Leary told the BBC that it was ridiculous for European law to force airlines to pay thousands of dollars to passengers who had perhaps only purchased a ticket for a US$12 flight. It does appear that EU Rule 261 effectively turned airlines into unwitting and unwilling insurance companies which was possibly not what the law was intended to do.

The insurance industry seemed quick to distance itself from the crisis and while a few companies did honour their commitments, most hid behind some form of 'Act of God' clause. Stephen Cross, CEO of Aon Risk Consulting, remarked that business interruption insurance was unlikely to be of any use as policies tend to respond when there has been some form of physical damage. Supply chain disruption is also likely to be excluded in the small print. Whereas airlines were sometimes able to look to governments for a form of compensation, other businesses which suffered could not.

There was some respite from the shackles of EU 261, however, delivered to the airlines by UK Prime Minister Gordon Brown. As Spanish airports were free from the ash cloud, he encouraged UK-bound travellers to make their way to Spain for onward transfer to the UK by sea. There Royal Navy ships were used as part of the rescue mission.

But in launching this initiative, Brown failed to mention that by taking this route home passengers would release the airlines from their EU 261 obligation. Consequently, many Britons taking this option would have found themselves out of pocket and with no means of recompense.

'We have been saying there's a volcanic threat from Iceland for years and we need an ash monitoring system.' – Dave Rothery, Open University.

We know we cannot influence Mother Nature and stop volcanoes erupting nor can we accurately predict when they will erupt, but the aviation industry is not ignoring the situation. The British airline easyJet is involved in a research project that will ultimately enable aircraft radar to see volcanic ash clouds, thereby preventing an aircraft flying blindly into one. To facilitate the experiment, they have transported one tonne of volcanic ash from Iceland to the UK. The radar system, known as AVOID (Airborne Volcanic Object Imaging Detector) is being jointly developed with Airbus and the Norwegian Institute for Air Research.

Impact on business

According to the BBC, only 1% of UK trade relies on air freight. *Der Spiegel*, conversely, claims that between 35% and 40% of international trade is dependent upon air freight. If correct, this would have made the German daily economic loss in the region of US$1.3 billion. But businesses relying on air freight for transporting perishable goods are most likely to have been seriously affected. Those businesses that operated a just-in-time supply chain strategy were also particularly vulnerable. Losses by the

13: Closing the European Airspace: Eyjafjallajökull and the Volcanic Ash Cloud – Robert Clark

Kenyan and Ecuadorian floricultural markets alone are estimated to be US$12 million and US$5 million respectively. Farmers in Kenya were dumping tonnes of flowers and vegetables every day that the European skies were closed. Moreover, international couriers such as FedEx and DHL were severely constrained throughout Europe. During the flight restrictions, Israel quickly reduced its loss exposure by shipping around 35% of its floral produce to the Dutch auction houses by sea.

'In terms of crisis management, a supply chain with no redundancy available is very difficult to maintain and manage.' – Simon Barth (Barth, 2010).

BMW and Nissan in Germany, Japan and the USA both temporarily suspended car production due to parts shortages caused by the interruption to their just-in-time supply chain operation. They were too reliant on low-weight, high-value electrical components normally shipped by air. An Airbus-commissioned report also estimates that around 2.8 million days of productivity were lost as a consequence of stranded travellers.

Had the crisis been prolonged, some economists saw a bleak outlook:

'A drop of between 1% and 2% for European economies is not being ruled out. That would mean a lot of European countries wouldn't get any growth this year.' – Vanessa Rossi, Senior Economic Fellow, Chatham House.

A number of high profile sporting events were disrupted, with the Japanese Formula One Grand Prix being cancelled. The Moroccan Golf Classic was postponed, while Barcelona Football Club switched to a coach for a lengthy two day journey to fulfil their Champions League fixture with Inter Milan.

Many employees on company business found themselves trapped in foreign parts. In some respects this was a repeat of the 9/11 situation when US airspace was closed. Companies need to provide their employees with clear instructions with regard to being stranded overseas. Companies should consider developing their own policies while making adequate provision for the continued welfare of their employees.

Impact on tourism

From a European perspective, the crisis did not happen in peak season and as the incident lasted no more than a few days, the impact on the industry was fairly minimal. Any lengthy interruptions to air travel, however, either now or in the future, could have a substantial impact particularly on those tourist-dependent economies that rely heavily on air transportation for their visitors. Even so, tour operator Tui attributed a £90 million loss to the ash cloud.

The island of Jersey in the English Channel estimated a US$2.3 million loss in the first six days of the crisis even though the island is not solely dependent upon air travel, as there are regular ferry services between Jersey and the UK Mainland and to France. Conversely, 98% of tourists visiting the Mediterranean island of Malta arrive by air. Even though Malta's International airport remained open, it still lost an estimated 90,000 bed-nights during the initial disruption. For a country where approximately 35% of GDP comes from tourism, a prolonged closure of the European skies would have been disastrous.

13: Closing the European Airspace: Eyjafjallajökull and the Volcanic Ash Cloud – Robert Clark

The author also observed that while there were many losers, there were some beneficiaries of the crisis. For a brief period, European railways were running at full capacity, ferry companies enjoyed a short renaissance, while car hire companies on continental Europe felt they could charge what they liked. The author himself received two quotes for two days' car hire, at over US$3,000 each. For some European hotels Christmas came very early in 2010. Reuters reported that many were taking full advantage of stranded travellers by raising their tariffs, with some reports of prices being doubled.

Impact on independent travellers

There was no evidence found to suggest that Britons who were on package holidays were not looked after by their tour operators. But from a first-hand perspective, the author experienced the plight of the independent travellers. Unless they remained where they were and waited for the flights to resume, they would have to fund their own way home. For some, just waiting was not an option as they had insufficient funds to cover their food and accommodation costs for what was potentially an indefinite period. Two couples the author met explained that they had approached their local British Consulate for financial assistance, which was provided. The other issue with waiting for the ash cloud to disperse was how long would the wait be. The previous Eyjafjallajökull eruption lasted for over 12 months.

Although the author made his own way back to the UK from Sardinia, had he waited for British Airways to have a vacant seat from Cagliari to London, he could have waited for up to two weeks before securing a seat home. The first weekly flight after the initial lifting on the flight ban was cancelled. As Ryanair's Michael O'Leary told the BBC, while airlines had no control over the airspace closure they still had to pay compensation while insurance companies in general were paying nothing.

Having secured a berth aboard a ferry from Sardinia to Genoa, the author headed for Milan. He spoke with many travellers who had flown from numerous non-European airports to anywhere they could in Europe in the hope of getting back to their destinations overland. Travellers heading for the UK and Ireland also had to contend with sea crossings too. But the French and Italian railways were at full capacity. Moreover, the train operators' websites were overloaded and booking tickets online was virtually impossible as the sites continually crashed. These websites could not cope with the sheer volume of visitors and behaved as though they were the victims of a DDoS (distributed-denial-of-service) cyber attack. The alternative was joining exceedingly lengthy queues for tickets and at Milan, electronic displays announced that all trains to Northern European destinations were full for the next three days.

The author saw evidence of travellers boarding trains without tickets, and they were prepared to stand on journeys of several hours across Europe. This practice was not possible on Eurostar due to the more vigilant ticket inspection plus tight immigration and security controls. At Gare du Nord Station in Paris, the wait for a Eurostar train was posted on the information bulletins as four days at the peak. The alternative to waiting for a Eurostar ticket was to travel by local trains to Calais and return to the UK by ferry. At Calais, the French were well organised. Coaches were ready to transport travellers from the town's railway station to the port. At the ferry terminal, bottled water and space blankets were available free of charge. At the time of joining the queue for ferry tickets, the author was told that there over 2,000 already waiting and the queuing time would be around two hours. They were spot on. Once at the cash desk, tickets were issued and within ten minutes the author had set sail.

Sea France were not so well organised at Dover, however, and it took far longer to disembark than it took to cross the channel. This key cause for the delay was entirely due to only one bus being available to transport around 1,200 foot passengers to the ferry terminal. And yet, Sea France were making tens of thousands of dollars extra each trip. What is more, there was no attempt by their staff to communicate with the passengers which only served to antagonise them further. After two hours police had to be called to deal with a very angry crowd. Ironically, less than two years later, a French court ruled that Sea France was officially bankrupt.

Impact on climate change

While volcanic ash that is blasted into the stratosphere will fall to earth, generally over a short period, volcanic gases such as sulphur dioxide do not. The gas oxidises and converts into tiny aerosol droplets of sulphate which reflect the sun's radiation back into space resulting in a cooling effect on the earth's surface.

'Volcanic eruptions are one of the major causes for climate change.' (Dhillon, et al., 2013).

The particularly cold winter conditions of 1991 were attributed to the eruption of Mount Pinatubo in the Philippines, with the worst of the harmful effects being noticed some 6,000 km away in the Red Sea area. In 1816, Europe and North America found themselves in the grip of a freezing summer coupled with an agricultural disaster. The effect was caused by the eruption in 1815 of Mount Tambora in Indonesia.

'Folks talk about a nuclear winter – this [Laki] eruption generated enough sulphuric acid droplets that it made the atmosphere reflective, cooled the planet for an entire year or more and caused widespread famine in many places around the globe.' – (O'Brien, 2011).

Eyjafjallajökull big sister Katla is part of a volcanic zone that includes the Laki craters. A volcanic winter, as they are sometimes referred to, was experienced in Europe following the eruption of Laki in 1783. All Iceland's livestock and half the population died with many succumbing to starvation. Laki is also believed to have discharged more toxic gases than any other eruption in the 150 years that followed. An estimated 20,000 people died from inhaling sulphur dioxide in the UK alone.

'It (Laki) actually changed the Earth's climate.' – Ford Cochran, National Geographic (O'Brien, 2011).

Despite its impact on Europe, the 2010 Eyjafjallajökull eruption was a comparatively small event compared with some of the more spectacular performances of its infamous peers. Consequently, any impact on climate change would have been minimal. We need to remain mindful that we can neither predict nor control these events, which history has taught us can have devastating consequences. In many respects a deadly volcanic eruption could have the same effect on a country's work force as a serious pandemic, including a high death toll. Asphyxiation and starvation are probably the two worst scenarios.

Lessons learned

This was a catastrophe that the world was simply not ready for, but it highlighted the level of dependence of businesses and travellers on the aviation industry. The European Union was quick to grasp the severity of the situation. It recognised that a major contributory factor of the crisis had been a lack of data about aircraft engines' tolerance of volcanic ash. It stressed that an EU position was urgently required for future risk assessments pertaining to aircraft engines and volcanic ash clouds. It also recognised that passenger rights legislation (EU 261) needed urgent review to:

'Strike the balance between the exceptional circumstances in case of natural disasters and the need to ensure that stranded passengers are afforded adequate treatment.' – (EU Transport Ministers Council, 2010).

EU Rule 261 should never have been allowed to expose airlines to the kind of liability that occurred during the volcanic ash disruption. The EU should not only review and revise this law, but also consider legislation that discourages insurance companies from using an 'Act of God' justification to avoid meeting claims of the kind arising from this crisis.

It has become very apparent that independent travellers within Europe would be wise to familiarise themselves with EU Rule 261, and any future amendments. A clear understanding of their rights is important should airlines be grounded again for an extended period, regardless of the cause. It is also sensible to be aware of the support that can be made available by their consulates and embassies in the event that they become stranded overseas.

In addition to leaving thousands of travellers stranded, the eruption's economic impact was felt globally. It is estimated that the airlines alone collectively lost US$1.7 billion, but it is more difficult to accurately quantify the total cost to businesses and individual travellers. Much of this disruption could perhaps have been avoided if the CAA had previously established levels of acceptable density for safe flight through ash clouds. Moreover, in the absence of such data, the delay in sending aircraft up to verify whether it was safe to fly delayed the resolution of the situation.

Statisticians and risk managers might claim that Eyjafjallajökull may not erupt again for another 200 years. On that basis it could be argued that revisions to business continuity arrangements based on this event might be rather pointless. They would do well to remember that Eyjafjallajökull is only one of 500 active global volcanoes. Any one of these volcanoes could cause multi-faceted disruption resulting in some form of global impact.

Some severe disruption was felt within aviation-dependent supply chains. Those businesses that had built their supply chain dependency around the aviation industry found themselves particularly vulnerable. Without viable alternatives, both upstream and downstream supply chain relationships suffered as routes to market became blocked. Any long term disruptions to supply chains could have become market differentiators which ultimately threatened organisational brand names and reputations.

13: Closing the European Airspace: Eyjafjallajökull and the Volcanic Ash Cloud – Robert Clark

Any future interference to air traffic may not necessarily be the result of volcanic activity; the paralysing effect of no-fly zones could be the same. The 9/11 terrorist attack on the World Trade Centre caused US and transatlantic air space to be closed. Even air traffic controllers are known to cause occasional disruption. Moreover, the 'Single European Sky' initiative plans to centralise Europe's 27 separate country air traffic control functions. While this may seem an obvious and sensible improvement, it remains unpopular with ATC staff and collective pan-European action could once again bring Europe's airspace to a standstill. Serious air traffic disruption was also experienced in the UK in December 2013 when a technical glitch reduced traffic to 80% of the daily norm.

Wars can also cause supply chain disruption. Even as long ago as the 1861–65 American Civil War, the UK cotton industry was starved of raw materials which were primarily sourced from the Southern States.

The following recommendations are made with a specific focus on supply chain management. They should be implemented to avoid the disruption that any future no-fly zone might create.

- Exporters of perishable goods that rely on air freight should consider alternative routes to market in the event of future aviation disruptions. Relying on a single route to market could prove unsustainable, placing such businesses in serious jeopardy.

- Companies relying on a just-in-time supply chain strategy should consider alternative strategies that would mitigate the risk of disruption to their supply chain.

13: Closing the European Airspace: Eyjafjallajökull and the Volcanic Ash Cloud – Robert Clark

- Business continuity plans should be discussed with air cargo handlers to ensure they have contingency plans for dealing with disruptions.

- Consider the implications to the business or having to switch to other modes of transport in both the short term and long term, both as a supplier and a customer.

- Contractual arrangements for alternative ground or sea transportation should be made well in advance. Demand for such services will invariably be higher in the event of more prolonged flight disruption.

- Understand what contingency plans both your upstream and downstream supply chain have in place.

What went well

- Following the eruption, steps have been taken to establish aircraft engine tolerance for volcanic ash. This might reduce the disruption caused by volcanoes in future.

- Icelandic tourist organisations successfully encouraged 'volcano tourism' to bring revenue to the island.

- French authorities shipped British travellers home efficiently.

What could have been done better

- Data on engine tolerance could have been gathered more quickly following the eruption.

- EU Rule 261 protected consumers, but caused financial issues for airlines. Had the crisis continued, it might have put some of them out of business. This was possibly due to the law being poorly drafted.

- UK Prime Minister Gordon Brown's rescue effort did bring British travellers home, but by accepting help they waived their right to compensation. This was not communicated at the time to those affected.

What did not go well

- No data was initially available regarding engine tolerance levels.

- Many airlines felt that the imposition of a no-fly zone was an overreaction.

- Suppliers of perishable often suffered massive losses due to the lack of an alternative route to market.

- Companies operating a just-in-time supply chain strategy experienced disruption to their operations.

- The websites of train operators crashed – they could not support the number of additional visitors.

Conclusion

So, could Eyjafjallajökull and the 500 or so other active volcanoes around the world be considered sources of 'Black Swan' events? They have the potential to generate a very high impact but individually have a low probability of erupting. Mother Nature of course does not conveniently publish a schedule of events and so we only have historical data to help us try and predict when and where any type of natural disaster may occur.

13: Closing the European Airspace: Eyjafjallajökull and the Volcanic Ash Cloud – Robert Clark

But let us not forget Eyjafjallajökull's big sister Katla. Not only does it historically erupt at about the same time as Eyjafjallajökull, but it has been known to erupt on its own every 50 to 100 years. These two cycles are now converging and, as of the beginning of 2013, Katla's condition was described as *'restless'*. Maybe Iceland's volcanoes have not finished with us just yet.

CHAPTER 14: THE ÅSTA TRAIN ACCIDENT, NORWAY, JANUARY 2000 – JON SIGURD JACOBSEN

'Most disastrous train wrecks occur in Asia and Africa. Fatalities there are on the rise, whereas such deaths are decreasing in Europe. But accidents still happen in modern Western countries.' – (Hammer, 2012).

The history books show that train crashes are nothing new and were regular events in the 19th century when the railways were in their infancy. Even now in the 21st century, accidents around the globe still abound. This case study looks at a head on collision shortly after the arrival of the new millennium, which resulted in one of Norway's worst rail disasters.

Development of the Norwegian Railway Network

Norway's first railway was commissioned in 1854 and it ran from Oslo to Eidsvoll, a distance of 68 km. The main part of the country's railway system was built in the period 1854 to 1920. During this time, the railway had no serious competition from any other land-based transport system and the various lines were often in private ownership.

The Norwegian state established the Norwegian Railway Company (NSB) in 1883, which set about extending the railway network throughout the entire country. The golden era was a 20 year period from 1890. Thereafter competition from cars, buses and air traffic started to grow resulting in a gradual loss of market share, weakening NSB's domination of the Norwegian transport industry. Still, the government continued to develop the railway system in the public interest, and in support of different district policy interests.

The network was maintained and upgraded, with the majority being completely electrified. A new signalling system was also introduced in this period although parts of the old infrastructure remained in situ.

Norwegian rail travel safety record

The safety of its passengers and staff are overriding objectives of NSB. In fact, in Norway, rail transport is considered safer than most other transportation systems and compares very favourably against car travel. In the ten year period immediately before the Åsta disaster, a total of 20 people had been killed on Norway's railways. During the corresponding period after the disaster, that number had halved. In a 2011 comparison against other European countries' rail network safety records, Norway also fared well. Taking account of the number of passengers and kilometres travelled against the number of fatalities, Norway came 8th across Europe. When considering the number of railway network incidents reported against the passenger/kilometres measure Norway was only average, coming in 15th. Even so, the 35 Norwegian incidents recorded in this 2011 review was double the number recorded the previous year.

Head-on collision

'A train driver's worst nightmare is being on a single-track line and seeing another train coming

14: The Åsta Train Accident, Norway, January 2000 – Jon Sigurd Jacobsen

straight at you.' – John Lillywhite, retired British Rail train driver.

On Tuesday 4 January, 2000 a head on collision occurred between two trains on a single-track line close to the Åsta station in Hedemark County, Norway. This stretch of railway goes through a sparsely populated part of the country to the north of Oslo. The line, named Rørosbanen, was managed by a centralised system although it did not incorporate an automatic train stop system (ATS). Unlike much of Norway's rail network, this line was not electrified, necessitating the use of diesel-powered trains. The train heading in a southerly direction was a diesel locomotive with three cars travelling from Trondheim to Hamar. The second, proceeding north, was a diesel multiple unit travelling from Hamar to Rena.

The official log shows that at 1:07 pm the southbound train left Rena station on a green light. Meanwhile at Rustad station the northbound train was scheduled to arrive at 1:06 pm and then wait until 1:10 pm, allowing the southbound train to pass. The train left three minutes early at 1:07 pm. The log does not show that a green light was showing at Rustad station, although it did record that the points north of Rustad were forcibly opened by this train as it left the station.

At 1:12 pm the accident happened. The northbound train remained on the track but was completely destroyed. The southbound train was seriously damaged. Its front car was derailed and plummeted down an embankment, the second was also derailed but remained on the tracks while the third stayed on the tracks. Of the 86 passengers and railway staff on board the two trains, 67 survived.

14: The Åsta Train Accident, Norway, January 2000 – Jon Sigurd Jacobsen

'The collision caused the fuel tanks on both trains to rupture and some 5,000 litres of diesel poured out and caught fire. The trains burned for several hours. 19 people were killed, some by the collision and some by the fire. Among these were the drivers of both trains.' – (Halvorsrud, 2002).

The unfolding disaster

The traffic controller at Hamar Station had not been following the Røros – Hamar line on the screens in the control room. He also was also responsible for the much busier Eidsvoll – Hamar line, which had been taking up his attention. Moreover, there was no acoustic alarm installed in the control room to warn the controller that two trains were on a collision course.

An 'imminent collision' warning was showing on the screens in the control room at 1:08 pm although the traffic controller did not notice this until 1:11 pm, one minute before impact. Although both drivers from the doomed trains had made their mobile numbers available in line with standard operating procedures, this information had not been passed to the controller. With no automatic train stop system installed on the line and no radios in the drivers' cabs, the controller was helpless to stop the tragedy unfolding. At 1:12 pm, the trains collided.

Subsequent investigation

The appointed commission considered that the accident could have been caused both by direct and indirect causes. The direct causes were most likely either human error or a malfunction in the signalling system. Numerous tests were conducted although no physical fault could be found with the signalling system. Moreover, with both drivers killed in the crash, establishing human error as the cause was always going to be difficult.

The level of safety, and the safety system, on the Rørosbanen were not considered satisfactory by the commission. For this reason alone the possibility of a short term operational malfunction could not be excluded. Furthermore, it was not possible to eliminate the prospect that the system had shown an incorrect green signal on the northbound line.

With no advanced train stopping system on the Rørosbanen, however, and no radios in the driver's cabs, the network controller was totally reliant on contacting each driver via mobile phone. But a failure in the NSB notification process meant that the correct numbers had not been passed to the controller.

'The direct cause of the accident is still not known and probably it never will be.' – (Halvorsrud, 2002).

The incomplete evidence available made arrival at a firm conclusion regarding the accident's cause virtually impossible. It was clear, however, that once that northbound train left Rustad the collision was inevitable. The Norwegian rail administration was heavily censored for its apparent lack of safety awareness and safety management, and for failing to have completed an effective risk assessment. It was also fined NOK 10 million (circa US$1.6 Million).

Trauma management

It is not unusual to find that survivors of life threatening disasters are traumatised and the Åsta incident was no exception. Crash survivors were found to be suffering from a variety of emotions including guilt and sorrow. A support group was created to provide counselling and afford the opportunity for members to share their experiences. An estimated 120 joined the group, approximately twice the number that actually survived the disaster.

Corporate manslaughter

Although corporate criminal liability was entered into the Norwegian Statute books in 1991, no record of prosecutions associated with the Åsta train crash can be traced. The law states that three conditions must be met for a prosecution to be successful:

- a crime has been committed
- a connection between the offender and the corporation is shown
- the offence formed part of the offender's work for the corporation

It can only be assumed that, as the results of the investigation were inconclusive, it would have been difficult to build a case against NSB which met these three criteria.

Insurance claims

Insurance claims resulting from injury or trauma are not uncommon. One female survivor pursued a claim through the courts for eleven years. She finally won her case against insurance company Tryg, which was covering NSB at the time of the crash. A court awarded her NOK 4.5 million (around US$700,000) plus costs.

Lessons learned

While the reason for the premature departure of the northbound train from Rustad remains a mystery, either human error or signal failure are considered to be the most likely cause. The failure to pass on the drivers' mobile phone details to the controller, however, was clearly a process failure. Moreover, with mobile phone communications not being possible, there were absolutely no other contingency measures in place to avoid the ensuing disaster.

It is debatable that in the one minute the Controller had between realizing a collision was imminent and the actual impact, whether he had sufficient time to warn both drivers even if he had had their correct mobile details. Perhaps if an audible alarm had been installed in the Control Room, or someone had been monitoring the Rørosbanen, those extra couple of minutes gained may have rescued the situation.

A report published in 1990 had recommended that all remote lines should have an automatic train stopping system installed. Due to other priorities nothing was done on the Rørosbanen and the Norwegian Rail Administration was duly criticised and fined. Following the Åsta crash, installation work for such a system did rather belatedly commence.

Given the prevailing circumstances, once that northbound train had prematurely left Rustad station the accident was inevitable. There was no way of stopping the collision.

What went well

- Norway's rail safety measures were generally good, as reflected by their record in comparison with other European countries.
- A trauma management support group was set up to help survivors.

What could have been done better

- The traffic controller was able to monitor the affected line remotely, but his attention was taken up by a busier line. Without an acoustic alarm it was easy for him to miss the impending disaster.
- Communications equipment was completely inadequate – mobile phones were used exclusively, with no backup.

What did not go well

- No advanced train stopping system: when communications failed there was no way for the traffic controller to prevent the disaster.
- The drivers' mobile numbers had not been passed on to the traffic controller – a clear failure of procedure.
- The safety systems on the line were later found to be unsatisfactory.
- An effective risk assessment had not been carried out prior to the crash. This might have identified some of the failings in NSB's systems and procedures and reduced the potential for a crash.

Conclusion

It is difficult to take any positives from this study except that Norway's rail safety record is one of the best in Europe. But clearly, had at least some of the various safety measures available to the rail industry been deployed on the Rørosbanen as elsewhere in the country, the tragedy could have been avoided.

CHAPTER 15: A TALE OF THREE CITIES: THE BOMBING OF MADRID (2004), LONDON (2005) AND GLASGOW (2007) – NEIL SWINYARD-JORDAN, TONY DUNCAN AND ROBERT CLARK

This case study examines and compares three terrorist attacks on European transport targets – the Madrid Railway Network (2004), the London Underground and bus network (2005), and Glasgow Airport (2007). It considers the comparative effects of the attacks, the respective reactions and the resultant economic impacts.

Terrorism overview

Terrorism is just one of the many threats that organisations need to consider as a part of their risk assessment process. As of 2011, over 6,000 armed and militant groups had been identified world-wide, an increase of 200% on 1988, which supports the argument that the threat is growing. The START Program has recorded around 100,000 global terrorist incidents since 1970. This equates to an average of approximately seven daily incidents.

Although acknowledging the existence of numerous terrorist organisations operating around the globe, it is not the intent of this case study to explore and understand their *raison d'être,* how they are financed or their individual objectives. Nor does the study make any attempt to distinguish between groups labelled as terrorists, guerrillas or freedom fighters.

'One of the depressing lessons from the history of terrorism is that it is always likely to be with us.'
(English, 2009, p. 120).

15: A Tale of Three Cities: The Bombing of Madrid (2004), London (2005) and Glasgow (2007)

Terrorism has been around for hundreds of years. Examples include the infamous Gunpowder plot of 1605, when Guy Fawkes and his cohorts attempted to kill King James I and his Parliament. The United Kingdom has been fighting Irish terrorism since the 1860s. Despite the apparent success of the Northern Ireland peace process, and the subsequent power-sharing arrangement between the various factions in the Northern Ireland Assembly, there is still a serious terrorist threat from dissident Irish Republicans. Meanwhile, the Spanish have been in conflict with the terrorist organization Euskadi Ta Askatasuna (ETA) for four decades.

Enter the suicide bomber

Personal self-sacrifice has become a way of operating for some terrorist groups. This was developed into a weapon of war during World War II with the advent of the Kamikaze. It was in Lebanon in 1983 that the first terrorist suicide bombing occurred, when terrorists targeted the US Embassy. As of 2005, over 350 suicide attacks had been executed in more than 20 countries. Suicide bombing is a powerful psychological weapon, surpassed in the 'fear factor' it generates only by weapons of mass destruction.

Terrorism and building design

'In a bomb blast, a square metre of glass can produce up to 1,800 razor sharp fragments. These flying glass shards cause more damage, injury and death than the explosion itself.' – (Advanced Glass Technology, 2014).

Modern architecture has for many years made extensive use of glass in building designs. One only has to observe the skyline of any modern city to note that, from a distance, many buildings appear to be made entirely of glass. Indeed, many railway stations that date back to Victorian times incorporate glass canopies in their design. This is a dream situation for terrorists as flying glass has the potential to greatly improve the effectiveness of their bombs.

Terrorist goals

While each terrorist group will have overarching objectives of a political, religious or nationalist nature, each individual terrorist strike will usually look to achieve three goals. Savitch defines these as 'Catalytic Terrorism, Mega Terrorism and Smart Terrorism' (Savitch, 2008, p. 38) as shown in *Figure 12*.

CATALYTIC TERRORISM	MEGA TERRORISM	SMART TERRORISM
In full view of the media	Maximise human casualties	Maximise damage to critical assets

Figure 12: The Savitch 'three goal' model

The 9/11 attacks achieved all three of these goals, whereas the subsequent attacks on the London Transport (7/7) and Madrid railway system (3/11) only achieved a Mega and Catalytic Terrorism effect. The Glasgow Airport bombing only achieved the Catalytic goal and while the Madrid bombing did not achieve a 'Smart' effect, it did succeed in bringing down the Spanish Government.

History shows that the three goal Model does not always apply. Evaluation of the IRA's 1990s UK Mainland bombing campaign demonstrates that the targets were primarily economic. The campaign did not aim to achieve a Mega Terrorism goal as prior warnings minimised human casualties. With an estimated 75,000 people evacuated from the city centre prior to the explosion, the casualties from the 1996 Manchester bombing could have been horrific without prior warning.

Terrorist threat to transport

The worst terrorist atrocity to date which also involved an act of self-sacrifice by the perpetrators was the calculated and sophisticated terrorist attack on the World Trade Centre in 2001. By flying hijacked aircraft into the World Trade Centre and the Pentagon, not only did they cause the deaths of almost 3,000 people, but close to another 600,000 also lost their jobs.

Major cities are often targeted and London is no stranger to terrorism. Local organisations take the threat very seriously. A London Chamber of Commerce survey revealed that its members rated terrorism seventh out of 17 threats in terms of being a risk to their finances. 44% of the respondents listed terrorism as a concern.

Traditional, or classic, terrorist weapons such as the bomb and the bullet have been available to terrorists for centuries. There is no reason to suggest that this approach to terrorism is likely to recede as these weapons are comparatively easy to obtain. The arrival of the suicide bomber has given terrorists a new, efficient and frightening means of delivering their attacks. In the case of the transport industry, with two recorded exceptions all types of attack have been traditional (see illustration below) and examples of suicide bombings abound.

While the Achille Lauro cruise liner hijacking (1985) and the Netherlands train hijackings (1970s) are exceptions, there have been examples of multiple terrorist attacks against the transport targets over the last 20 years as shown in *Figure 13*, below.

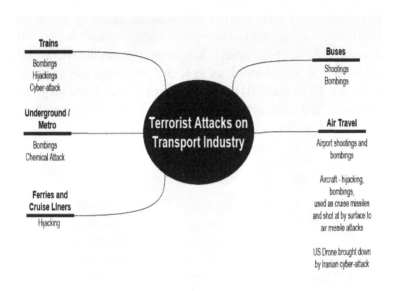

Figure 13: Examples of terrorist attacks conducted against transport and tourism targets

The preceding illustration provides an overview of the type of terrorist attacks that have targeted the transport sector. This overview is by no means definitive and excludes areas such as air and maritime cargo, road haulage and private air travel.

Whilst the annual Glasgow Airport annual passenger count is around eight million, London Underground carries in excess of one billion travellers annually utilising over 200 stations. The Spanish rail network has many hundreds of stations and transports in excess of 500 million passengers per annum. Apart from a plethora of security cameras, both forms of rail transport along with buses are considered to be 'open' to terrorist attack while UK airports are considered as 'secure', despite the fact that between 1970 and 2010, global terrorist incidents targeting airlines and airports numbered 1,044. This excludes thwarted attacks.

Madrid Train Bombings, 2004

On 11 March 2004, an example of mass-casualty terrorism occurred in Spain. Terrorists prepared 13 bombs inside plastic bags and backpacks, and placed the devices in twelve passenger carriages, spread across four different trains. They expected the bombs to detonate when the trains would be packed with rush hour commuters. Ten of the bombs exploded, killing 191 and injuring 1,841.

Within days of the bombings CNN reported knowledge of an alleged Al-Qaeda document claiming responsibility for the attacks. One of the statements made was: '*We think the Spanish government will not stand more than two blows, or three at the most, before it will be forced to withdraw* [from Iraq] *because of public pressure on it. If its forces remain after these blows, the victory of the Socialist Party will be almost guaranteed – and the withdrawal of Spanish forces will be on its campaign manifesto.*' This is exactly what happened. Al-Qaeda was seeking regime change in Spain in an effort to '*separate Spain from its allies by carrying out terror attacks.*'

15: A Tale of Three Cities: The Bombing of Madrid (2004), London (2005) and Glasgow (2007)

Examination of this these attacks identifies a number of issues relating to business continuity management, security and emergency planning. The impact of the bombings on businesses was immense in addition to the unexpected change of government, with hospitality and tourism bearing the brunt of the impact.

> *'For the first forty eight hours or so after the bomb blasts there was an intense debate around the authorship of the attack. . . Figures in the governing party, the Pardito Popular, made it clear from the outset that they believed the Basque separatist movement, Euskadi ta Askatasuna ('Basque Fatherland and Liberty') or ETA was responsible.'* –
(Garvey & Mullins, 2009).

Within days of the Madrid train bombings, eight million Spaniards had taken to the streets to march against terrorism. Controversy regarding the handling and representation of the bombings by the government arose with Spain's two main political parties, the Partido Socialista Obrero Español and the Partido Popular, accusing each other of concealing or distorting evidence for electoral reasons.

The timing of the bombings was also significant as they occurred three days before general elections and this had a direct influence on the defeat of the incumbent José María Aznar's Partido Popular, which had obtained a small but narrowing lead in the opinion polls. The party was anticipated as highly likely to win the general election but was voted out of office following the attacks.

The victorious Partido Socialista Obrero Español advocated a withdrawal of Spanish troops from Iraq, regarding this as a strong vote winner, because it would appease the terrorists and hence minimise the risk of future attacks in the home nation. The presence of Spanish troops in Iraq and the Spanish prime minister's support for the 'War on Terror' were identified as the motivating factors for the bombings. In the face of the terrorist pressure Spain, for all intents and purposes, capitulated.

A second business continuity issue was the significant negative impact of the attacks across the European financial arena. The financial markets' response to the Madrid bombings was initially negative and virtually all European stock markets fell following the news of the explosions. It is clear that as the day progressed the issue of the authorship of the attacks was seen as important and that doubts over whether or not ETA carried out the attack weighed heavily on the market.

The attacks reawakened fears of terrorism, with most European stock markets falling between 2% and 3% on 11 March 2004. Stocks dropped in London and in New York, with the Dow Jones diving after speculation of involvement by Al-Qaeda. In Tokyo, stocks opened lower the next day. Reuters summarised the fall in the markets in a series of interviews across several organisations: on 11 March 2004 Cema Marti, a manager at Ata Investment, was quoted as saying *'Sales came with the fall in European bourses because of fears Al-Qaeda is behind the blasts in Madrid.'* Similarly Anita Griffin, investment director for European equities at Standard Life, stated, *'This is a reaction on the day to terrible news of the bombs,'* and Jeremy Batstone of the brokers Fyshe Group said, *'The market's greatest fear was the Al-Qaeda network responding to the US led invasion of Iraq.'*

15: A Tale of Three Cities: The Bombing of Madrid (2004),
London (2005) and Glasgow (2007)

The main security management issue identified by this incident was the need to closely monitor the link between terrorism and crime. Experts had identified that a convergence of international terrorism and transnational organised crime might take place somewhere in Western Europe. Police terrorism investigators had highlighted marked similarities in the behavioural and operational methods of terrorists and organised criminals. Unfortunately it was not regarded as sufficiently important to change the long-held view that the different goals of the two groups would prevent them working together, i.e. personal profit was the key determinant for criminals whereas terrorist were focused primarily on achieving political upheaval. The Spanish bombings showed this was no longer valid, as terrorist and criminal organisations were willing to co-operate over specific matters, in order to gain the benefits of economies of scale through working together.

> *'One of the central members of the Madrid terror cell, Jamal Ahmidan, was a former international drug dealer who converted to Islam while in prison and tapped his criminal past after his release to supply the cell's logistical needs—including the exchange of drugs for the explosives used in the attacks.'* – (Shelly, et al., 2005, p. 41).

A number of key issues emerged after the attacks – the reduction in immigration constraints, the need for effective communication networks and the need for good international cooperation. These are discussed in turn below.

The first area to consider was the need to re-examine the existing immigration laws because the Madrid bombings alerted the world to the proliferation of jihadi networks in Europe since 11 September 2001. Al-Qaeda had moved from focusing on African/Middle East operations to the European arena. It now actively provided encouragement and strategic orientation to scores of relatively autonomous European jihadi networks. These networks were marshalled for specific missions, drawing operatives from a pool of professionals and apprentices, and then dispersed. The Madrid bombers received radical teaching, advice, and assistance from imams and colleagues in Britain, Denmark, France, Germany, Italy and Norway as well as North Africa.

Based on secret recordings of militants and the arrest of suspects internationally, senior counterintelligence officials believe that post-9/11, wider support for the jihadi movement has allowed Islamic terrorists to significantly extend their European operations. The Spanish authorities expressed concern that liberal western immigration laws facilitate easy movement of potential jihadi terrorists and their arms. Minimal European international borders allowed Al-Qaeda and allied groups to travel freely across the continent, and relaxed immigration laws constrained the ability of the government to deport suspected terrorists. Such laws needed to be reviewed and effective movement controls established without creating a negative impact on the genuine movement of EU nationals for business and pleasure.

It is also evident that efficient communication between members of the emergency response teams is essential. The Madrid bombings clearly demonstrated the need for effective, speedy, adaptable, high volume communications networks which would operate on designated emergency channels. Quick and effective communication networks are vital to help reduce chaos and minimise the impact on the immediate environment and the wider economy, both during and after the incident.

15: A Tale of Three Cities: The Bombing of Madrid (2004), London (2005) and Glasgow (2007)

The incumbent NATO chairman, General Harald Kujat, reported that the Spanish emergency medical response team reacted quickly and efficiently to the attacks. Disaster response and life-saving vehicles arrived within minutes and emergency response personnel made efforts to distribute the injured among a number of nearby hospitals. The third and fourth explosions caused some resource and personnel strain because almost all available resources had been devoted to dealing with the first two. The later explosions exceeded capacity for the emergency response teams, and this has become the aim of terrorist groups seeking to create maximum disruption. Kujat noted that the communications system must also allow for broadcast of clear messages from the emergency services and media to the wider public to minimise panic and control movement.

Finally for effective security and emergency planning there must be close co-operation between national and international law enforcement agencies. Mutual concern and discussion following incidents such as the Madrid bombings have resulted in the establishment of formal international agreements, including conventions, treaties, and memoranda of understanding. It is clear, however, that these agreements are not self-enforcing. Without law enforcement and judicial cooperation that results in investigation, prosecutions, and crime prevention, international agreements lack meaning in practice. The key point is that the implementation of such agreements is the real measure of the success of international cooperation.

'The Madrid bombings led to attempts to galvanise Europe's response to terrorism.' – (BBC News, 2007).

15: A Tale of Three Cities: The Bombing of Madrid (2004), London (2005) and Glasgow (2007)

One crucial outcome of the Madrid bombings was the conference organised by the United States Mission to NATO and the George C. Marshall Centre, supported by the Slovenian Foreign Ministry. From 27 June 2005 to 1 July 2005, an expert conference was held in Slovenia under the NATO-Russia Council (NRC) with the intent of identifying 'Lessons Learned from Recent Terrorist Attacks: Building National Capabilities and Institutions'.

Following on from the NRC report, nine expert working groups were established. Composed of professionals working on specific areas related to the fight against terrorism, each group addressed in greater technical detail national policies and priorities in those areas, allowing for a unique exchange of information regarding what might be improved. Taking each subject area in turn, the groups reached the following recommendations and conclusions:

- Site security: while there is no single approach that can guarantee site security, enhanced and comprehensive intelligence gathering and sharing, improved use of available technologies (such as biometrics), and frequent training, exercises and simulations including both public and private sector agencies would be very beneficial.

- Medical preparedness and response: participants discussed ways in which NRC nations might wish to concentrate on improving training and qualifications for emergency medical personnel, such as producing operational guidelines based on common operative principles.

- Civil law enforcement and investigations: legal norms and the role and investigative methods of enforcement agencies in terrorist cases were discussed. Emphasis was placed on the need to share information and resources among both agencies and governments. The group analysed preventive measures aimed at anti-terrorism law enforcement, such as improving immigration laws, confronting hostile reconnaissance and fighting organised crime.

- Military roles and tasks: most participants noted that the military should play a supporting role in combating terrorism, including explosive detection, Chemical, Biological, Radiological & Nuclear (CBRN) defence, or training of relevant personnel.

- Airspace control & monitoring: experts exchanged views on specific anti-terrorist measures undertaken by NRC member states, such as improved radio and radar coverage, new procedures for intercepting airborne threats, visual warning systems and ground-based defence assets.

- Interagency and vertical co-ordination: the importance of devising a comprehensive approach to emergency planning, so as not to under-invest in non-terrorist emergency situations, the need to designate a lead agency early in the process and the importance of efficient communication was discussed.

- Building responsive legislation and institutions: legal experts discussed possible enhancements to national and international legal frameworks on terrorism, including existing export controls, transport and site security, regulation of financial transactions, immigration laws and extradition agreements, as well as terrorism-related UN Conventions and the EU Action Plan.

- Nature of terrorist organisations and operations: experts examined their national experiences and the evolution of terrorist cells and networks operating on their territory, their financing and resource management, as well as trans-border links.

- Hostage negotiation and rescue: psychological experts addressed this. They pointed to the tension between the general principle of refusing to negotiate with terrorists and the need to employ all available means to safeguard the lives of hostages.

The Madrid bombings hit Spain unexpectedly and led to a change of government. The incident negatively affected the European financial markets and demonstrated the willingness of terrorists and criminals to work together to mutual benefit. A review of immigration laws was demanded to reduce free movement of terrorist suspects and arms across Europe. It also highlighted the need for effective emergency communication networks and good cooperation between law enforcement organisations. The attack was the focus of the NATO conference of 2005 in Slovenia and it encouraged all European states to review their business continuity, security and emergency management plans and procedures.

London Underground and bus bombings, 2005

On Wednesday 6 July 2005 it was announced that the 2012 Olympic Games would be held in the UK. The whole country was celebrating an unexpected win in the close fought contest, and planning began almost immediately for this high profile, international event. Hardly had the announcement been made when more sinister and negative news dominated the headlines. The following day a series of bomb blasts in the heart of London killed 52 people and injured more than 700. Shortly before 9:00 am on the 7 July 2005, death and destruction resulted from the biggest terrorist attack in Britain since Lockerbie in 1988. It brutally punctured the Olympics euphoria. As a result Thursday 7 July, 2005 can be regarded as one of the darkest days in British history since the Second World War.

The Economist reported police statements that at least 33 people had been killed and hundreds injured by three explosions on London's Underground. Eyewitnesses described huge explosions that sent glass flying and filled carriages with acrid smoke. Rescue workers had to use pickaxes to reach trapped passengers.

A further attack on a bus in Tavistock Square blew the roof off a double-decker which was travelling through Woburn Place in Bloomsbury. A previously unknown group calling itself the Secret Organisation, Al-Qaeda's Jihad in Europe, claimed responsibility for the attacks citing the action as revenge for the British 'military massacres' in Iraq and Afghanistan.

In justifying the attack, the terrorists provided a 200 word statement published on an Islamic website. This group was previously unknown before the bombings and their website purported to carry statements from Al Qaeda. In short, the message said that:

> *'The attack was against the British Zionist Crusader*
> *government in retaliation for the massacres Britain*
> *is committing in Iraq and Afghanistan.'* – (BBC
> News, 2005).

Time and again military and political leaders had predicted that an attack on the United Kingdom's mainland was inevitable – a case of when, not if. By striking at London, the heart of international transport and finance, Al Qaeda hoped to achieve a three-pronged success which would damage continuity:

- First, it looked to disrupt the Group 8 summit meeting, attended by the most powerful leaders in the Western world. This was being hosted by the British prime minister at Gleneagles, Scotland. That aim failed.

- Second, Al Qaeda hoped to reproduce the 'Spanish effect' and alienate the public from its government, as it had so successfully done after the Madrid train bombs the previous year. Here, too, it failed, as is clear from the results of the next election.

- Third, it wanted to fracture the 'special relationship' between America and the United Kingdom, to break the partnership in Iraq by making the price of co-operation with America too costly to bear. This was never going to happen as the ties between both nations are too strong.

Although the attack was grave the economic impact was not even close to the devastation of the 9/11 attacks, mostly because of lessons learned from the 9/11 attacks but also for a number of other reasons. The foremost explanation is that the London attacks did not damage the financial infrastructure. There was limited immediate disruption to the national and world economy. There was no significant impact on trading in either the London Stock Exchange or the London Financial Futures, and the Options Exchange was not affected. In order to assess the result of the attacks on the financial system, calls were made within the central banks, finance ministries and leading financial institutions. Precautionary assessment was also conducted in the United States as British Treasury officials communicated with the US Federal Securities and Exchange Commission. Their initial findings were ratified by the Financial Services Sector Co-ordinating Council, a private-sector group set up after the 9/11 terrorist attacks to examine possible threats to the United States' financial infrastructure.

The attacks understandably caused massive disruption to travel in and around London. The Underground and bus services were suspended and overland mainline railway stations closed. With the exception of Kings Cross, which was used as a makeshift hospital to treat casualties, and neighbouring St Pancras, mainline stations services along with London Transport buses restarted later in the day. The majority of the underground network reopened on 8 July. Use was made of river vessels as an alternative means of transport although many commuters making their way home had to walk to mainline stations.

The Kings Cross and St Pancras mainline stations reopened on 9 July. Disrupted underground services were gradually restored over the following four weeks with the Piccadilly line being the last to fully reopen on 4 August.

In April 2005, the London Resilience Team published the UK's Strategic Emergency Plan (Version 2.1). Since the introduction of the Civil Contingencies Act 2004 in 2005, all regions in England and Wales have been required to establish and maintain a Generic Regional Response Plan enabling the activation of regional crisis management when needed. In order to comply with the requirements of the Act this document performs as a signposting authority. It links to other relevant emergency plans, thus establishing a comprehensive and holistic Generic Regional Response Plan.

In effect, this plan is the basis upon which the UK first responders react to any major emergency or crisis, although this is not terrorism specific. After years of preparing for the

worst, or something very close to it, the unexpected terrorist
attack happened. Emergency planning proved crucial in the
response to the London bombings. The emergency services
were widely praised – by the Queen and the prime minister,
among others. The opinion of the overwhelming majority
was that their response had been swift and effective.

It is always possible to identify areas for improvement and
a Home Office report partially published by the BBC
summarises the emergency response. It identifies a number
of shortcomings in the manner in which the emergency
services responded to the situation. There was evidence that
some information was suppressed; the police casualty
bureau was overwhelmed by calls which were made worse
by technical difficulties.

Investigative journalists found it extremely difficult to
obtain reliable information about the number of casualties
and their associated injuries, especially with regard to
foreign nationals. Only the obviously injured were treated
and there was little consideration of the emotional trauma
associated with such an event. Details of what had
happened were not collected from people caught up in the
events and there was no mechanism to provide those
involved with details of avenues for advice and support.
Many individuals were left feeling forgotten or unimportant
and there were limited medical emergency supplies
available at rail and Underground stations for general first-
aiders to treat minor injuries.

The report also reflects on the success of the response to the
incident by the emergency and security agencies. It
concluded that the emergency response was extremely
good; but makes three key recommendations:

15: A Tale of Three Cities: The Bombing of Madrid (2004), London (2005) and Glasgow (2007)

- Firstly with regard to communications, future emergency responders should not rely on mobile phone networks, which became heavily congested. The disabling of mobile phones to all but 999 calls could be counter-productive as calls to family can stop widespread panic and also pre-empt calls enquiring about the location and status of individuals. It was suggested that a dedicated digital communications network for emergency services across London was urgently needed.

- Secondly, it was apparent that there were insufficient medical supplies. The report recommended that a cache of supplies be placed at major transport hubs and regularly checked and maintained.

- Finally those responding to the attacks received a large number of requests for information from the government. To improve coordination in future it was suggested that all requests should go through senior coordinators, leaving those on the ground able to focus on their support to the crisis.

The suicide bombings were carried out by Muslim extremists, all of whom were British and none of whom had previous convictions. Only one, Mohammad Sidique Khan, had come onto MI5's radar; their interest was taken up with what they considered to be more urgent and dangerous targets. Khan along with two of the other bombers, Hasib Hussain, and Shehzad Tanweer, had reportedly received terrorist training and religious instruction in Pakistan several months before. The fourth, Jamaican-born Jermaine Lindsey is believed to have converted to Islam in Afghanistan. All had been recruited or influenced deeply by Al Qaeda. This highlighted the need to consider 'home-grown' potential threats to the security of the UK when conducting security and emergency planning, rather than solely anticipating any terrorist activity to originate with external groups.

Within minutes of the bombings in London, ambulance, fire and police sirens could be heard throughout the city. The high visibility vests worn by rescue teams would subsequently dominate the images in international media coverage. Behind the scenes, ministers and security, emergency and health service officials executed a highly structured emergency strategy. As planned, the Home Office took primary responsibility for combating terrorism within the UK and the Home Secretary chaired the cabinet committees on terrorism, bringing together the work of ministers across the government.

Agreed emergency management and planning procedures made establishing the nature of the threat and tending to the injured the priority. The preparation for terrorist attacks which had already taken place proved vital in ensuring an effective and coordinated response. The security and emergency planning paid off and while 'no plan survives contact with the enemy', it became apparent on the day that the time spent 'exercising' and training for such an atrocity ensured that casualties and disruption across the city were kept to a minimum.

In conclusion, the tragic loss of life and the injuries sustained to those directly caught in the 7 July 2005 bombings touched the city, the nation and beyond. London is a historically resilient city. The disruption, however, both in terms of business continuity and the capital's infrastructure, was minimal. The introduction of the UK's Strategic Emergency Plan promoted swift and effective responses by the emergency services.

15: A Tale of Three Cities: The Bombing of Madrid (2004), London (2005) and Glasgow (2007)

It is perhaps worth noting that London only had four explosions to deal with whereas Madrid had ten. Moreover, the London death toll was just 25%, and the injury rate only 30%, of Madrid's. While the emergency services in London were commended for their effective response, could they have managed as well had the city been hit by as many bombs as Madrid? The Spanish emergency services did cope with the situation until the fifth bomb exploded.

Glasgow Airport bombing, 2007

The British Airports Authority (BAA), now rebranded Heathrow Airport Holdings, owns and operates a number of airports including Glasgow. This part of the study examines the bombing of Glasgow International Airport in 2007 by two men using a Vehicle Borne Improvised Explosive Device (VBIED). The terrorists Bilal Abdullah, a British born Muslim of Iraqi descent, and Kafeel Ahmed, a Muslim of Indian origin, were al Qaeda affiliated. Abdullah was a doctor based at the Royal Alexandria Hospital, Paisley, while Ahmed was studying for a PhD at Anglia Ruskin University. A suicide note subsequently discovered by the authorities indicated that the two men expected to die in the attack. This incident followed a failed attempt less than 24 h earlier by the same terrorist cell to explode two VBIEDs outside a popular London night club.

The day of the attack

On Saturday 30 June 2007 at 1:34 am, Kafeel Ahmed uploaded a suicide note and his will to his e-mail account.

At 8 am Ahmed and Abdullah constructed the VBIED at Houston near Glasgow by packing a four-wheel drive Jeep

15: A Tale of Three Cities: The Bombing of Madrid (2004), London (2005) and Glasgow (2007)

Cherokee with fuel, gas canisters and makeshift shrapnel before driving north to Loch Lomond. They remained there until 2 pm. During this time Ahmed sent a text message to his brother describing how his will could be retrieved.

Closed circuit television cameras situated around Glasgow International Airport recorded the terrorist's vehicle arriving at 3:04 pm.

At approximately 3:13 pm and with Ahmed behind the wheel the suspects drove the Jeep into the doors of the main terminal building of the airport. The vehicle would have penetrated the terminal building had it not been for the security bollards outside the main doors. Ahmed tried to free the Jeep without success. Abdullah threw petrol bombs from the vehicle while Ahmed doused himself in petrol and set himself alight. Ablaze and with both the vehicle and terminal building now also on fire, Ahmed emerged from the Jeep and attempted to enter the terminal building on foot. Officers from Strathclyde Police supported by members of the public restrained him, along with his accomplice. After a brief struggle both Ahmed and Abdullah were detained by the police.

The terminal and additional areas of the building were efficiently cleared. Strathclyde Fire and Rescue Service initially attended the fire before being joined by BAA rescue and firefighting units. It was discovered that the vehicle contained several propane gas canisters with the intent of creating an incendiary bomb effect. Both the terminal and vehicle fires were brought under control within 15 min and had been extinguished after 30. A sprinkler system was activated by the fire, but the isolation valve could not be reached due to the close proximity of the fire and the existence of a crime scene. Consequently, large volumes of water continued to be pumped into the building for several hours. Neither the water nor smoke damage could be dealt with until the following day.

The crime scene was finally wrapped up by the emergency services and handed back to BAA after 54 h. Crichton notes that shortly before this incident an exclusion zone around a murder scene in Glasgow was in place for four weeks, but the airport reopened just 23 h and 59 min after the incident, with BAA initially working around the exclusion zone. It is worth noting that the emergency services will only lift an exclusion zone when they consider it safe to do so and the crime scene activities have been completed. In Glasgow's case this was achieved in just over two days. In the case of the 1996 IRA Manchester bombing, the exclusion zone lasted for months and within six months of the incident, 250 companies were declared bankrupt.

'Had the cargo detonated, a huge fireball would have swept through the building, with shrapnel killing and maiming many victims.' – (Edwards, et al., 2007).

The airport handles over eight million passengers each year. With the school holidays having just started, they day of the attack was one of its busiest days on the calendar. In addition to the injured terrorists, fortunately no more than five members of the public were hurt in the incident. They were all taken to the Royal Alexandria Hospital, Paisley for treatment, approximately 3.5 miles away from the airport. A suspicious device was discovered on Ahmed when he was being treated and the hospital was partially evacuated. It was later found to be harmless. Ahmed suffered 90% burns to his body during the attack and died from his injuries two days later.

There were approximately 1,100 passengers held on board incoming aircraft for several hours after the incident occurred. This allowed the emergency services to evacuate circa 4,500 members of the public from the terminal building and transfer them to an emergency holding area. This location had been previously identified in the continuity plans and evacuees were relocated to the Scottish Exhibition and Conference Centre in central Glasgow, approximately 8.5 miles from the airport. Crime scene and police investigation protocols dictated that each person transferred to the holding centre had to be interviewed before being released by Strathclyde police.

Glasgow airport's response

It is not unusual to find business continuity plans that are designed to deal with single incidents. Glasgow airport was no exception and it had no one plan that dealt with this particular scenario. Instead it had a series of integrated plans that addressed situations such as mass evacuation, closure of airport approach roads and mobilisation of off-duty staff. Within 45 min of the initial incident, the BAA crisis management team had become operational, with the recovery team in place one hour later.

Efforts had to be made to reopen the airport as early as possible and a system of communication and coordination had to be established with other key stakeholders to accomplish this. Some airlines had already decided to cancel flights into and out of the airport and this had to be incorporated into these communications.

Each business unit within the airport environment is required to have a documented and clear contingency plan, all of which have been incorporated into the main BAA contingency planning. BAA's strategy is centred on the '7 Rs' method that incorporates:

- **Risk**: an evaluation of the financial, operational and strategic risks to BAA and its key stakeholders.

- **Resilience**: the ability to positively adapt to change, transform experiences or situations to the organisation's advantage, and emerge stronger from doing so.

- **Rehearse**: the various drills and test situations that key stakeholders have to incorporate into contingency planning in order to hone reaction times and methods.

- **Responses**: a documented, measured set of constantly reviewed strategic, tactical and operational reactions to given risk-assessed situations.

- **Recovery**: these are the various activities and tasks necessary to resume normal operations.

- **Review**: the cyclic system of re-examination of risk assessments, the allocation of resources and the involvement of key stakeholders within the contingency planning systems within the organisation.

- **Reputation**: every business needs to be aware of how they are perceived. A negative perception can affect areas of business such as recruitment and investment as well as the sales performance of the organisation.

Media

Any organisation that ignores the importance of positive media relations can suffer as a result. This can hinder the return to normal operations. Air transport is regarded as immensely newsworthy by the editors of newspapers, magazines and television broadcasts. During the first 24 h after the incident, the BAA media relations team handled somewhere in the region of 800 calls.

'The week following the incident, Glasgow Airport website received 130,000 visits compared to 6,000 the previous week.' – (Crichton, 2007, p. 4).

It follows that, during this high profile media incident, BAA would look to pro-actively protect the image of Glasgow International Airport. Despite being the victim of a terrorist attack, it would want to avoid any undue criticism over its handling of the situation. It achieved this very effectively by maximising the use of a number of media channels including its own website, e-bulletins, a local radio campaign plus using the Glasgow city centre big screens. It also ensured that Scottish members of parliament were kept well briefed.

Impact on travellers

Commercial flight cancellation is something of an occupational hazard for airlines and can happen for any one of a number of reasons. Usually only individual flights are affected. In addition to terrorist attacks, however, other scenarios such as adverse weather, volcanic ash clouds or air traffic control strikes can seriously disrupt aviation operations or even cause complete airport shutdowns.

'The problem for a lot of people whose flights have been cancelled is that you don't automatically go on the next plane, you actually go to the back of the queue.' – Simon Calder, Travel Editor, *The Independent.*

Anyone booking their flights and hotels separately may find that while the airline is legally obliged to refund them or offer a suitable alternative, hotels may insist on being paid. Package holidays do provide better protection as travel companies must either give you a full refund or offer an appropriate alternative.

The immediate aftermath

Both Liverpool's John Lennon airport and Blackpool airport were initially closed and security was tightened at other UK airports. Security at airports in the USA was also intensified in response to the Glasgow incident. The attack resulted in wide-ranging global changes regarding vehicle access to airports which included extensive deployment of hostile vehicle mitigation measures.

'We have a long way to go before airports here in the UK are secure enough to prevent the prospect of another terrorist attack.' – Chris Yates, security consultant (BBC News, 2008).

Despite the severity of the attack, the airport reopened 24 h later. Twelve months on, a reported £4 million of additional funds had been spent improving the airport's security. This included around 300 steel hostile vehicle mitigation barriers. Even so, security specialist observed that although some weak points in airport security had been addressed, others remained.

The economic cost of terrorism

The Israel Interdisciplinary Centre in Herzliya, Israel has been studying the effects of terrorist attacks on the economy for many years. The centre has determined that although one single event such as the London bombings cannot be used to gauge economic impact, there is enough data to draw some conclusions. One of their conclusions tells us that terrorism as a global trend is having an impact on the economy.

> *'From an economic point of view, terrorism works. For a relatively small investment terrorists obtain a large economic impact. . . Gradually the global economy is being hurt by the constant threat of terrorism and the attacks.'* – (International Institute for Counter Terrorism, 2010).

The economic cost of terrorism can be divided into short, medium and long term. In the short term there are several direct costs such as the loss of human life, victim support, loss of property, cost of the attending emergency services, cost of removing debris and losses due to economic activites interrupted by an attack. He further identifies short term indirect costs such as the effect on tourism, hotel occupancy, theatre and cinema attendance figures and reduced restaurant bookings generated by a consumer fear of further attacks.

In the medium and long term there is reduced investment and economic growth, not to mention the ever-increasing cost of anti-terrorism measures. Sustained attacks (as experienced in Northern Ireland and Israel) can effectively destroy the tourism industry while one-off incidents tend to be quickly forgotten.

> *'During the Troubles, tourism just died.'* – Martin Mulholland, Concierge Europa Hotel, Belfast, 2012.

The economic costs relating to the Glasgow attack are the least complex of the three incidents. The cost of policing the attack was put at £1.7 million while physical damage to the airport is reported to be in the order of £4 million. The actual loss of business was considered minimal as the airport reopened within 24 h of the incident. We must not, however, lose sight of the fact that the terrorists' incendiary device failed to detonate.

No figures are available regarding the loss of income for the shopping outlets, bars, cafes and restaurants based at Glasgow, or for any airlines or airline-dependent suppliers such as caterers. It is assumed that their respective operations will have resumed when the airport reopened for business.

In Madrid, the attacks caused material damages of about 17 million Euros but the additional economic cost has been estimated at more than 282 million Euros. The Madrid train bombings were not only the most devastating act of terrorism in modern Spain but also across Western Europe.

In London, it was London Transport that bore the brunt of the attacks, resulting in a negligible immediate impact to the broader economy. It is clear that the British economy was affected by these bombings in the long term, with an estimated subsequent cost to the capital's tourist industry of approximately £4 billion, although tourism across the remainder of the UK witnessed an increase in its 2006 revenue figures. Confidence in London tourism was probably further dented by the subsequent failed attacks on the London Underground network only two weeks later.

Figure 14 is based upon the Al Qaeda attacks on Madrid (2004), London (2005), Glasgow (2007) plus the 9/11 World Trade Centre attack. It illustrates that while the cost of terrorist attacks is generally reducing, the resulting economic cost is soaring. The expenditure required in financing a terrorist attack is also generally small in comparison with the resultant economic damage.

Event	Year	Casualties	Terrorist Costs in US$	Economic Costs in Million US$	Comments
Attack on World Trade Centre	2001	2,973 killed	500,000	83,000	An estimated 598,000 workers lost their jobs as a result of this terrorist attack, including 279,000 from the tourist trade alone.
Madrid railway bombings	2004	200 killed 1,800 injured	10,000	282	This attack is credited with bringing down the Spanish government.
London Transport 7/7 bombings	2005	52 killed	2,000	4,000	This is primarily the estimated loss of tourism revenue to London although the number of tourist

					visitors to the UK rose in 2005 by 6% over 2004 and then by a further 9.2% in 2007.
Glasgow Airport	2007	1 killed, 5 injured	5,000	6	The only fatality was one of the terrorists. The major terrorist expense was procuring the vehicle used to construct the VBIED.

Figure 14: Cost of terrorism versus related economic costs

The exception in terms of terrorist costs is the 9/11 operation. In this instance, however, the number of casualties was far higher than any previous attack and the economic impact was unprecedented.

When considering the 'terrorist costs' and the corresponding 'economic costs', people could be forgiven for thinking that the best return on investment (ROI) for the terrorists in recent times was the 9/11 attacks. *Figure 15*, overleaf, demonstrates that while the 9/11 attack achieved a 166,000 to 1 ROI, the London 7/7 bombings generated a staggering 2,000,000 to 1 return. Meanwhile, Glasgow hardly registers when compared with the other featured attacks.

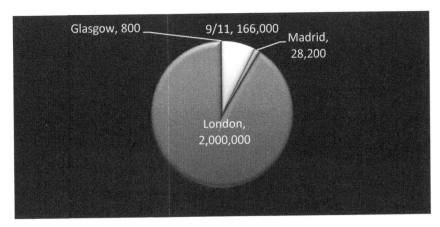

Figure 15: Terrorist's return on investment -v- economic costs of attacks

While the cost of terrorism can be quantified in terms of casualties and economics, the intangible terrorist objective of generating fear cannot.

Conversely, on a positive note, 7/7 did witness some business beneficiaries, especially security firms, taxis and bicycle stores. In fact, as one observer noted: 'safety and security seem to be converging.'

Lessons learned

Terrorism is considered a Tier One threat by the UK and it is taken just as seriously in many other countries. In general, transport presents a soft terrorist target and there is no single method of guaranteeing the protection for more open modes such as trains and buses.

15: A Tale of Three Cities: The Bombing of Madrid (2004), London (2005) and Glasgow (2007)

Glasgow Airport was the first terrorist attack on Scottish soil. Conversely, London has been dealing with terrorism for over 150 years while Spain has had to tolerate the unwanted attention of ETA for decades. The Madrid bombing also demonstrated that terrorist and criminal elements are prepared to cooperate with each other to further their own ends, with explosives being traded for drugs.

Both the London and Glasgow bombings were suicide attacks. Moreover, when you take account of the failed attack on the London Underground on 21 July 2005, at least eleven jihadists have been prepared to martyr themselves at the expense of the British travelling public. This of course excludes other foiled plots such as that of Richard Wright, the shoe bomber, and the liquid bomb plot, both of which intended to blow up transatlantic flights.

While businesses may not be the specific target of a terrorist attack, they can still suffer from collateral damage. The impact could be in the form of exclusion zones, damaged property, injured, killed or traumatised staff, transport disruption, supply chain failures, etc. Furthermore, with so much glass used in the design of modern buildings, a relatively small explosion could still cause substantial casualties from flying glass. The deployment of comparatively inexpensive anti-shatter plastic film would certainly help mitigate the risk. Businesses could also suffer if they are located in areas considered to be at a high risk from terrorism. The tourism and hospitality industries both suffered in London and Madrid following the bombings.

Following the failed Glasgow attack, hostile vehicle mitigation (HVM) measures have been deployed at airports within the UK and beyond, sometimes in the form of ugly steel barriers or concrete blocks, sometimes designed to appear like attractive seats or planters. But whatever their appearance, the vital criteria is that they work. In fact HVM solutions are becoming more widespread as companies also look to negate the efforts of ram-raiders.

It is clearly not the responsibility of individual businesses to detect or apprehend terrorists – that is the work of the national security services. It is their responsibility though to protect their businesses and staff as effectively as is possible. Moreover, we must not forget that while they were at the forefront of each of the three terrorist attacks, the emergency services are not just there to react to such events. In addition to their respective 'day jobs', they are also expected to respond to other, non-terrorist situations such as natural disasters.

It could have been worse

While all four bombs were successfully detonated in London on 7/7, the bomb targeting Glasgow Airport and three of the 13 Madrid bombs did not. With the emergency services in Madrid over extended after the fourth explosion, not only would there have been more fatalities had all bombs detonated, but scores of additional injured would have been left unattended.

As for Glasgow, we can only speculate. With hundreds of travellers in the terminal building it would be reasonable to assume many potential casualties. In the aftermath, Glasgow Airport would probably have needed rebuilding rather than repairing and its recovery plans would have been tested to the limit.

15: A Tale of Three Cities: The Bombing of Madrid (2004), London (2005) and Glasgow (2007)

What went well

- The Spanish emergency services had effective, adaptable, high volume communications networks which operated on designated emergency channels.

- The Madrid bombings resulted in better international cooperation to help plan against and prevent future attacks.

- The emergency services in London were very highly praised for their efforts.

- Glasgow Airport's plan went well. Much benefit was derived from the extensive testing of their plans, as the reopening of the airport within 24 h demonstrates. With key staff effectively on round-the-clock emergency call-out, mobilising additional resources to deal with the incident was particularly successful. Easy access to appropriate contact details was of paramount importance. Their media plan was well thought out and they were pro-active in their communications. The airport's vehicle access denial plan was also implemented in the aftermath to restrict access to the terminal's inner forecourt until necessary security measures were applied.

What could have been done better

- The Spanish Government fell, probably as a result of the attack.

- Spanish emergency services struggled to cope with the number of casualties across multiple locations.

- The Spanish authorities should have more closely monitored the link between terrorism and crime.

- The financial markets reacted badly when it was discovered that al Qaeda and not ETA was behind the Madrid attacks.

- Both the Spanish and British governments should have paid more attention to the risk from home-grown Islamic terrorists. Glasgow Airport coped well with the crisis. Had the device brought by the terrorist gone off, however, it could have been a very different story.

What did not go well

- The Spanish emergency services coped well with the initial blasts, but were unprepared to deal with the scale of the Madrid bombing attack.

- In London, communications proved nigh on impossible as the Underground network lacked any mobile phone or wireless facilities. The police phone network proved unable to deal with the volume of calls.

- Insufficient medical supplies were available in locations close to the London attacks.

Conclusion

Every business, large or small, needs to embrace business continuity taking account of any potential terrorist threat they may face. They should keep in mind the damage caused by a terrorist bombing may be similar to that of an accidental explosion or a fire, potentially resulting in business inhibitors like denial of access and temporary or permanent loss of staff through fatalities, injuries or trauma.

CHAPTER 16: HURRICANE KATRINA – OWEN GREGORY AND NEIL SWINYARD-JORDAN

'Judges can show mercy, but against the laws of nature, there is no appeal.' – Arthur C. Clarke.

The annual American hurricane season officially runs from 1 June to the end of November. In recent years forecasting has been much improved via the National Hurricane Center (NHC). A broader range of scientific and statistical information has been collected annually, refining the evolving forecasting model. It contains data from 1954 onward and not only facilitates longer-range forecasting but a greater degree of accuracy over the intensity of the storms.

As early as May 2005 scientists from the National Oceanic and Atmospheric Administration (NOAA) suggested that the 2005 hurricane season would be active with, a 70% chance of above-normal activity. They were proved right, with 26 named storms that year, 13 of which were hurricanes – seven of which were considered major. Three of the major storms were Category 5 including Katrina, the subject of this case study. Specific attention will be paid to its effects on New Orleans.

The Saffir/Simpson Scale categorises hurricanes from 1 to 5 as illustrated in *Figure 16*.

Category	Damage	Pressure (milli bars)	Max Wind Velocity (mph)	Peak Gusts (mph)	Surge (metres)	Examples	Year	Fatalities	Cost (US$ Billion)
1	Minimal	>980	94	119	1	Noel	2008	163	0.58
2	Moderate	980-965	112	139	2	Juan	2003	5	0.20
3	Extensive	964-945	130	161	3	Fran	1996	26	4.16
4	Extreme	944-920	155	193	4 – 5	Frances	2004	49	9.85
5	Catastrophic	<920	>155	>193	>5	Rita	2005	62	12.00

Figure 16: Hurricane categories and statistics

Despite being a devastating hurricane resulting in almost 2,000 fatalities, Katrina was by no means the worst ever to make landfall in the USA. The 1900 hurricane which hit Galveston in Texas killed over 8,000 people, amounting to around 20% of the population, while destroying a third of the city. Katrina, however, was the most costly in terms of widespread damage.

Birth of Katrina

Formed over the Bahamas on 23 August 2005, Katrina was officially declared a tropical depression on the same day. It developed into a tropical storm and by 25 August, it had attained hurricane status as it passed over south Florida, heading into the Gulf of Mexico. 14 fatalities were recorded in the state with damage estimates exceeding US$1 billion.

Crossing the Gulf of Mexico

During Katrina's transit over the Gulf of Mexico the NHC forecast that it would make landfall in the bayous of Louisiana, and even pinpointed the town of Buras as the most likely place it would strike. The forecast was a mere

18 miles out, which in terms of hurricane prediction is highly accurate.

In anticipation of the inevitable widespread destruction that would result from Hurricane Katrina, on 27 August Max Mayfield, Director of the National Hurricane Centre, telephoned New Orleans Mayor Ray Nagin to express his extreme concern. The following day Mayfield made a video call to U.S. President George W. Bush at his farm in Crawford, Texas about the severity of the storm. This action served as the catalyst for detailed and rapid refinement and implementation of existing security and emergency management and planning in the region.

With the hurricane threat to the Gulf Coast rising, evacuation warnings were issued. Many New Orleans residents started taking precautions to secure their homes and prepare for possible evacuation. By mid-morning on the 27 August there were long queues outside of those petrol stations which had not yet run out of fuel. It was reported that the mayor of the city, after initially called for a voluntary evacuation at 5:00 pm, subsequently ordered a citywide mandatory evacuation at 9:30 am on the following morning, the first such order in the city's history. In a news conference, Nagin predicted that, '*the storm surge most likely will topple our levee system,*' and warned that oil production in the Gulf of Mexico would be shut down.

Warnings by the city mayor were reinforced by a national address from President Bush who made a televised appeal for residents to heed the evacuation orders.

'*We cannot stress enough the danger this hurricane poses to Gulf Coast communities.*' – George W. Bush.

By mid-afternoon, officials in the neighbouring areas of Plaquemines, St. Bernard, St. Charles, Lafourche, Terrebonne, Jefferson, St. Tommany and Washington, had also called for voluntary or mandatory evacuations.

On the available evidence, it would be reasonable to accept that both the NOAA and the NHC had warned of Katrina's potential to cause seriously damage to the infrastructure in Louisiana and Mississippi well in advance of the landfall, at city, state and federal level.

The impact

> *'New Orleans is a disaster waiting to happen.'* – *Mark Fischetti, Senior Editor at Scientific American* (Fischetti, 2001).

Rated as a Category 3 hurricane, Katrina hit New Orleans on the 29 August 2005 with sustained winds of 125 miles per hour. The subsequent official report of December 2005 from the NHC described Katrina as:

> *'. . .an extraordinarily powerful and deadly hurricane that carved a wide swath of catastrophic damage and inflicted large loss of life. It was the costliest and one of the five deadliest hurricanes to ever strike the United States. . . After reaching Category 5, over the central Gulf of Mexico, Katrina weakened to Category 3 before making landfall on the northern Gulf coast. Even so, the damage and loss of life inflicted by this massive hurricane in Louisiana and Mississippi were staggering. . . Katrina was one of the most devastating natural disasters in United States history.'* – (Knabb, et al., 2005, p. 1).

16: Hurricane Katrina – Owen Gregory and Neil Swinyard-Jordan

The primary areas that were affected were south-eastern Louisiana including the city of New Orleans and the counties of Jefferson, Plaquemines, St. Bernard and St. Tammany, as well as the Mississippi Coast. Hurricane Katrina was one of the deadliest natural disasters in the history of the United States and claimed 1,836 lives of which 1,577 were in Louisiana.

Katrina has since been dubbed 'the most anticipated natural disaster in modern American history' by some commentators. The Federal Emergency Management Agency (FEMA) listed a hurricane strike on New Orleans as 'one of the direst threats to the nation.' The increasing temperature in the Gulf and areas of Atlantic Storm formation are significant as they could lead to more powerful hurricanes in the future. The increased threat should have raised awareness regarding the high risk of flooding in New Orleans, as the levees along the south shore of Lake Pontchartrain were built as a result of the previous flooding of the Jefferson parish of New Orleans in 1947.

The levee height was raised to twelve feet after Hurricane Betsy in 1965 and again after the 'near-miss' of Hurricane Georges in 1998. Hurricanes will repeatedly impact New Orleans. The sea level is rising which reduces the effectiveness of any levee system over time. This is particularly true of the complex 350 mile levee system that exists around New Orleans, the city is subsiding and this also reduces levee effectiveness. In addition, the current levee system is vulnerable to terrorist attack at many points. The cross-section map in *Figure 17* shows the difficulty of protecting New Orleans from a storm surge tide due to its position below the mean sea level.

'Hurricane Katrina was one of the worst natural disasters in our nation's history and has caused unimaginable devastation and heartbreak throughout the Gulf Coast Region. A vast coastline of towns and communities has been decimated.' – George W. Bush, 8 September 2005.

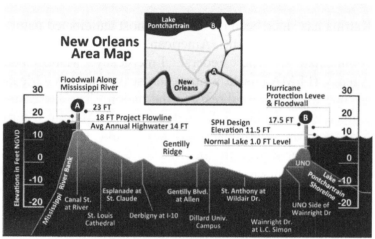

City of New Orleans Ground Elevations
From Canal St. at the Mississippi River to the Lakefront at U.N.O.

Figure 17: City of New Orleans ground elevations

'The Federal Response to Hurricane Katrina: Lessons Learned' lists 125 recommendations to address the lessons learned from Katrina's landfall. The FEMA-funded Southeast Louisiana Catastrophic Hurricane Planning Project was established in the summer of 2004 as a result of a report released four years previously by the US Army Corps of Engineers (USACE), detailing a possible inundation of up to 20 feet of flood water in the event of certain slow-moving hurricane types in the region.

The response to this USACE report led to the initial planning group meeting and after-review workshops – the last of which took place a few weeks before Katrina's landfall – but no physical solution was carried out to address the issues raised. A quicker response to the USACE 2000 findings might have had a positive impact on hurricane preparedness. The Southeast Louisiana Catastrophic Hurricane Functional Plan did have some beneficial effects regarding inter-jurisdictional relationships and capabilities, identification of issues and rudimentary concepts for handling the consequences of a disaster but no positive effect on the physical protection of New Orleans.

The response

> *'Those who cannot remember the past are condemned to repeat it.'* – George Santayana.

The majority of the recommendations in the 'Lessons Learned' report deal with the interaction of mitigation planning, communication and emergency response from the numerous identified agencies that were involved – the majority of which are sub-agencies of the Department for Homeland Security (DHS). Attention was drawn especially to post-event search and rescue, accommodation, sanitation, evacuation and health concerns. The *New York Times* firmly places the blame for the US$100-US$200 billion of damage caused by Katrina at the doors of the DHS and FEMA. When Hurricane Katrina hit New Orleans and its levees collapsed, DHS director Michael Chertoff was, by his own later admission, slow to focus on the domestic disaster as it developed. He even flew off to Atlanta for a terrorism conference as the city flooded. The head of FEMA at the time, Michael Brown, later furiously criticized Chertoff and blamed him for the dilatory federal response, but reports by investigative committees in the House and Senate found enough to blame both men for. Chertoff was subsequently cited in particular for delays in activating the federal emergency plan that could have rushed aid more quickly to the Gulf Coast.

It is clear that the hurricane season cannot be prevented until mankind learns to control the weather, but the capability to hold back a storm-surge, and emergency responses once the storm has passed, need urgent attention. Political commentators such as Lauren Mauser are keen that FEMA be returned to its pre-2003 Cabinet Level, as this would help to deal with natural disasters that might befall the USA. It would leave the DHS to concentrate on the security of the USA regarding the fight against terrorism and other man-made emergency events. The alternative, communications across a number of agencies influenced by two separate Cabinet-level organisations, has proved to be very difficult to control – it would also preclude adequate control when multiple events occur simultaneously. The Lessons Learned report does contain two paragraphs that neatly sum up what is needed to improve the American system:

'Hurricane Katrina and the subsequent sustained flooding of New Orleans exposed significant flaws in Federal, State, and local preparedness for catastrophic events and our capacity to respond to them. Emergency plans at all levels of government, from small town plans to the 600-page National Response Plan. . . were put to the ultimate test, and came up short. . . We must routinely revisit our plans and reassess our capabilities in order to account for evolving risks and improvements in

technological capabilities, and preparedness innovations.' – (White House, 2006, p. 1, p.74).

Katrina has intensified the way the American public look at the Government response to any event that occurs on their home soil, in the same way as 9/11 focused them on the fight against terrorism. The events of 9/11 – instigated by external terrorists – were new to the agencies on home soil. Conversely, the systematic failures that occurred when Katrina struck should have been prepared against as the threat was familiar:

> '. . .hurricanes have hit before, exposing weaknesses in the plans that were formed by the government in the years past. This time, we have the opportunity to prevent this sort of destruction from happening ever again. We cannot let the people in this country forget the lessons of the past.' – (McCarragher, 2011).

A key issue was the failure to consider in advance the most damaging impact of the hurricane which was flooding. This resulted from the excessive rainfall which accompanied the hurricane. The river level rose to the point where the city's levees were unable to contain the immense amount of water. The Mississippi River Gulf Outlet (MRGO) breached its banks in approximately 20 places, flooding much of eastern New Orleans, nearly all of Saint Bernard Parish and Plaquemines Parish. The collapse of the levees left approximately 80% of the city flooded with the associated constraints on transport and communications, and the longer-term threat to health.

It was evident that the emergency planning was inadequate to cope with the aftermath of Hurricane Katrina, which left the Gulf Coast in desperate need of resources and assistance. Nearly a million people were forced to live outside of their homes and relied on shipments of ice, food and water to meet their basic needs. Hospitals, shelters, and other critical facilities required diesel fuel to run their back-up generators and many evacuees lacked access to medical providers and supplies. Some hospitals had patients on life support machines and had as little as three days' fuel to run generators.

Emergency responders conducting life-saving operations demanded additional supplies and fuel, but FEMA's pre-positioned supplies were unable to meet the demand. FEMA simply could not procure enough resources to match the rate at which commodities were being consumed. To fill this gap, the federal government sent more resources to Louisiana in the first two weeks after Hurricane Katrina than it had sent to Florida for all of the previous year's hurricanes combined.

No sooner had additional resources been allocated than the FEMA personnel discovered that the quantity of material requested post-landfall outstripped their logistical capabilities. The agency's contracts with private companies, though sufficient for smaller disasters, were incapable of supplying and moving the enormous quantities of resources needed. The lack of transport infrastructure meant that shortages plagued the affected area.

> *'There was a huge gap between what we required on the ground and what they were sending us.'* – William Carwile, Federal Co-ordination Officer for Mississippi.

Later review of the response identified that the logistical failure was a key issue. In testimony before the United States Senate Homeland Security and Government Affairs Committee, members of the academic staff of Harvard University stated that the inability to respond adequately to

16: Hurricane Katrina – Owen Gregory and Neil Swinyard-Jordan

Hurricane Katrina resulted from '*failures of systems and of failures to construct systems in advance that would have permitted and helped to produce better performances and outcomes.*'

The Katrina disaster cannot be classified as a surprise. Ample warning of the coming disaster was met with insufficient preparation even though the emergency responders also had adequate warning. As Hurricane Katrina developed, the National Weather Service issued grave warnings, which were severe enough to convince the governors of Mississippi and Louisiana to declare states of emergencies on Friday, three days before landfall. The failure to take adequate action following these early warnings also characterised the federal response, where emergency teams lacked urgency, treating Katrina as if it was a normal storm. Senior White House staff had not reconvened in Washington when the disaster appeared imminent, and seemed out of touch with what was happening. Even after landfall, the response was marked by an astonishing degree of inertia.

Human impact

Despite instructions to evacuate the city, as many as 100,000 residents remained in New Orleans. Some chose to stay whole others had no means of transport to escape the impending disaster. The subsequent widespread flooding resulted in many becoming stranded. With average daytime August temperatures hovering around the 30° Celsius mark, plus no fresh water or power, conditions were often desperate. Some were rescued from their rooftops but others remained trapped in their attics.

16: Hurricane Katrina – Owen Gregory and Neil Swinyard-Jordan

The Louisiana Superdome in New Orleans was designated a place of last resort, having been used on two previous occasions when hurricanes had threatened. With no power and limited food, water or toilet facilities available in the complex, the authorities were heavily criticised for being ill-prepared. Conditions quickly became squalid as search and rescue teams brought in more and more survivors. The number seeking shelter in the Superdome exceeded 20,000.

Mass exodus

The monthly labour review published by the U.S. Bureau of Labor Statistics reported that Hurricane Katrina resulted in the relocation of over one million people from the central Gulf coast to elsewhere across the United States. This became the largest diaspora in the history of the country. Population movement resulted in an increase of 35,000 people in Houston. The state of Alabama gained over 24,000. Baton Rouge, Louisiana grew by over 15,000 and Hammond, Louisiana received over 10,000. The single largest growth of a non-southern city occurred in Chicago, which received over 6,000 people.

By late January 2006, about 200,000 people were once again living in New Orleans, but this was less than half of the pre-storm population. By 1 July 2006, when new population estimates were calculated by the U.S. Census Bureau, the state of Louisiana showed a population decline of 219,563, or 4.87%. The economic effects of Hurricane Katrina were widespread, comprehensive and impacted on national agencies/businesses including the National Oceanic and Atmospheric Administration (NOAA) and the US Military.

16: Hurricane Katrina – Owen Gregory and Neil Swinyard-Jordan

Economic impact

Immediately before Katrina struck, the states of Louisiana and Mississippi accounted for around 2% of the total national GDP. The local economies depended heavily upon oil and gas production and importation, oil refining plus transport, particularly because five of the twelve largest US ports are located on the Gulf Coast. The area is responsible for supplying 6.5% of the nation's domestic crude oil and 16% of its natural gas.

The effect of Hurricane Katrina on New Orleans from a business continuity perspective was shattering, particularly in terms of loss of employment, cost of repair work, increased insurance costs and relocation of population.

From a national economic perspective, oil and gas production and refining were both victims of the hurricane. Some 37 offshore platforms were destroyed while others were damaged and local refineries were shut down before landfall. Some of these companies had difficulty in tracking down their employees, who in fairness probably had more pressing priorities on their minds. This was to the detriment of their recovery efforts. Other refineries were unable to resume operations until power had been restored. The situation also witnessed the price of crude oil jump from US$66 to US$70 per barrel, before it eventually returned to its pre-Katrina level. The situation was eased by President Bush releasing 30 million gallons of oil from the strategic petroleum reserve. The country has a contingency reserve of circa 700 million barrels – amounting to 24.5 billion gallons.

One industry that turned out to be a beneficiary of Katrina was construction, with substantial repair and rebuilding required across the region.

16: Hurricane Katrina – Owen Gregory and Neil Swinyard-Jordan

The storm devastated the economy, with only tourism, port operations and educational services surviving. These proved essential in providing the city with a base of industry to assist in the recovery. Ten months after the hurricane the city of New Orleans had suffered around 95,000 job losses, with employment falling 105,000 below the previous year's total. Similarly, the broader economic effects were far reaching. By April 2006, the Bush Administration had provided over US$105 billion for repairs and construction in the region and it is estimated that the total impact exceeded US$150 billion.

These figures do not account for damage to the economy caused by the interruption of the oil supply, destruction of the Gulf Coast highway and damage to exports such as grain. The forestry industry in Mississippi was also affected, as 1.3 million acres of forest land was destroyed. Furthermore, hundreds of thousands of local residents were left unemployed; this had an effect as fewer taxes were paid to local governments. Additionally, some insurance companies have since stopped insuring homeowners in the area because of the high cost of claims resulting from Hurricanes Katrina and Rita, or have raised homeowners' insurance premiums to cover their risk.

Utilities

Local power supplier Entergy faced a serious challenge, attempting to restore normal service after back-to-back hurricanes – first Katrina and then Rita less than a month later.

Katrina saw 1.1 million customers lose power across Louisiana and Mississippi. Power was also cut off from refineries plus the Plantation and Colonial oil pipelines.

Severe flooding had occurred at substations and transmission lines across the entire region were seriously damaged. Recovery was hampered by a shortage of locally available gasoline and diesel in addition to some employees' homes being destroyed. Other employees had been despatched to Florida to support Katrina related power restoration work in that state. Moreover, locally domiciled recovery contractors' equipment had been damaged or destroyed, giving rise to fears of their possible bankruptcy.

By 23 September 2005 power had been restored to around 75% of customers, before Hurricane Rita caused further disruption. Some isolated settlements in the region were without power for several months.

Less than a month after Katrina's landfall, facing massive rebuilding costs plus serious revenue losses, Entergy New Orleans filed for bankruptcy protection.

Emergency management

The security and emergency services' response to Hurricane Katrina involved an inter-governmental cross-sector network of agencies. The introduction of a National Response Plan in 2004 had sought to formalise the role and responsibilities of at least some of the main players in crisis response. This plan identified a series of emergency support functions for different agencies to provide support to FEMA. FEMA's traditional role for large-scale disasters is to act as a coordinator, orchestrating the activities of federal government agencies while working with state emergency services.

As a crisis builds, more emergency response is required in terms of numbers of personnel and equipment and complexity; as the crisis grows and expands more tasks arise demanding a greater variety of capabilities and skill sets. The Hurricane Katrina network was so large that there was a failure by the emergency response control centre to realise the number of agencies actively involved, the differing skills and resources they offered and how to use these to maximum effect. One study counted over 500 different local, national and international organisations involved in the weeks after landfall. Planning for major incidents must consider the depth and complexity that could arise and ensure adequate resourcing accordingly.

Despite the potential financial impact, loss of life, and devastation caused by hurricanes, their economic effects tend to be only short term.

Media

Despite still essentially being business entities, the media has the chance to perform a unique and vital role before, during and after an emergency situation arises. They have the opportunity to work with authorities to transmit timely and effective communication for the good of the community, which could even save lives. To achieve this, however, they too must have tried and tested business continuity plans which, certainly in the instance of a hurricane strike, assume a worst case multiple scenario situation. They may be ready to cover other peoples' disasters; but they also have to be prepared to deal with their own. Many of the companies that had developed contingency plans actually found that they were inadequate.

In New Orleans, many TV and Radio stations found they had become the news. Flooded or wrecked studios, no power, missing outside reporting vehicles, stranded reporters, damaged transmitters – the list of problems goes on. Most struggled on although only one station, the New Orleans-based CBS affiliate WWL-TV, never went off the air as it relocated its operation to Baton Rouge.

However, with widespread power failures across the region, it does beg the question: 'was anyone listening?'

Insurance

'Nearly half the people whose houses were damaged or destroyed by Hurricane Katrina did not have flood insurance, yet the federal flood insurance program did not have enough funds to pay claims worth about $25 billion by those who were insured.'
– (Drew & Treaster, 2006).

Operational factors

- Complex agency relationships – especially those of responders.
- FEMA, as the historical responder to natural disasters, absorbed into DHS in 2003.
- Emergency planning priorities based around the terrorist threat after 9/11.
- Vertical reporting (stovepipes) prevent immediacy of actions.
- Local, state and federal levels apply to emergency response for resourcing and budget.
- Agency response delayed.
- Physical barriers to flooding (levees) not updated since 1998.

Technical factors

- The capability of the forecasters is improving with improving data analysis.

- Historical information provides data analysis possibilities.

- Early forecasting and accuracy indicated landfall although storms do not always permit such accurate definition.

- Forecasters warned that 2005 would be an above normal year for activity.

- Reports from 2000 not acted upon by the Katrina landfall date.

Lessons learned

The analysis of risk, and any mitigation of the risks that can be identified, is the primary function involved in business continuity management and emergency planning. In each of the case studies above the absence of levels of risk management either caused or increased the impact of a particular event.

Failure to update the emergency plan, and to align agency efforts more thoroughly with the National Response Plan (NRP) and Emergency Support Functions (ESF), were highlighted after an investigation into the event. Katrina became a rallying cry against the Bush presidency due to its tardy initial response to the displacement of the population and the subsequent delayed recovery of southern Louisiana's infrastructure.

From the case of Katrina we can see that risks must be constantly monitored to ensure that the correct actions can be carried out for their immediate mitigation. As part of risk mitigation a sound business continuity plan, emergency plan or combination of the two must be in place to cover both the public and private interests as necessary.

What went well

- Tourism, port operations and educational services survived the disaster. This helped the city to recover.

What could have been done better

- The slow-moving process of making adjustments to existing US Government plans, guaranteed by the labyrinthine nature of policies and agencies, meant that necessary improvements to the protection of New Orleans – first identified in the year 2000 – had not been updated by the start of the 2005 hurricane season. Five years that could have been spent on planning and restitution was wasted.

- Emergency planners were blindsided by Katrina due to the post 9/11 obsession with the terrorist threat. Priorities were arguably not correct.

- Evacuation planning was clearly not sufficient. This was the first ever mandatory evacuation of New Orleans. By contrast, Florida has had many such evacuations and, thus, planning is more advanced.

- Coordination of recovery efforts was poor. The sheer number of different organisations involved resulted in a high degree of complexity.

- Recovery of services including electricity was often slow, especially for isolated areas.

- Although emergency supplies were in place, the quantity was far from adequate to deal with a disaster on this scale. This made logistical problems and congestion worse.

What did not go well

- Failure to consider flooding in advance was critical – this caused more damage than the hurricane itself.
- Poor media handling by the Bush Administration, which came to be seen as the cause of delays to post-storm response by many people. Areas most affected by Katrina were seen as 'poor' and 'majority black'.
- Despite the order to evacuate, thousands of residents remained in New Orleans.
- Displacement of population poorly handled, with conditions in temporary habitations deteriorating.
- Failure to deal with unemployment and other issues in the aftermath resulted in a significant population decline.
- Most organisations, including Energy New Orleans, seem to have found their contingency plans inadequate.

Conclusion

Any consideration of Hurricane Katrina must acknowledge that its impact was immense, not solely as a result of human failures, but because of the size and scope of the task. Good security and emergency management can help to minimise the negative impact of such natural disasters, but it cannot eliminate them. Hurricane Katrina highlights the need to produce comprehensive business continuity management plans to address the maintenance of oil supplies, the movement of exports such as grain, and the need to fund repair work. It is vital to maintain employment or the population will not return, or will be forced to move to find work. When conducting emergency planning it is important to consider the requirement for close cooperation and coordination between a large number of internal and external agencies and the likelihood of temporary and permanent movement of affected persons. The impact of Hurricane Katrina was more pronounced due to subsequent flooding which damaged communications networks, and due to the inability of authorities to rapidly import additional resources from outside the immediate area when emergency stocks ran out. It is clear that better coordination among the network of emergency response agencies, a greater sense of urgency, and more successful management of related risk factors would have minimised some of the losses caused by the hurricane. As Robert R Latham stated, the right course is to *'Hope for the best but prepare for the worst.'*

CHAPTER 17: ARRIVA MALTA: BUSINESS CONTINUITY WITHIN A CHANGE MANAGEMENT PROGRAMME – ROBERT CLARK

Malta is a former British colony which lies in the centre of the Mediterranean Sea. Located less than 100 km to the south of the Italian island of Sicily, the Maltese archipelago is made up of a small group of islands, three of which are inhabited – Malta, Gozo and Comino. Malta is the largest of the islands and is approximately 27 by 19 km, giving it a land mass of 316 km^2. Its 2012 GDP was in excess of US$8 billion. With a combined population of over 400,000, Malta is the most densely populated member state of the European Union. It is considered by International Living Magazine to have the best climate worldwide.

Owned by Deutsche Bahn, Arriva is a leading transport services provider and operates buses and trains across 12 European countries. In 2010, the company was awarded a 10 year contract to replace the vintage bus service on the Mediterranean islands of Malta and Gozo. The company was expected to operate 264 buses and employ around 920 people. The following year Arriva announced that it had deployed 285 buses and was employing 1,230 staff, making it one of the top five employers across the islands.

Having lived in Malta for several years, the author has first-hand experience of the foibles of public transport across the archipelago both before and since Arriva's appearance on the scene. In this case study he considers the events since the commencement of Arriva's operation and the business continuity management issues for a contract that he believes became something of a poisoned chalice.

Tourists returning from a trip to Malta would more often than not talk fondly of the old buses. Although on average they were 35 years old, the chassis of the oldest operational bus amongst those classics is alleged to have been built in 1919. Some of the models in service were no longer used anywhere else in the world. While loved by tourists, they were not much fun for the locals who had to travel on them day in and day out, but the service worked.

There were over 500 buses registered although not all were used every day. The service was centred on the capital Valletta; consequently, with the vast majority of journeys either starting or ending at the capital's bus terminus, relatively local journeys could take far longer by bus than by using a more direct route by car. Belching out noxious black plumes of exhaust smoke, the buses were recognized as major contributors to local air pollution. None were fitted with air conditioning to cater for the scorching hot summer days, nor was the seating designed with any thought for people with long legs. Moreover, the vast majority were not user friendly for anyone with a physical disability, as there were often several steps up to the vehicle's deck. But at midnight on 2 July 2011 all that changed.

The dawning of the Arriva era

> *'We totally underestimated the resistance to change. It was now up to the operator (Arriva) to deliver the service under contract.'* Austin Gatt, Former Minister of Transport, Malta.

By 3 July 2011 these relics from a bygone era had disappeared from Maltese roads and were replaced by the aquamarine-liveried buses of Arriva. They were air conditioned, had comfortable seating with ample legroom and the low floors were wheel chair friendly. Route changes meant every district in Malta now had direct access to the main hospital, Mater Dei, and the airport was also served by seven direct express bus routes, whereas before travel via Valletta was a necessity.

The new fleet was primarily made up of King Long buses constructed in China, supported by Mercedes Benz O530G Citaro articulated buses that were formerly operated by Arriva in London and could carry three times the passenger load of the largest King Long vehicles. The King Long buses met the European 'Euro V' engine standard while the articulated buses were in line with 'Euro III'.

The departure of the old buses meant that Maltese tourism lost a much loved icon – but it also heralded the start of a new sport across the islands, 'Arriva Bashing'. Where did this resistance to change come from?

One third of drivers never turned up

The new service did not get off to an auspicious start. Approximately one third of the contracted and trained drivers, many of whom had driven the old buses, did not turn up for work. Arriva had invested time and money training these drivers prior to the changeover, with both sides entering into a contractual agreement. Even so, the writing had been on the wall at least two days before changeover as drivers expressed their dissatisfaction with shift rosters.

Choice changeover dates

Arguably one of the key mistakes was the changeover date. Even though schools had closed for the summer, the islands were full of tourists. With the vast majority of new bus shelters still to be constructed, there was little protection from the sun for the many people waiting for buses that either turned up full or never turned up at all.

Arriva website crashes

To compound the day-one chaos Arriva's website crashed, making bus timetable information inaccessible.

While computer techies were left to sort the website, within a day or two British Arriva bus drivers started appearing. Not speaking Maltese was not a problem as English is an official language on the island, and many overseas students in fact travel to Malta to learn English. These drivers did not know the routes, however, and had to be given a crash course on arrival.

Passengers and drivers totally confused by new routes

Transport Malta worsened the situation by introducing a new set of bus routes. This caused much confusion among passengers used to the old system, and many felt the changes were unnecessary. Although the Arriva bus fleet now boasted a carrying capacity of 6,000 more passengers than the old buses, the actual number of buses was almost halved. Consequently, new routes were needed to reflect the reduced size of the fleet. Despite several changes to routes and schedules since the changeover, this issue has never gone away and criticism from the travelling public persists.

17: Arriva Malta: Business Continuity within a Change Management Programme – Robert Clark

'The disastrous launching of the service was partly down to the lack of proper planning of routes and partly due to the no-show of a third of Arriva's drivers on the first day of service. Adding this with the country's intrinsic propensity to oppose change did not make it easy for the Anglo-German transport company.' – Jurgen Balzan, MediaToday.

Complaints about various aspects of the new service came thick and fast, although it was unfair to blame Arriva for them all. For example, the company was not responsible for the new routes. Other complaints could be placed fairly and squarely at Arriva's door. Drivers would often take advantage of their new and more powerful vehicles by speeding, particularly if they were running late. Some would accelerate away from bus stops before passengers had chance to seat themselves, others would brake hard at the last moment when approaching bus stops. Reports of passenger injuries were not uncommon.

Why can't the buses stay on schedule?

Delays were the source of many grievances, although to be fair they were caused by a variety of circumstances which were sometimes outside of Arriva's control:

- Congestion, particularly during rush hours and school term time. With the Arriva buses in the main much larger than their classic predecessors, negotiating narrow and busy streets was never going to be easy

- Passengers stopping buses just to ask where the bus is going (both locals and tourists), despite the fact that comprehensive route information was provided at each stop.

- Time delays in issuing tickets. Other countries insist that you must have purchased a ticket before you board the bus.

- Badly or illegally parked cars – a problem endemic in Malta despite the recent introduction of traffic wardens

- Some drivers ignored passengers at bus stops who are quite clearly flagging them down, even when the buses were not full.

Road traffic accidents (RTAs) are a major cause of delays for all Maltese motorists, including Arriva. Malta has a number of pinch-points on its roads and even the smallest of RTA's can lead to very lengthy delays. Such an incident was experienced by the author on 1 October 2013, involving a journey from his home in Ta l'Ibragg to the bus stop at Mater Dei Hospital. The Arriva timetable estimated the journey time as 11 min but it took 95 min. The cause was an RTA that occurred on a roundabout approaching the hospital, where two vehicles had had a minor collision in which no one was hurt. Because this took place on a feeder road for an industrial estate, however, the resulting congestion in all directions was substantial.

Maltese law actually slows down the process of clearing the roads after an accident. In general, the respective drivers cannot move their vehicles until after a traffic warden has attended the scene and taken details and photographs. By comparison, UK, drivers are only obliged to exchange details for insurance purposes while the police do not need to attend the scene unless someone has been injured. Except when a vehicle needs recovering, once details are exchanged the drivers are free to go about their business.

These delays not only affect Arriva passengers but all road users and the lost productivity has a cost to the local economy. To aggravate the author's own frustration, the bus was stationary for two or three minutes outside the building he was visiting but the driver would not let him exit the bus as it was not an official bus stop.

It's just not good enough!

Four months after the cutover, the governing body Transport Malta was less than satisfied with the new service, and issued a stark warning to Arriva:

> *'It slammed the 'unacceptable' service of the public transport operator and gave it until the end of November to bring it up to scratch. Otherwise, it would deploy its own buses at Arriva's expense.'* – (Peregin, 2012).

Arriva acknowledged that the service on some routes was not reaching the contractual requirement and stated that it would deploy additional buses. Twelve months on and Parliament heard that in the first 16 months since the Arriva operation had started, Transport Malta had received 2,917 complaints. But let us put this into perspective; during that same period, over 30 million passengers used public transport. Those complaints represent an incredibly small percentage (0.01%) of those who used the service. The author overheard one elderly Maltese lady grumbling about the Arriva service. He enquired if would she have been happier if the old buses had stayed and was very firmly told 'no way!'

Did the Arriva fiasco cause the government's downfall?

In March 2013, the country held a general election. The 'Partit Nazzjonalista' had been in power for 25 of the previous 27 years, but suffered a resounding defeat at the hands of Joseph Muscat's 'Partit Laburista'. Although there may be many reasons for the size of the defeat, some argue that the Arriva catastrophe had a large part to play. One Partit Nazzjonalista MP said after the defeat:

> *'The public transport reform, introducing Arriva on our streets, was a massive disaster.'* – Hon. Beppe Fenech Adami MP.

Racism on the buses

Once a Maltese male dominated profession, it would appear that anyone can now become a Maltese bus driver. It is not unusual to see women behind the wheel while the workforce is becoming multinational. This has led to another serious issue, however – racism. The author has witnessed racially motivated verbal abuse directed at black drivers and passengers. The local media has also reported both verbal and physical abuse against drivers, with a black woman driver being insulted because of the colour of her skin. A second bus driver, an Italian national who came to her aid, was also physically abused which necessitated police intervention. In a separate incident, a Polish expat witnessed a verbal attack carried out by Arriva employees against a black passenger.

The saga of the 'Bendy-Bus'

A further bone of contention in Malta has been articulated buses, otherwise known as 'Bendy-Buses'. Rejected by Mayor of London Boris Johnson, over 60 of these bendy-buses became the backbone of the Arriva fleet. But at the end of August 2013 three bendy-buses caught fire on consecutive days, although Arriva suspected at least one instance of arson. Fires in bendy-buses are certainly not unprecedented – in London they were nicknamed 'chariots of fire'.

At the insistence of the government, the entire fleet was withdrawn from service while safety checks were performed. With a carrying capacity of 140 passengers, they transported over 40% of the Maltese travelling public. Their withdrawal presented Arriva with a huge logistical nightmare. This also occurred at about the same time that Arriva Malta posted a €35 million loss for its first two years of operation.

Contingency plans were put into action. Several of the old buses were brought back into service and a number of local coach firms were used to fill the gap. Putting this into perspective, it needed approximately three 52-seater coaches to replace one bendy-bus. The daily cost to Arriva was reported as being in the order of €30,000 per day, which was not sustainable in the longer term. None of the replacement coaches had machines for issuing tickets to passengers. Although Arriva made it clear that no one should travel without a valid ticket, it was simply not possible for many passengers to pre-purchase a ticket unless they happened to start their journey where an Arriva official was available. With 850 bus stops on the island of Malta alone, there were simply too many for the company to man them all. Consequently, revenue was lost as many passengers enjoyed free rides.

*'Unfortunately they (bendy-buses) have become the
butt of many jokes.'* – Joe Mizzi, Transport Minister,
Malta.

The transport minister and Transport Malta have made no secret of the fact that they want to see the back of the bendy-bus. They are considered too big for the islands' narrow roads, despite meeting the original dimension criterion laid down by the governing body. Unless Arriva fails to satisfy the minister over the safety concerns, however, the government is contractually tied and can do little about them short of renegotiating the contract. Many people feel that the sheer size of bendy-buses causes traffic congestion. Since their withdrawal congestion has eased, a point which even Arriva have acknowledged. Further research has, however, attributed the reduced congestion to the inability of replacement coaches to issue tickets, with the result that they are stationary for less time.

It all ended in tears

In December 2013, the local press reported Transport Minister Joe Mizzi's statement that the bendy-bus fires were not caused by arson. This was immediately met by a counter claim from Arriva that they were. The reality is that the safety inquiry report was inconclusive and provided no firm proof either way; the jury is still out on the matter.

With Arriva continuing to make big losses in Malta, the company had already hinted that it might simply pull out of the country all together. Transport Minister Joe Mizzi claims to have an effective contingency plan in place, but creating a replacement public transport system overnight would be no mean feat.

> *'But what about a Plan B? There isn't any and present chaos would be nothing compared to the situation if Arriva pulls out without an acceptable substitute. And this is not something one invents within a couple of months.'* – Richard Caruana.

The bankruptcy option

Negotiations between the government and Arriva continued for weeks. It seemed that Arriva was seriously considering the option of putting its Maltese operation into the hands of the receiver. This would have resulted in all its assets, and in particular the buses, being frozen, leaving the country with no public transport system. Malta would have fallen foul of only having one supplier, without any viable alternative replacement options waiting in the wings. With many people totally dependent upon public transport to get to work, the impact on the local economy would have been horrendous. But those Maltese citizens who wished Arriva gone finally got their way when the company officially announced its departure from Malta in January 2014.

Reflection by Transport Malta

> *'The radical, overnight change of the public transport system; its operator, route network, drivers, infrastructure, information, ticketing etc. was not without planning, technical and operational problems. The past 12 months, will serve as an important learning experience for the planning and execution of any future transport changes at a*

*national level. Now that the new public transport
bus services are in place and the first year of
operation indicates a growth in patronage levels full
operation, the main challenge facing both
government and the operator will be how to
improve of reliability of bus services in traffic and
how to encourage further modal shift away from the
private car.'* – (Transport Malta, 2013).

What does the future hold for Maltese public transport?

An objective of Malta's 'Intelligent Traffic Solution' action
plan is to encourage car drivers to switch over to public
transport, an objective shared by many developed nations.
This in turn will put more pressure on Arriva's successor to
provide a fully comprehensive and reliable service. With
buses on busy routes already often full at peak times, the
public transport system is presented with a potentially
insurmountable challenge. Congestion charging along the
lines of London has already been implemented in the
capital city, Valletta, and could be rolled out across the
country.

The bendy-buses are to play no part in this initiative, having
been sold to an African country. Each one will need to be
replaced with at least three of the largest King-Long buses
(or an equivalent), plus the corresponding number of
drivers to operate them. Arriva were constantly looking for
new drivers during their tenure, despite searching far
beyond Malta for staff, so whether this objective is really
achievable remains in doubt. Advertisements have been
spotted in both the UK and Spain for English speaking bus

drivers. Even the Irish social services apparently alerted at least one job seeker to bus driving opportunities in Malta.

Yet, was Arriva really doing such a bad job, especially when Transport Malta has acknowledged that 90% of all services are now working as per contract? Arriva Malta carried 18 million people in its first six months of operation, a 2 million increase on the same period the previous year. When it comes to encouraging car drivers to switch to public transport, this was certainly a major step in the right direction.

Lessons learned

Unlike other operations that Arriva has taken over across Europe, in Malta they started with a blank canvass. No buses to take over, a new set of routes and a very high expectation of how good the service was going to be. There was no softly-softly approach, no incremental change; it was a massive big bang switch from the old order to the new. Anything short of perfection was going to be seen as a failure by the Maltese travelling public. This was not so much a business continuity exercise as a massive change management programme, but there was a distinct need for business continuity to be an integral part of the plan.

What went well

- With only two-thirds of the drivers initially reporting for work, Arriva got off to a disastrous start. The speedy deployment of UK bus drivers certainly took some of the strain off the situation.

- The day after the bendy-buses were withdrawn from service, local coach firms were used to successfully plug the gap. While this contingency plan worked, however, the €30,000 daily cost would not be sustainable in the long term. Every local coach deployed not only represented a cost to Arriva, it also resulted in lost revenue as they were not equipped with ticketing machines.

Would could have been done better

- The expectations of public transport users in Malta could have been much better managed by the government and Transport Malta. Many believed a total transformation for the better would happen overnight.

What did not go well

- One third of the trained and contracted drivers did not report for work on day one of Arriva's new operation. Most of the missing drivers never showed up at all. Compared with the service being run up to 2 July 2011, Arriva immediately found itself on the back foot.
- To add to the misery, the Arriva website, complete with timetable information, failed on day one with no apparent fall-back options.
- The revamped bus routes turned out to be a disaster. Even though the travelling public tended to blame Arriva, this change was actually instigated by Transport Malta.
- Buses were often found to be too big to negotiate narrow Maltese streets and were frequently delayed by inconsiderate local parking habits.

Other observations

There are other pressing safety issues that whoever replaces Arriva will need to address. The local press frequently carries reports of road traffic accidents involving buses. Many of these incidents are caused by bad driving practices that make disasters inevitable. The author has personally observed:

- That new buses are more dangerous because they are bigger and can be driven faster than their archaic predecessors. Speed limits are frequently ignored, as roadside speed indication monitors often demonstrate.
- Drivers will often drive away from a bus stop while still issuing tickets and dispensing change, without their full attention on the road ahead
- Drivers regularly use mobile phones while driving which is both illegal and dangerous
- Despite regulations to the contrary, drivers often allow passengers to travel on the footplate beside them and frequently engage in conversation. The author has even observed one driver steering the bus single-handed with one arm wrapped around a young lady standing beside him

Arriva seemed to be continually recruiting drivers, although perhaps some attrition is to be expected with a workforce of 800. The company is also employing part-time drivers to allow better flexibility in shift patterns for full-time drivers.

Conclusion

Whoever replaces Arriva has to learn the lessons from their failure; but they will also have to win the hearts and minds of the Maltese people. Not an easy task. When the author has chatted with fellow passengers, however, he has never found one that preferred riding on the old buses!

The Maltese archipelago is no stranger to miracles. From the biblical record of St Paul's shipwreck to a World War II bomb that failed to explode when it fell amongst a packed congregation in the Church of the Assumption of Our Lady in Mosta. Maybe Arriva were also expected to deliver a miracle too. Perhaps a fitting epitaph marking their exit from Malta should be: 'the impossible we can do immediately but miracles were always going to take a little longer'.

CHAPTER 18: THE DEVIL IS IN THE DETAIL – ROBERT CLARK

It is reasonable to assume that most organisations gravitate towards 'big ticket' threats when preparing their BCM arrangements. All the same, the reality is that even the little things that often might go unheralded in the media can also cause us grief if left unattended. Rather than a full blown case study, this chapter is a cornucopia of little, seemingly unimportant items which could still have a big impact on your business continuity's effectiveness.

Have you considered the workforce?

I was invited to review the business continuity arrangements for a Netherlands-based company whose operation was contained in a single multi-story building. On discovering the cafeteria and kitchen were on the ground floor underneath the data centre, I deemed it a rather inauspicious start.

Mindful that their premises were a concentration of risk, it was their intention to relocate their key workers, about 50% of the workforce, to their offices in Brussels if they were denied access for an extended period. On a good day the trip would take about two hours each way. On a bad day. . .

Many of these key employees were young mothers who dropped their children off at kindergarten or school before work and collected them afterwards, which very much governed the hours they could work. It had been assumed that they would all be prepared to either commute daily or temporarily relocate to Brussels. I suggested that they briefed these individuals of the firm's intentions and not surprisingly they were met with a resounding 'no way'.

But the relocation saga did not end there. I later spent time in their Brussels office and I asked the question, *'If a few coach loads from the Dutch office arrive looking for somewhere to work, what plans do you have to accommodate them?'* It transpired that the Belgians were totally unaware of the Dutch plans, meaning that a Dutch disaster could have become a Belgian disaster too.

Flooding

With frequent media reports on major flooding incidents around the globe and concerns about climate change abounding, one could be forgiven for focusing on the enormity of the threat. But it does not need to rain for flooding to occur.

It was a Friday afternoon and the office was emptying rapidly. Suddenly one of my colleagues noticed a trickle of water running down the office wall and the trickle soon became a torrent. The server room was on the ground floor – and much of the ICT equipment was actually on the floor. As electrical equipment does not react particularly well to water, we persuaded a couple of techies still in the building to perform an emergency power-off and get the equipment off the floor. Fortunately they succeeded as there was no IT disaster recovery in place at the time.

It transpired that a workman had drilled through a water pipe on the top floor which came directly from a large tank on the roof. While the water supply to the tank could be isolated, it was not possible to stop the tank draining its contents into the office.

On another occasion I was reviewing a Lisbon-based organisation's risk assessment and noticed that they had flagged flooding as a major risk. Since they were located at the top of a hill, I challenged this. It emerged that their concern centred upon the swimming pool on their office roof. With Lisbon susceptible to earthquakes, they quite rightly argued that if the pool cracked, the consequences could be disastrous. Local knowledge won the day!

Information security

With Internet-facilitated information theft increasing in prominence, we must not forget that the age-old physical threat still exists and can still cause companies grief. One NGO I visited was reeling from the theft of several PCs from a ground floor office. An emergency exit was forced open by thieves and they helped themselves to some easy pickings. The PCs were quickly replaced and some more effective security measures put in place but that was not the real issue. Each of the stolen PCs contained data which had not been backed up to the NGO's file server and the loss of this data was causing some acute embarrassment.

Taking effective backups of all your vital data, whether server, PC or tablet-based could make the difference between recovering or not after a serious incident.

In the UK, the BBC has regularly reported stories of missing laptops, pen drives, CDs, DVDs, external hard drives, etc. containing sensitive data. Local authorities appeared to be the worst offenders, with over 1,000 cases of data loss reported by 132 local councils between 2008 and 2010.

The private sector is little better. HSBC were fined £3 million in 2009 and Zurich Insurance were fined £2.3 million in 2010 for customer data loss. Even the BBC itself admitted in 2010 to losing £240,000 worth of laptops and mobiles.

Of particular concern is the reported loss of laptops from the Ministry of Defence, including unexplained disappearances from high security areas. Over a four year period, this amounted to more than 650 machines, some of which contained classified information.

The UK is not the only source of such worrying losses – and the theft of hardware is not confined to laptops, pen drivers and other easily moveable hardware. The following example, from Australia, caused much embarrassment:

> *'Australian authorities have ordered an urgent review of security at Sydney's international airport after the theft of two mainframe computers from a restricted customs area.'* – (Mercer, 2003).

Airport security guards had been fooled into allowing the dismantling and removal of the two mainframe computers from a high security zone. Did no one notice the response time degradation?

Closer to home, two friends were reading for university degrees and each had a laptop to aid their studies. Every day they unfailingly backed up their work onto pen drives. One night, however, a burglar helped himself to the laptops and their pen drives too. In short they both lost all their data. But it did not have to be so. With simple and inexpensive Cloud-based backup solutions available, worrying about losing data in this way should become a thing of the past.

Employee fraud

> '*A typical organization loses 5% of its annual revenue to employee fraud. Applied to the estimated 2009 Gross World Product, this figure translates to a potential global fraud loss of more than $2.9 trillion. . . Employee Theft Solutions, a division of The Shulman Center for Compulsive Theft and Spending, estimate that one-third of all U.S. corporate bankruptcies are directly caused by employee theft.*' – (Russakoff & Goodman, 2011).

Fiducial notes that there are many ways in which employees can defraud their employers. For example :

- '*Opening a checking account in a nearby community under the same name as the employer company.*

- *Overpaying the payroll taxes or large suppliers and asking for refunds which are then deposited in the employee's new company account.*

- *Convincing the employer that the independent accountant is an expensive luxury which the company can do without now that the employee is available to do financial statements.*

- *Soliciting the help of a supplier's employee, then overpaying the supplier and sharing the overpayment.*

- *Opening a checking account with the same name as the employer's major suppliers and then paying invoices twice. The first payment is sent to the supplier, and the second is deposited in the employee's extra supplier account*'.

Succession planning

It is not unusual for organisations to undertake succession planning, but this is generally aimed at identifying replacements for the more senior members of staff. For example, having realised he was losing his battle against cancer, Steve Jobs resigned from Apple, naming Tim Cook as his successor. There can be situations though when 'lesser' members of staff are just as vital to the company because there is no one else who can perform the critical role that they undertake. For example, the loss of the payroll clerk could mean that no one gets paid if nobody else understands how the payroll process works.

I came across a situation where one computer programmer in an organisation of around 400, was the only employee with expertise in 'MUMPS'. He alone had in depth knowledge of several massive and unstructured monolithic programmes written in that language. He had also been allowed over several years to accrue 12 months leave by combining time-off-in-lieu instead of overtime payments and untaken annual leave. With his intention of taking a round-the-world-cruise the company was facing a massive exposure of their own making. First by allowing him to accrue the leave and second by not providing a stand-in for him to cover for his absence.

Fire

Large building fires will often catch the imagination of the media and business continuity planners will invariably have the threat well and truly on their radar. But an electrical fire that started in a small storage room in a large office complex did not even rate a mention by the local press.

This was largely due to an alert security guard extinguishing the blaze before the fire brigade's arrival. Sounds like job done – except that was not the end of the drama. It transpired that all the fire debris and soot had been sucked up into the air conditioning system and for the next month it was being circulated around the building making it uninhabitable. As soon as a layer of debris was removed by face-mask wearing cleaners, it was duly replaced by more deposits from the air conditioning.

In another case, an off duty fireman friend was rather surprised to get a call from his cousin, especially now that Health and Safety are quite rightly demanding our attention more and more in the workplace. The conversation went something like *'Our office wall is getting very hot, what should we do?'* *'Get out now,'* came the response. Apparently the building was shared by several small companies and one section was ablaze. Regardless of the size of a company, it is eminently sensible to ensure an effective fire alarm is installed and frequent building evacuation drills are held. Do you know how quickly you can evacuate your premises?

Keeping your contact details up to date

Keeping your contact details current is a key BCM task. I learned this lesson the hard way almost 30 years ago. I was managing a team of IT techies trying to sort out a serious system failure and we concluded that we needed the specialist skills of a colleague who was not on duty at that time. Even though it was 3 am I duly telephoned him. When the phone was answered I was horrified to discover that he no longer lived there. On reflection, I cannot believe what I did next. I actually asked the gentleman I had erroneously dragged out of bed if he had our man's new telephone number, which he politely gave me before bidding me goodnight. Needless to say, it was some time before I was allowed to forget that rather unfortunate faux pas, but rest assured I never did it again.

Trauma management

Including some trauma management arrangements in your BCP is not uncommon, but these would usually be invoked in response to a serious life threatening incident in the work location. A recent event in Malta suggests that we should consider extending trauma management for events outside the workplace, too. Two employees of a multinational company were outside of their office enjoying a cigarette break. They found themselves just a few feet away from an attempted armed robbery and witnessed a victim being shot in the face. The event resulted in traumatisation of the employees.

The cyber threat

'There are two types of company – those that have been hacked and those that are going to be hacked.' – Robert Mueller III, Director of the FBI, 2012.

When people talk of the cyber threat they appear to believe that it is a single threat. The reality is that it is multi-faceted, comes in many different forms and continues to evolve.

Another false impression is that only large organisations are at risk of attack. This is sadly untrue, as in reality SMEs are looked upon by perpetrators as 'low-hanging fruit' and therefore easy pickings. In 2012, 31% of all attacks targeted companies with 250 or fewer employees. Similarly, the government departments of small countries do not escape the attention of cyber criminals, as this 2011 quote from Rodney Naudi, Government of Malta Information Security Department Manager, reveals:

> 'We're currently seeing more [cyber] attacks addressing specific audiences including a surge in precision targeting such as phishing e-mails in Maltese. People need to be aware of the implications of a simple click. We might be small, but we experience the same threats that larger countries face.'

Ignorance concerning ICT security can be an organisation's Achilles' heel. The FBI report that over 80% of cyber attacks could have been easily prevented. An email with a Malware attachment is one of the most common routes used to infect computers, although often an effective Antivirus program would prevent such infections.

What did the press really say?

People will often take seriously what they learn through the media, so companies should be prepared to respond quickly to any inaccurate reporting about them. Sometimes, this reporting could be considered irresponsible. A case in point occurred after a fire broke out at Malta-based Drop Chemicals. With clouds of black smoke billowing from the site, safety fears were heightened when a local paper reported the presence of cyanide. In the end, it transpired that the threatening-looking green substance observed in the vicinity was nothing more sinister than washing-up liquid, one of the company's products.

A less spectacular example with broader economic implications is provided by Northern Rock. There is little doubt that the bank was in trouble, although the catalyst that triggered the run on the bank has been much debated. Many commentators implied that media remarks, and in particular those of the BBC's Robert Peston, caused the run, a charge vigorously denied. Ultimately taken into public ownership, Northern Rock was not the only bank in the UK to request support from the Bank of England. It was, however, the only bank to need Tripartite Authority rescue (i.e., The Bank of England, the FSA and HM Treasury).

Your fiercest competitor could also be your best friend

Just a few days after the NatWest Tower in London was bombed in 1993, I had a meeting with my bank manager. We talked briefly about how brilliantly NatWest had recovered. He explained that everything was up and running in 24 h except foreign currency handling which took an extra day or so. Whenever a client came into a branch requesting foreign currency, all the other high street banks helped out. After all, any of them could have been in a similar position to NatWest.

Safety in numbers

For a time, I worked for a small consultancy company in the City of London where the workforce numbered around 70. One day the managing director got wind of a lottery syndicate being formed. Although the odds of the syndicate scooping the jackpot were miniscule, the thought of 10% to

20% of his workforce taking early retirement filled him with trepidation. So he persuaded around 85% of the work force to join the scheme, thereby substantially reducing the individual share of any winnings and effectively mitigating the risk. Furthermore, the cost of this mitigating action was zero.

Malicious damage

When you think of malicious damage you may picture smashed windows, damaged vehicles, graffiti or perhaps even arson. You might think of the perpetrators as mindless individuals perhaps under the influence of drugs or alcohol. Sometimes, however, a disgruntled employee on the inside of your organisation has the motive and means to cause considerable harm to the company.

In one such instance, a middle-aged credit controller was denied a pay rise and took his revenge over a three-year period by spraying the company's computer equipment with the highly corrosive cleaner 'Cillit Bang'. He was only caught after CCTV cameras were installed in the office.

In another case, a SCADA (Supervisory Control and Data Acquisition) expert applied for a position with the Maroochy Shire Council in Queensland, Australia, but his application was unsuccessful. His revenge attack made headlines:

> *'He caused 800,000 litres of raw sewage to spill out into local parks, rivers and even the grounds of a Hyatt Regency hotel. Marine life died, the creek water turned black and the stench was unbearable for residents.'* – (Abrams and Weiss, 2008)

He was subsequently caught and a judge handed down a two-year prison sentence plus the costs incurred by the council for the clean-up. This attack became the first widely known example of someone maliciously breaking into a control system. Since then the vulnerability of SCADA has become more widely apparent, accentuated by the high profile Stuxnet cyber attack on the Iranian nuclear programme.

CHAPTER 19: CONCLUDING THOUGHTS – ROBERT CLARK

In Hindsight has dexterously reflected on a series of disasters from a business continuity perspective. Some had positive outcomes while others did not. Five of the companies featured were unprepared and never recovered from the catastrophes they faced, while a sixth only survived because it was 'unbelievably lucky'. Some of the incidents were very high profile and had global consequences. Others were localised affairs but, to the companies affected, they were still major catastrophes that threatened their very survival.

The causes of the disasters are varied. However, a theme of poor management practices and ill-preparedness often featured with the occasional finger of blame pointed at human error. In at least three instances profitability arguably took priority over health and safety, resulting in avoidable injuries and fatalities. In fact, around half of the case studies record loss of life – some people died while at work whereas others were simply the victims of being in the wrong place at the wrong time – even though only one chapter, 'A Tales of Three Cities', focuses on terrorism.

This book investigates several incidents that caused environmental damage, which in some cases resulted in hefty fines being levied. Health and safety litigation is not uncommon in these case studies; early examples of corporate manslaughter are also touched upon; and there are instances of substantial compensation being paid out to victims. The prosecution of the defendants indicted in connection with the 'Love Parade' tragedy was still ongoing when the book was printed while other incidents saw the culpable individuals tried, convicted and imprisoned for their parts in the respective disasters.

There are examples of exclusion zones where one company's disaster has had a direct impact on other companies located in the immediate vicinity. This includes the worst ever peacetime explosion in the UK at the Buncefield oil depot, which had an effect not only on nearby businesses but also on the downstream supply chain. The conditions created by this incident resulted in the 'best recovery' award for 2006 being presented to Northgate Information Services, a victim of collateral damage.

Mother Nature features in four of the case studies, demonstrating just how helpless we humans are to prevent these natural disasters occurring. We have no control over hurricanes, pandemics, flooding, tsunamis, earthquakes or volcanic eruptions, nor do we know where or when these events will strike. At best, we can plan and prepare for natural disasters in order to limit the damage, quickly bring aid and relief to the victims and facilitate a swift and efficient recovery. Each of these four case studies looks at the dramatic and far reaching consequences of events beyond our control.

- The 2010 closure of much of the European airspace resulting from Eyjafjallajökull's volcanic ash cloud reminded us just how dependent the world has become on the aviation industry. This Icelandic volcano is just one of 500 active throughout the world. Travellers were left stranded and many companies with supply chains based upon a just-in-time strategy dependant on air transport discovered the vulnerability of a single route to market. In closing the airspace, aviation authorities were accused of over-reacting – in retrospect a justifiable claim. Its blanket policy to forbid passage through volcanic ash clouds was inappropriate in this case; it had no established model to distinguish between the various volcanic ash cloud compositions, which would have made it possible to ascertain which presented a threat to aircraft and which did not. This ultimately cost the aviation industry alone an estimated US$1.7 billion.

- Described as the worst UK civil disaster since World War II, the country's response to the 2007 Gloucestershire flooding was commendable. Potable water in bottles and bowsers was supplied to 300,000 consumers who were denied tap water for a period of two weeks. Even so, the failure to recognise that the clearly vulnerable Mythe water treatment works was also a massive single point of failure was scandalous and perhaps even contravened the Civil Contingencies Act (2004). Moreover, the situation provided ample evidence that expecting a population to use only a thirteenth of their normal water consumption was not sustainable.

- When hit by natural disasters, the poorer nations of the world have little option but to turn to the international community for help. Yet, when one the richest countries in the world, both in terms of finance and available resources, struggles to deal with the effects of a hurricane, asking 'why' is not unreasonable. The USA's disaster management before, during and after Hurricane Katrina's landfall in New Orleans drew significant and justifiable criticism from various quarters. The USA frequently experiences hurricane landfalls and generally manages the situation, including population evacuations, efficiently and effectively. The need for improved protection for New Orleans, including the reinforcement of the city's levee system, had been identified five years before Katrina and yet no action had been taken by the time the hurricane finally struck. Despite a rather late evacuation order, thousands of residents remained in their homes – some through choice but others with no means of transport had no choice but to stay. The city's levee system broke and the resultant flooding caused more damage than Katrina itself, while the coordination of the recovery was poor and the media handling by the Bush administration was weak.

- The final study from the natural disaster quartet considered the impact that the 2002 SARS pandemic outbreak had on the tourism industry. Even though history warns us to periodically expect life-threatening pandemics, there is no doubt that the industry was not prepared for what occurred. The whole experience was subsequently described as an 'economic tsunami', with South East Asia bearing the brunt of the costs. The World Health Organisation successfully activated its war plan to deal with such contagions. Under the direction of the WHO, expert microbiologists, usually in competition with each other, took the unprecedented step of working together to isolate and identify the virus that we now know as SARS. But this study is not just about what happened. It also takes account of how both SARS and the 2004 Indian Ocean tsunami galvanised the tourism and aviation industries into better organising themselves and preparing for future natural disasters.

Consideration in the book was also given to a number of supply chain issues and, in particular, the vulnerability of the single route to market. In the case of the Republic of Malta, the country was dependent upon one supplier for its public transport system. From the start of its ten-year contract in July 2010, Arriva Malta began losing revenue at an alarming and unsustainable rate. Contract renegotiations with the Maltese Government were protracted as the Maltese Government demonstrated a strong reluctance to yield ground over the contract's terms and conditions, with the result that Arriva considered the bankruptcy option as a means of extricating itself from the untenable position. This would have resulted in the seizure of its Malta-based assets including the buses. Some Maltese citizens went on record via the local press expressing their delight at the prospect of Arriva's demise. What seems to have been overlooked by this element of the local community, however, was the inevitable horrendous chaos Arriva's bankruptcy would cause to both an already strained local transport infrastructure and the local economy, as there simply was no viable 'Plan B'.

The inherent dangers associated with the off-shore oil industry were examined by comparing the plight of Piper Alpha and the Alexander L. Kielland North Sea rigs. Although the causes of the disasters differed (human error and structural failure respectively), poor management and an apparent indifference towards the health and safety of the crews undoubtedly led to many avoidable deaths. In both instances, a lack of safety training compounded the situation. Around 80 men died of carbon monoxide poisoning in the Piper Alpha accommodation block while they waited for management to direct them. Moreover, it is also believed that most of the 123 fatalities on the Alexander L. Kielland could have survived had someone taken charge of the situation.

The final chapter, 'The Devil is in the Detail', looks at a collection of small, seemingly insignificant possible events which could result in serious repercussions for companies struck by one or more of them. The chapter includes several examples including a lack of BCM awareness, succession planning, information security, data loss, employee fraud and malicious damage. The major lesson to be learned here is that it can be unwise to focus solely on the big ticket items when it comes to your BCM arrangements.

The collective cost of dealing with the case studies covered in this book runs into hundreds of billions of US dollars. The cost of introducing effective business continuity programmes to mitigate the risks and introduce resilience and contingency is likely to have been substantially less. Moreover, had they embraced BCM, the five companies that succumbed to their respective disasters might still be in business today. With those five companies in mind, perhaps it is fitting to close with the words of the late former American Footballer, Vince Lombardi: *'It's not whether you get knocked down; it's whether you get up'*.

GLOSSARY

ABBREVIATION	EXPLANATION
3/11	11th March 2004 bombing of Madrid's railway system
7/7	7th July 2005 London bombings
9/11	Terrorist attack on the USA resulting in the destruction of the New York World Trade Centre Twin Towers, 11 September 2001
ALK	Alexander L. Kielland
APO	Asian Productivity Organisation
ATS	Automatic Train Stop
BAA	British Airports Authority
BBC	British Broadcasting Corporation
BCM	Business Continuity Management
BCI	Business Continuity Institute
BCMS	Business Continuity Management System
BCP	Business Continuity Plan
Big Bang Day	26th October 1986, the UK Government deregulated the financial market

BS	British Standard
CAA	Civil Aviation Authority
CCTV	Closed-Circuit Television
CEO	Chief Executive Officer
CIO	Chief Information Officer
CM	Crisis Management
CMT	Crisis Management Team
COMAH	Control of Major Accident Hazards
COSCO	China Ocean Shipping Company
DDoS	Distributed Denial of Access: a type of cyber attack which attempts to make a network or computer(s) unavailable to legitimate users
DEFRA	Department for the Environment, Food and Rural Affairs
DHS	Department of Homeland Security
EA	Environment Agency
EC	European Community
ESF	Emergency Support Functions
ETA	Euskadi Ta Askatasuna: Spanish based separatist terrorist group

	formed in 1959 with the objective of securing an independent Basque homeland
EU Rule 261	European Union regulation regarding passenger compensation entitlement for delayed or cancelled flights
FBI	Federal Bureau of Investigation
FEMA	Federal Emergency Management Agency
FRS	Fire and Rescue Service
FSA	(UK) Financial Services Authority
GCC	Gloucestershire County Council
GDP	Gross Domestic Product: the value of all the goods and services produced by a country each year
GMT	Greenwich Mean Time
HFE	*Herald of Free Enterprise*: a roll-on / roll-off ferry which capsized outside the Belgian port of Zeebrugge
HOSL	Hertfordshire Oil Storage Ltd.
HSE	Health and Safety Executive
HVM	Hostile Vehicle Mitigation: a means mitigating the risks

	associated with vehicle born improvised explosive devices
IATA	International Air Transport Authority
ICT	Information and Communication Technology
Intifada	An Arabic word literally meaning 'shaking off', referring to the two Palestinian uprisings against Israel in 1987 and 2000.
IRA	Irish Republican Army: Terrorist Group formed in 1916 with the objective creating a united Ireland, independent of the United Kingdom
IS	Information Services
ISO	International Standards Organisation
ISP	Internet Service Supplier
IT	Information Technology
ITOPF	International Tankers Oil Pollution Federation
IUA	(Norwegian) Local Authorities
Just-in-time	A supply chain model that keeps inventory levels to a minimum while depending upon having the right materials in the right place at

	the right time.
LA	(UK) Local Authorities
LNG	Liquefied Natural Gas
LPG	Liquid Petroleum Gas
MI5	Military Intelligence Section 5: UK Security Services
MIC	Methyl Isocyanate: a pesticide
NATO	North Atlantic Treaty Organisation
Nautical mile	1 nautical mile = 1.151 miles or 1.852 km
NEP	National Emergency Plan
NFSA	Norwegian Food and Safety Authority
NGO	Non-Governmental Organisation
NHC	National Hurricane Centre
NOAA	National Oceanic and Atmospheric Administration
NOFO	Norsk Oljevernforening For Operatørselskap: a Norwegian energy company
NOK	Norwegian Krone (Norwegian currency)
NRC	NATO-Russian Council

NRP	National Response Plan
NSB	Norwegian Railway Company
OIM	Offshore Installation Manager
OP	Occidental Petroleum
PA	Piper Alpha
PAS	Publicly Available Standard
PC	Personal Computer
PhD	Doctor of Philosophy degree
PTW	Permit to Work
ROI	Return On Investment
Ro-Ro	Roll-on / Roll-off ferry
RTA	Road Traffic Accident
RTO	Recovery Time Objective
SARS	Severe Acute Respiratory Syndrome
SCADA	Supervisory Control And Data Acquisition system
SME	Small and Medium size Enterprise
Stuxnet	A computer virus discovered in 2010 which is credited with seriously disrupting Iran's nuclear programme

SWT	Severn-Trent Water Limited
TASW	Towards a Safer World
TERN	Tourism Emergency Response Network
UCC	Union Carbide Company
UCIL	Union Carbide India Limited
UNWTO	United Nations World Tourism Organisation
UPS	Uninterruptable Power Supply: batteries that keep computers running in the event of a power failure
VBIED	Vehicle Borne Improvised Explosive Device
WHO	World Health Organisation
WTTC	World Travel and Tourism Council

WORKS CITED

Abrams, M. & Weiss, J., 2008. *Malicious Control System Cyber Security Attack Case Study – Maroochy Water Services, Australia.* [Online]
Available at:
csrc.nist.gov/groups/SMA/fisma/ics/documents/Maroochy-Water-Services-Case-Study_report.pdf
[Accessed 02 03 2014].

Accident Investigation Board Norway, 2009.
INVESTIGATION OF THE GROUNDING OF MV FULL CITY – IMO No. 9073672 AT SASTEIN JULY 31st 2009.
[Online]
Available at: *www.aibn.no/Sjofart/Rapporter/09-533?iid=7530&pid=SHT-Report-Attachments. Native-InnerFile-File&attach=1.*
[Accessed 14 06 2013].

Allen, B., 2011. *The Herald : For Want of a Green Light.*
[Online]
Available at: *www.healthandsafetyatwork.com/hsw/herald-disaster*
[Accessed 14 01 2014].

Ambedkar, B., 2013. *National Seminar on Contemporary tourism planning : introspecting problems and prospects.*
[Online]

Available at:
*www.bamu.net/workshop/acad2012/contemporaryplanning_
tourism.pdf*
[Accessed 04 01 2014].

Aragon, J. & Messner, T. A., 2001. *Master's handbook on
ship's business.* Cambridge: Cornell Maritime Press.

Baker, C. & Seah, A., 2004. *Maritime Accidents and
Human Performance : The Statistical Trail.* [Online]
Available at: *www.google.co.uk/url?sa=t&rct=j&q=
&esrc=s&source=web&cd=1&ved=0CC0QFjAA&url=
https%3A%2F%2Fwww.eagle.org%2FeagleExternalPortal
WEB%2FShowProperty%2FBEA%2520Repository%2FRef
erences%2FTechnical%2520Papers%2F2004%2FMaritim
eAccidentsHumanPerformance&ei=*
[Accessed 17 01 2014].

Balzan, J., 2012. *Everything's gonna be O-Kaye.* [Online]
Available at:
*www.maltatoday.com.mt/en/newsdetails/news/interview/
Everything-s-gonna-be-O-Kaye-Dave-Kaye-20120303*
[Accessed 17 09 2013].

Barth, S., 2010. *Managerial Perception and Assessment of
Catastrophic Supply Chain Risks: An Empirical Study.*
Norderstedt: Druck und Bindung : Books on Demand
GmbH.

BBC News, 2005. *Statement claiming London attacks.*
[Online]

Available at: *BBC News (2005) Statement claiming London attacks [online]. BBC News. Available from: http://news.bbc.co.uk/2/hi/uk_news/4660391.stm* [Accessed 12 11 2010].

BBC News, 2007b. *Floods bring chaos across county.* [Online] Available at: *http://news.bbc.co.uk/1/hi/england/gloucestershire/6911490.stm* [Accessed 15 01 2014].

BBC News, 2007. *Floods force thousands from homes.* [Online] Available at: *http://news.bbc.co.uk/1/hi/uk/6239828.stm* [Accessed 04 01 2010].

BBC News, 2007. *The legacy of the Madrid bombings.* [Online] Available at: *http://news.bbc.co.uk/2/hi/europe/6357599.stm* [Accessed 16 11 2013].

BBC News, 2008. *Airports 'vulnerable' to attack.* [Online] Available at: *http://news.bbc.co.uk/2/hi/uk_news/scotland/glasgow_and_west/7476112.stm* [Accessed 12 09 2013].

BBC News, 2011. *Oil cyber-attacks could cost lives, Shell warns.* [Online]

Available at: *www.bbc.co.uk/news/technology-16137573*
[Accessed 09 06 2013].

BBC World, 2003. *SARS – The True Story.* [Online]
Available at: *www.youtube.com/watch?v=MXPaee0uEQM*
[Accessed 14 01 2014].

Becker, S. et al., 2010. *The Love Parade Files: Looking for Answers in Duisburg.* [Online]
Available at: *www.spiegel.de/international/germany/the-love-parade-files-looking-for-answers-in-duisburg-a-709763.html*
[Accessed 15 01 2011].

Behar, M., 2008. The Volcano Tracker. *Popular Science,* 273(No 1), p. July.

Bellona, 2009. *Bellona and Norwegian authorities work to contain oil leak from Friday ship accident.* [Online]
Available at:
www.bellona.org/articles/articles_2009/cargo_ship_oil_clean_up
[Accessed 31 08 2013].

Bhalla, A. S., 1995. Collapse of Barings Bank: Case of Market Failure. *Economic and Political Weekly Vol 30 No 13*, p. 660.

Bird, L., 2013. *Horizon Scan 2013 – Survey Report,* Caversham: Business Continuity Institute.

Bouissou, J., 2012. *Why The Bhopal Disaster Site, 28 Years Later, Is Still A Toxic Killer.* [Online]
Available at: *www.worldcrunch.com/culture-society/why-the-bhopal-disaster-site-28-years-later-is-still-a-toxic-killer/india-bhopal-dow-contamination-toxic/c3s9764/#.UrHjzMTQA1I*

Carmichael, C. et al., 2012. *Health impacts from extreme events water shortages,* s.l.: Health Protection Agency.

Cassels, J., 1993. *The Uncertain Promise Of Law: Lessons From Bhopal.* Toronto: University of Toronto.

Chemical Industry Archives, 2009. *A Project of Environmental Working Group – Bhopal India.* [Online]
Available at:
www.chemicalindustryarchives.org/dirtysecrets/bhopal/index.asp
[Accessed 19 12 2013].

Clean Caribbean and Americas, 2004. *OIL SPILL EFFECTS ON FISHERIES.* [Online]
Available at:
www.google.co.uk/url?sa=t&rct=j&q=&esrc=s&source=web&cd=1&ved=0CCAQFjAA&url=http%3A%2F%2Fww w.cleancaribbean.org%2Fdownload_pdf.cfm%3FcF%3DIT OPF%2520Technical%2520Information%2520Papers%25 20(TIPS)%26fN%3DOil-Spill-Effects-on-Fisheries.pdf&ei=rgSjU4C3M-rJ0QWX-ICYCQ&usg=AFQjCNHCMPCYjBD1GZ8qH64HdfjoXx-9uA
[Accessed 14 06 2013].

Connor, M., 2010. *Toyota Recall : Five Critical Lessons.* [Online]
Available at: *http://business-ethics.com/2010/01/31/2123-toyota-recall-five-critical-lessons/*
[Accessed 14 01 2011].

Crewe Chronicle, 2007. *Smoke clears to reveal a company in tatters.* [Online]
Available at: *www.crewechronicle.co.uk/crewe-news/local-crewe-news/2007/06/06/smoke-clears-to-reveal-a-company-in-tatters-96135-19254721/*
[Accessed 20 12 2010].

Crichton, G., 2007. The Glasgow airport attack from a business continuity and crisis management point of view. *Business Continuity Journal,* Two(Three), pp. 18 – 23.

Crichton, G., 2013. *Head of Assurance, Glasgow Airport* [Interview] (13 09 2013).

Crookes, D., 2013. *Tourists visiting Malta driven round the bend by the unpopular buses that Boris Johnson rejected.* [Online]
Available at:
www.independent.co.uk/news/world/europe/tourists-visiting-malta-driven-round-the-bend-by-the-unpopular-buses-that-boris-johnson-rejected-8819734.html
[Accessed 17 09 2013].

Crowd Management Strategies, 2010. *Love Parade Disaster – Titanic Error.* [Online]

Available at: *www.crowdsafe.com/new.asp?ID=2049*
[Accessed 19 01 2014].

Dale, G., Marvel, A. & Oliver, H., 2005. *Travel and Tourism.* Oxford: Heinmann.

Der Spiegel, 2010. *Disaster Investigation: Love Parade Report Calls Organizers to Task.* [Online]
Available at:
www.spiegel.de/international/germany/disaster-investigation-love-parade-report-calls-organizers-to-task-a-710381.html
[Accessed 12 01 2011].

Dhillon, G. et al., 2013. *Cilmate Change Modeling, Mitigation and Adaption.* Reston, VA: American Society of Civil Engineers.

Diehl, J., Gathmann, F., Hans, B. & Jüttner, J., 2010. *Analysis of the Love Parade Tragedy: The Facts Behind the Duisburg Disaster.* [Online]
Available at:
www.spiegel.de/international/germany/analysis-of-the-love-parade-tragedy-the-facts-behind-the-duisburg-disaster-a-708876.html
[Accessed 13 01 2011].

Drew, C. & Treaster, J., 2006. *Hurricane Katrina Demonstrated the Weaknesses of U.S. Flood Insurance.* [Online]

Available at: *www.worldwatch.org/node/4384*
[Accessed 12 01 2013].

Dutta, A., 2009. *Disaster tourism plan for Bhopal gas leak site.* [Online]
Available at:
http://indiatoday.intoday.in/story/Disaster+tourism+plan+for+Bhopal+gas+leak+site/1/72899.html
[Accessed 18 12 2013].

Economist, 2005. The Attack on London: Murder in the rush hour. *Economist,* 09 07, p. 4.

Edwards, R., Bunyan, N. & Cramb, A., 2007. *Airport bombers hoped to murder hundreds.* [Online]
Available at:
www.telegraph.co.uk/news/uknews/1556263/Airport-car-bombers-hoped-to-murder-hundreds.html
[Accessed 14 09 2013].

English, R., 2009. *Terrorism – How to Respond.* Oxford: Oxford University Press.

Environment Agency, 2010. *The costs of the summer 2007 floods in England,* Bristol: Environment Agency.

EU Transport Ministers Council, 2010. *Report on the actions undertaken in the context of the eimpact of the volcanic ash cloud crisis on the air transportation system.* [Online]
Available at: *http://ec.europa.eu/transport/doc/ash-cloud-*

crisis/2010_06_30_volcano-crisis-report.pdf
[Accessed 12 06 2013].

Fay, S., 1996. *The Collapse of Barings.* London: Cohen Books.

Fiducial, 2012. *Protect your business from employee theft.*
[Online]
Available at:
www.fiducial.com/Entrepreneur/StrategicPlanning/emp_theft.asp
[Accessed 02 03 2014].

Fischetti, M., 2001. New Orleans. *Scientific American.*

Garvey, J. & Mullins, M., 2009. *An Examination of 'New'
and 'Old' Terrorism Using High-Frequency Data.* [Online]
Available at: *www.economics-of-security.eu/publications*
[Accessed 04 11 2010].

Gislason, S. et al., 2010. *Characterization of
Eyjafjallajökull volcanic ash particles and a protocol for
rapid risk assessment.* [Online]
Available at:
www.pnas.org/content/early/2011/04/22/1015053108.full.pdf
[Accessed 10 06 2013].

Glaessar, D., 2010. *Toward a Safer World: The Travel,
Tourism and Aviation Sector.* [Online]
Available at:
*www.google.co.uk/url?sa=t&rct=j&q=&esrc=s&source=
web&cd=1&cad=rja&ved=0CCwQFjAA&url=http%3A%
2F%2Fdtxtq4w60xqpw.cloudfront.net%2Fsites%2Fall%2F*

files%2Fdocpdf%2Funwtotowardasaferworld.pdf&ei=RMn
8UveOGu-v7Aa-poGgAg&usg=
AFQjCNF6VqD3ocZxSU1hO8pjsKoEyYLd
[Accessed 13 01 2014].

Global Security, 2014. *Ro-Ro Ship Saftey.* [Online]
Available at:
www.globalsecurity.org/military/systems/ship/ro-ro-
safety.htm
[Accessed 17 01 2014].

Gloucestershire County Council, 2006. *A Guide to Business*
Continuity Management in Gloucestershire County
Council. 2nd ed. Gloucester: Gloucestershire County
Council.

Gloucestershire County Council, 2007. *Summer 2007.*
[Online]
Available at:
www.gloucestershire.gov.uk/index.cfm?articleid=18621
[Accessed 20 12 2010].

Gloucestershire County Council, 2010. *Gloucestershire*
County Council BCM Arrangements. [Online]
Available at:
www.gloucestershire.gov.uk/index.cfm?articleid=22732
[Accessed 06 01 2011].

NBC, 2010. Crisis Events in Tourism: subjects of crisis in
tourism. *Current Issues in Tourism,* 13(5), p. 401.

Halvorsrud, G., 2002. *The Åsta Train Crash, its Precursors and Consequences, and its Investigation.* [Online]
Available at:
http://link.springer.com/chapter/10.1007%2F978-1-4471-0173-4_2
[Accessed 10 11 2013].

Hammer, J., 2012. *Ber tog lære av biler.* [Online]
Available at:
www.forskning.no/artikler/2012/november/341122
[Accessed 12 11 2013].

Hammer, L., 2012. *A Swedish researcher rails against hazardous luggage systems.* [Online]
Available at: *http://sciencenordic.com/trains-should-be-more-cars*
[Accessed 10 11 2013].

Hansard, L., 1995. *Publications and Records.* [Online]
Available at: *www.parliament.the-stationery-office.co.uk/pa/ld199495/ldhansrd/vo950721/text/50721-14.htm*
[Accessed 27 11 2013].

Hayward, T., 2010. *BP CEO Tony Hayward: 'I'd Like My Life Back'* [Interview] 2010.

Health and Safety Executive, 2011. *Companies in court over major chemical fire in Crewe.* [Online]
Available at: *www.hse.gov.uk/press/2011/coi-nw-*

18greenway.htm
[Accessed 14 07 2013].

Helbing, D. & Mukerji, P., 2012. Crowd disasters as systemic failures: analysis of the Love Parade disaster. *EPJ Data Science,* 1(7).

Henning, D., 2011. *Germany: One year after the Love Parade disaster.* [Online]
Available at: *www.wsws.org/en/articles/2011/07/love-j25.html*
[Accessed 18 01 2014].

Hertfordshire Fire and Rescue Service, 2006. *Buncefield: Hertfordshire Fire and Rescue Service's review of the fire response,* London: The Stationery Office.

Information Age, 2006. *Getting back to business after Buncefield. Northgate Information Services' miraculous recovery from the oil depot explosions..* [Online]
Available at: *www.information-age.com/industry/uk-industry/284331/getting-back-to-business-after-buncefield*
[Accessed 09 06 2013].

Ingrassia, P., 2009. *Toyota Isn't Immune From the Recession.* [Online]
Available at:
http://online.wsj.com/news/articles/SB123112023622652953
[Accessed 05 01 2011].

International Institute for Counter Terrorism, 2010. *International Institute for Counter Terrorism. About Us.*

[Online]
Available at:
www.ict.org.il/AboutICT/AboutUs/tabid/55/Default.aspx
[Accessed 12 11 2010].

Khan, F. & Abbasi, S., 1998. *Risk Assessment In Chemical Process Industries.* New Dehli: Discovery Publishing House.

King, P., 2013. *Oil and gas deaths reached record high in 2012.* [Online]
Available at: *www.eenews.net/stories/1059986375*
[Accessed 12 01 2014].

Knabb, R., Rhome, J. & Brown, D., 2005. *Tropical Cyclone Report Hurricane Katrina.* [Online]
Available at: *www.nhc.noaa.gov%2Fpdf%2FTCR-AL122005_Katrina.pdf&ei=pDPRUpHbD-v07Ab5lYHYCw&usg=AFQjCNEWEujElloRlMfWCtQ2hv1r8aCtHQ&bvm=bv.59026428,d.d2k*
[Accessed 06 01 2011].

Lambert, R. & Gapper, J., 1995. A low-risk business until the fraud says Barings chairman. *Financial Times,* 28 02.

Lancet, 1989. Round The World: India--Long Term Effects of MIC. *The Lancet,* 29 April, p. 952.

Ling, G., 2013. *Witness: SARS – the epidemic that shook Hong Kong.* [Online]

Available at: *www.youtube.com/watch?v=ZgBEQZNbGrc*
[Accessed 18 01 2014].

Lockett, J., 2007. *From IT strategy to IT Reality : Coping with Disaster,* London: Caspian Publishing Ltd.

Malta Politics, 2013. *Malta u l-politika – Ittri ċċensurati u punti ta' riflessjoni politika..* [Online]
Available at: *www.maltapolitics.com/arriva.htm*
[Accessed 29 09 2012].

Malta Sunday Times, 2013. *Arriva indicates it could quit.* [Online]
Available at:
www.timesofmalta.com/articles/view/20131020/local/arriva -warns-it-could-quit.491044#.UmQwjT9QjaI
[Accessed 20 10 2013].

McCarragher, B., 2011. *New Orleans Hurricane History.* [Online]
Available at:
web.mit.edu/12.000/www/m2010/teams/neworleans1/hurric ane%20history.htm
[Accessed 06 01 2011].

Mercer, P., 2003. *Airport theft shocks Australia.* [Online]
Available at: *news.bbc.co.uk/2/hi/asia-pacific/3083228.stm*
[Accessed 02 05 2012].

Michels, B., 2013. *Toyota recall crisis was a failure in risk management.* [Online]

Available at: *www.adr-international.com/news-media-pr/press-releases/april_press_release/*
[Accessed 06 01 2014].

Minahan, T., 2010. *Risk management lessons from Toyota.* [Online]
Available at: *www.forbes.com/2010/05/10/toyota-suppliers-managing-technology-risk.html*
[Accessed 14 01 2011].

Moreorless, 2011. *Bhopal Industrial Incident.* [Online]
Available at: *www.moreorless.net.au/killers/bhopal.html*
[Accessed 18 12 2013].

News in English, 2009b. *Grounded ship's oil spill called the 'worst ever' in Norway.* [Online]
Available at: *www.newsinenglish.no/2009/07/31/grounded-ships-oil-spill-calledthe-worst-ever-in-norway/*
[Accessed 16 08 2013].

News in English, 2009. *'Oil spill ship' finally leaves Norway.* [Online]
Available at: *www.newsinenglish.no/2009/09/14/oil-spill-ship-finally-leaves-norway/*
[Accessed 19 08 2013].

O'Hehir, M., 2007. What is a business continuity planning (BCP) strategy?. In: H. A., ed. *The Definitive Handbook of Business Continuity Management.* 2nd ed. Chichester: Wiley & Sons.

O'Brien, J., 2011. *New Icelandic volcano eruption could have global impact.* [Online]
Available at: *www.bbc.co.uk/news/world-europe-15995845*
[Accessed 10 06 2013].

Officer of the Watch, 2013. *Alexander L. Kielland Platform Capsize Accident – Investigation Report.* [Online]
Available at:
http://officerofthewatch.com/2013/04/29/alexander-l-kielland-platform-capsize-accident/
[Accessed 14 03 2014].

Paté-Cornell, M., 1992. *Learning from the Piper Alpha Accident: A Post-mortem Analysis of Technical and Organizational Factors. Risk Analysis.* [Online]
Available at:
http://onlinelibrary.wiley.com/doi/10.1111/j.1539-6924.1993.tb01071.x/abstract
[Accessed 12 01 2011].

Peregin, C., 2012. *Arriva deadline moved to the Budget vote day.* [Online]
Available at:
www.timesofmalta.com/articles/view/20121205/local/Arriva-deadline-moved-to-the-Budget-vote-day.448219
[Accessed 28 09 2103].

Peterson, M., 2009. *Bhopal Plant Disaster – Situation Summary.* s.l.:University of Massachusetts.

Pitt, S. M., 2008. *National Archives – Cabinet Office.* [Online]
Available at:
http://webarchive.nationalarchives.gov.uk/20100807034701/
http:/archive.cabinetoffice.gov.uk/pittreview/thepittreview/
final_report.html
[Accessed 15 01 2014].

Radley, L., 2012. *Disaster at Sea.* [Online]
Available at:
http://archive.commercialmotor.com/article/8th-march-
2012/31/disaster-at-sea
[Accessed 17 01 2014].

Regester, M. & Larkin, J., 2008. *Risk Issues and Crisis
Management in Public Relations. A case book in best
practice.* 4th ed. London: Kogan Page.

Roberts, C., 2012. *Why are some places vulnerable to
extreme flood events : Focus England.* [Online]
Available at: *http://cgge.aag.org/WaterResources1e/cs-*
3/cs-3_print.html
[Accessed 15 01 2014].

Russakoff, R. & Goodman, M., 2011. *Employee Theft: Are
You Blind to It?.* [Online]
Available at: *www.cbsnews.com/news/employee-theft-are-*
you-blind-to-it/
[Accessed 02 03 2014].

Sandelson, M., 2009. *Langesund oil tanker disaster update.*
[Online]
Available at: *theforeigner.no/pages/news/langesund-oil-tanker-disaster-update/*
[Accessed 15 06 2013].

Sansone, K., 2013. *Driving the country round the bend.*
[Online]
Available at:
www.timesofmalta.com/articles/view/20130922/local/Driving-the-country-round-the-bend.487134
[Accessed 28 09 2013].

Savitch, H., 2008. *Cities in a time of terror: space, territory, and local resilience.* New York: M.E Sharpe Inc.

Schaer, C. & Crossland, D., 2010. *The World from Berlin: Love Parade Stampede 'Was a Tragedy Waiting to Happen'.* [Online]
Available at: *www.spiegel.de/international/germany/the-world-from-berlin-love-parade-stampede-was-a-tragedy-waiting-to-happen-a-708474.html*
[Accessed 12 01 2011].

Schmid, B. et al., 2010. *Disaster Plan: Love Parade Documents Reveal a Series of Errors.* [Online]
Available at:
www.spiegel.de/international/germany/disaster-plan-love-parade-documents-reveal-a-series-of-errors-a-710834.html
[Accessed 12 01 2011].

Sheen, B., 1987. *Herald of Free Enterprise: Report of Court No.8074 Formal Investigation,* London: Her Majesty's Stationary Office.

Shelly, I. et al., 2005. *Methods and Motives: Exploring Links between Transnational Organized Crime & International Terrorism.* [Online]
Available at: *www.ncjrs.gov/pdffiles1/nij/grants/211207.pdf*
[Accessed 21 11 2010].

Slywotzky, A., 2011. *The Upside of Strategic Risk : How Toyoyta Turned Its Greatest Threat Into a Growth Breakthrough.* [Online]
Available at:
www.mmc.com/knowledgecenter/viewpoint/Slywotzky2007.php
[Accessed 14 01 2011].

Spedding, L. S., 2009. *Due Diligence Handbook – Corporate Governance, Risk Management and Business Planning.* First ed. Oxford: CIMA Publishing.

St John, G., 2010. *Party, Love and Profit: The Rhythms of the Love Parade.* [Online]
Available at:
dj.dancecult.net/index.php/dancecult/article/view/304/290
[Accessed 17 01 2014].

Stein, M., 2000. The Risk Taker as Shadow: A Psychoanalytic View of the Collapse of Barings Bank. *Journal of Management Studies 37: 8,* p. 1217.

TASW, 2011. *BEYOND PANDEMICS: A WHOLE-OF-SOCIETY APPROACH TO DISASTER PREPAREDNESS.* [Online]
Available at: *www.towardsasaferworld.org*
[Accessed 12 01 2014].

The Hindu, 2010. *Bhopal gas disaster has nothing to do with pollution at plant site.* [Online]
Available at: *www.thehindu.com/news/bhopal-gas-disaster-has-nothing-to-do-with-pollution-at-plant-site-neeri/article506214.ece*
[Accessed 18 12 2013].

Thor, R., 2009. *Boat Design.* [Online]
Available at: *www.boatdesign.net/forums/all-things-boats-and-boating/where-17014-130.html*
[Accessed 15 06 2013].

Times of Malta, 2011. *Arriva was twice threatened with contract cancellation.* [Online]
Available at: *www.timesofmalta.com/articles/view/20111016/local/gatt.389278*
[Accessed 17 09 2013].

Toyota Learning, 2010. *Toyota Crisis Management.* [Online]
Available at: *www.ineak.com/toyota-crisis-management/*
[Accessed 12 01 2011].

Toyota, 2010. *Toyota European – Sustainability Report 2010.* [Online]
Available at: *www.toyota.eu/sustainability/social_performance/corporate_ citizen/Pages/default.aspx*
[Accessed 04 01 2011].

Transport Malta, 2013. *The National ITS Action Plan for Malta 2013-2017.* [Online]
Available at: *www.transport.gov.mt/admin/uploads/media-library/files/National%20ITS%20Action%20Plan%20for% 20Malta%20_2013%20-%202017_.pdf*
[Accessed 22 09 2013].

UK Cabinet Office, 2008. *National Risk Register,* Norwich: Stationery Office.

UK Cabinet Office, 2010. *A Strong Britain in an Age of Uncertainty:,* Norwich: Stationery Office.

UK Government, 2005. *The Civil Contingencies Act 2004 (Contingency Planning) Regulations 2005.* [Online]
Available at: *www.ifrc.org/docs/idrl/783EN.pdf*
[Accessed 09 06 2013].

UNWTO, 2006. *About the Tourism Emergency Response Network (TERN).* [Online]
Available at: *http://rcm.unwto.org/content/about-tourism-emergency-response-network-tern-0*
[Accessed 04 03 2014].

UNWTO, 2014. *Why Tourism.* [Online]
Available at: *www2.unwto.org/content/why-tourism*
[Accessed 17 01 2014].

White House, 2006. *The Federal Response to Hurricane Katrina: Lessons Learned.* [Online]
Available at:
http://library.stmarytx.edu/acadlib/edocs/katrinawh.pdf
[Accessed 10 12 2010].

Wilson, A., 2010. *BP's Disaster: No Surprise to Folks in the Know.* [Online]
Available at: *www.cbsnews.com/news/bps-disaster-no-surprise-to-folks-in-the-know/*
[Accessed 23 01 2014].

ITG RESOURCES

IT Governance Ltd sources, creates and delivers products and services to meet the real-world, evolving IT governance needs of today's organisations, directors, managers and practitioners.

The ITG website (_www.itgovernance.co.uk_) is the international one-stop-shop for corporate and IT governance information, advice, guidance, books, tools, training and consultancy. On the website you will find the following page related to the subject matter of this book:

_www.itgovernance.co.uk/bc_dr.aspx_.

Publishing Services

IT Governance Publishing (ITGP) is the world's leading IT-GRC publishing imprint that is wholly owned by IT Governance Ltd.

With books and tools covering all IT governance, risk and compliance frameworks, we are the publisher of choice for authors and distributors alike, producing unique and practical publications of the highest quality, in the latest formats available, which readers will find invaluable.

www.itgovernancepublishing.co.uk is the website dedicated to ITGP. Other titles published by ITGP that may be of interest include:

- Disaster Recovery and Business Continuity

  www.itgovernance.co.uk/shop/p-520-disaster-recovery-and-business-continuity-third-edition.aspx

- A Manager's Guide to ISO22301

  www.itgovernance.co.uk/shop/p-331-a-managers-guide-to-iso22301.aspx

- Business Continuity Management: Choosing to Survive

  www.itgovernance.co.uk/shop/p-412-business-continuity-management-choosing-to-survive.aspx.

We also offer a range of off-the-shelf toolkits that give comprehensive, customisable documents to help users create the specific documentation they need to properly implement a management system or standard. Written by experienced practitioners and based on the latest best practice, ITGP toolkits can save months of work for organisations working towards compliance with a given standard.

For further information please review the following pages:

- ISO22301 BCMS Implementation Toolkit

  www.itgovernance.co.uk/shop/p-1039.aspx

- Full range of toolkits

  www.itgovernance.co.uk/shop/c-129-toolkits.aspx.

Books and tools published by IT Governance Publishing (ITGP) are available from all business booksellers and the following websites:

www.itgovernance.eu　　　*www.itgovernanceusa.com*

www.itgovernance.in　　　*www.itgovernancesa.co.za*

www.itgovernance.asia.

Training Services

IT Governance offers an extensive portfolio of training courses designed to educate information security, IT governance, risk management and compliance professionals. Our classroom and online training programme will help you develop the skills required to deliver best practice and compliance to your organisation. They will also enhance your career by providing you with industry standard certifications and increased peer recognition. Our range of courses offer a structured learning path from foundation to advanced level in the key topics of information security, IT governance, business continuity and service management.

ISO22301:2012 is the International Standard for business continuity within organisations and defines the best practice for developing and executing a robust business continuity plan. Our ISO22301 Foundation, Lead Implementer and Lead Auditor training courses are designed to provide delegates with a comprehensive introduction and guide to the implementation of an ISO22301 management system.

For further information please review the following webpages:

ISO22301 Certified BCMS Foundation:
www.itgovernance.co.uk/shop/p-694-iso22301-bcms-foundation-training-course.aspx.

ISO222301 Certified BCMS Lead Implementer:
www.itgovernance.co.uk/shop/p-695-iso22301-bcms-lead-implementer-training-course.aspx.

ISO22301 Certified BCMS Lead Auditor:
www.itgovernance.co.uk/shop/p-1264-iso22301-certified-bcms-lead-auditor-training-course.aspx.

Full details of all IT Governance training courses can be found at *www.itgovernance.co.uk/training.aspx*.

Professional Services and Consultancy

IT Governance consultants have the expertise to help you apply intelligent approaches to disaster recovery and business continuity. We can show you how to operate smartly so that you and your organisation are prepared for the worst scenarios and can recover IT resources quickly and efficiently. We can show you how to put in place processes that satisfy detailed organisational requirements and mission objectives – making resilient thinking part of every employee's responsibility.

To further ensure your total preparedness in the event of a disruptive incident, we can also show you how to create a Business Continuity Management System (BCMS) certified to ISO22301. With a robust BCMS in place, your organisation can continue trading and return to normal operations as quickly and efficiently as possible, protecting your turnover and reputation.

For more information about how IT Governance consultancy can help improve the resilience of your whole organisation, please visit *www.itgovernance.co.uk/business-resilience.aspx*.

Newsletter

IT governance is one of the hottest topics in business today, not least because it is also the fastest moving.

You can stay up to date with the latest developments across the whole spectrum of IT governance subject matter, including; risk management, information security, ITIL and IT service management, project governance, compliance and so much more, by subscribing to ITG's core publications and topic alert emails.

Simply visit our subscription centre and select your preferences: *www.itgovernance.co.uk/newsletter.aspx*.

Lightning Source UK Ltd.
Milton Keynes UK
UKOW06f0043070315

247428UK00001B/26/P

9 781849 285919